HOPI
VOICES

Recorded, Transcribed,
and Annotated
by Harold Courlander

UNIVERSITY OF NEW MEXICO PRESS
Albuquerque

HOPI VOICES

Recollections, Traditions,

and Narratives of

the Hopi Indians

Library of Congress Cataloging in Publication Data

Main entry under title:

Hopi voices.

   Bibliography: p.
   1. Hopi Indians—Legends.   2. Hopi Indians—Religion and
mythology.   3. Indians of North America—Arizona—Legends.
4. Indians of North America—Arizona—Religion and mythology.
5. Hopi Indians—History.   I. Courlander, Harold, 1908–
E99.H7H69   1982   306′.08997   82–8413
ISBN 0–8263–0612–8   AACR2

Contents

Acknowledgments

My debt to the people of the Hopi villages who gave so generously of their time, thoughts, and feelings in providing these records of their traditions and way of life is obvious. But I want to let them know once more of my profound appreciation for their friendship and confidence. I believe they have contributed much that is valuable to our understanding of their outer and inner lives. To list all of those who helped in one way or another would be impossible. Indeed, to my regret, there were some whose names I did not know. There were those who provided narrations, explanations, or commentaries, and others who guided me to extinct villages, received me in their homes, or merely stopped to talk on some mesatop or trail.

Each of the texts is signed with the name of its contributor, except in three instances in which the speakers felt more comfortable using pseudonyms, along with the name of his or her home village.

I express special appreciation to the following persons: Albert Yava,* Dewey Healing, and Juanita Healing of Tewa Village; Ned Zeena* and Kilaoka (pseudonym) of Walpi; Wallace Lomakena, Jr., of Sichomovi; Stuart Tuvengyamtiwa* of Polacca; Peter Nuvamsa, Sr.,* and Porter Timeche of Shongopovi; Bert Puhueyestewa of Mishongnovi; Homer Cooyama and Eugene Sekaquaptewa of Kikeuchmovi; Don C. Talayesva of Oraibi; Percy Lomahquahu of Hotevilla; Louis Numkena, Sr.,* Stanley Honahni, Sr., Tsakap-

*Now deceased.

tamana (pseudonym), and Uwaikwiota (pseudonym) of Moencopi; and Estelle Fisher of Parker, Arizona.

I am also grateful to my friend and colleague, Dr. George Eaton Simpson, Professor Emeritus at Oberlin College, and Professor Joann W. Kealiinohomoku of the University of Northern Arizona, both of whom reviewed this book in manuscript and made many valuable suggestions. Abbott Sekaquaptewa, who was Tribal Chairman for a number of years while I was at work on the Hopi Reservation, was invariably generous with his help whenever I needed it, for which I express special thanks. Dallas Johnson and Bessie Condrey of Albuquerque, likewise, are due gratitude for assisting me in countless ways during my working trips to Arizona and New Mexico.

I acknowledge with appreciation a grant-in-aid from the Wenner-Gren Foundation for Anthropological Research which helped me in the collecting and transcribing of a number of these texts.

Introduction

The Hopis

The Hopi Indians today occupy a dozen villages situated between Keam's Canyon and Tuba City in northern Arizona. Eleven of the villages are located at the southern tips of three fingerlike projections of Black Mesa, and the twelfth, fifty miles farther west, is an enclave within the Navajo Reservation. On top of the easternmost projection, known as First Mesa, are the older settlements of Walpi (originally on a lower mesa shelf, where it was called Keuchaptevela), Sichomovi, and Tewa Village (also known as Hano). The modern village of Polacca is at the base of the mesa near the blacktop road that intersects the Hopi Reservation. Farther to the west, on Second or Middle Mesa, are Mishongnovi, Shipaulovi, and Shongopovi. The most westerly projection, called Third Mesa, contains the villages of Oraibi, Hotevilla, Bakavi, and, on lower ground, the village of Kikeuchmovi or New Oraibi. The enclave village near Tuba City is called Moencopi.

Shongopovi is generally regarded as the earliest of the Hopi settlements. It is believed to have been established in the thirteenth century, though its original site was not on the mesatop but on a lower knoll called Masipa. Oraibi, settled by people from Shongopovi, claims to be on a site close to its original one, and to be the oldest continuously occupied Hopi village. Hotevilla and Bakavi are early twentieth-century offshoots of Oraibi, which today is mostly in ruins and largely a ghost village, most of its families having moved down to Kikeuchmovi where the Hopi Tribal Government has its headquarters.

Anthropologists tend to regard the Hopis, along with the Eastern Pueblos of New Mexico, as descendants of the so-called Basketmaker peoples who occupied the San Juan Valley until about the thirteenth century, when an extended drouth forced them into southward migrations. According to this belief it probably was a group of wandering Basketmakers that founded the Second Mesa Hopi settlement at Masipa—the original Shongopovi—under the banner of the Bear Clan. But there is no conclusive evidence that they were the first inhabitants of Hopiland. On the contrary, Bear Clan traditions say that when they arrived at Masipa they saw smoke rising from Antelope Mesa in the east and discovered that the village of Awatovi was already established there. Furthermore, the countryside around the present Hopi villages in all directions contains hundreds of small ruins, few of which have been investigated and dated, and there is at least a possibility that some of them predated Masipa. On Third Mesa only a few miles from Oraibi there are ruins of small cave dwellings suggesting the antiquity of human presence in this area. Whether the earliest inhabitants actually derived from the San Juan Basketmaker culture is not known.

Anthropological investigations, as well as Hopi traditions, indicate that numerous groups and clans traveled considerable distances from the north, east, and south before joining and integrating with the Hopis.[1] Traditions speak of the migrations of

---

[1]Jesse Walter Fewkes, in his "Tusayan Migration Traditions," lists the main immigrant groups as follows—

From Tokonave (Navajo Mountain): Snake, Horn, and affiliated clans.

From Palatkwa (southern Arizona) and the Little Colorado River area: Squash, Flute, Cloud (Water), Lizard, Tobacco, Sand, Rabbit, and affiliated clans.

From the Rio Grande Valley in New Mexico: Bear, Firewood (Fire), Reed, Tansy-Mustard, Butterfly, Badger, and affiliated clans.

Fewkes's groupings do not correspond in all details with those indicated by various present-day Hopi informants.

the Water, Sun, Tobacco, and related clans from a place called Palatkwa, or Palatkwapi, far to the south of the Little Colorado River. Some accounts say that these groups brought Apaches and Pimas to Hopi country with them.[2] Numerous clan groups came from Muyovi, the Rio Grande Valley of New Mexico, while the Snake, Horn, and related clans are said to have come from the region of Navajo Mountain in the north, where they had settled after a previous migration from the west. Hopis also speak of the coming of at least some Plains Indians who were caught up in the concentric movements toward the mesas.

Eastern Pueblo people who came to settle in Hopi country included Tewa, Keresan, Zuni, Towa, and Tiwa language groups. Lagunas (traditionally called Kawaikas) and Zunis are believed to have made up a consequential part of the populations of Awatovi and the other Antelope Mesa villages, one of which was named Kawaika. Another village in this region, Meusiptanga, on the Jeddito Wash, is thought by Hopis to have been settled by Lagunas and Zunis. All of these settlements are now extinct. Another Eastern Pueblo village, Payupki on Second Mesa, had a Tiwa-speaking population. After a relatively brief stay in Hopi country, its inhabitants returned to the Rio Grande and settled in Sandia. A Third Mesa Eastern Pueblo village, Chimonvasi, was vacated when its Towa-speaking inhabitants moved back to the Rio Grande and joined the Jemez (more properly spelled Hemis) Pueblo. Only one Eastern Pueblo settlement continues to exist in Hopi country, Tewa Village on First Mesa adjoining Sichomovi and Walpi. It was founded by a large party of Tewas who had been invited by the leaders of Walpi to come and help defend that village against marauding Utes, Paiutes, and Apaches.[3] According to First Mesa recollections, there were at least two later Tewa settlements, one near Five Houses south of Walpi, the other near Wepo Spring to the north, both of them short-lived.[4]

The amalgam of cultures resulting from the influx of vari-

---

[2]Sitaiema of the Walpi Water Clan believed that his group was of Uche (Apache) origin. See Albert Yava, *Big Falling Snow*, p. 36.

[3]See text 36. Yava, ibid., pp. 26 ff., gives the First Mesa account of the coming of the Tewas.

[4]Ibid., p. 34.

ous groups over a half-dozen or more centuries is reflected in diverse, sometimes conflicting, traditions. One observes, for example, that the basketry techniques on Second and Third mesas are different, though the settlements are only a few miles apart. On Second Mesa, in the villages of Shongopovi, Mishongnovi, and Shipaulovi, only the old Basketmaker coiling technique is found, while on Third Mesa, in Oraibi and its offshoot villages, only the plaiting or wicker method is used.[5] Systems of counting likewise demonstrate diversity of cultural inheritance. On First and Second mesas, the decimal system was standard, while Third Mesa Hopis traditionally used the vigesimal system (counting by twenties)[6] as did the ancient Maya. While on First Mesa the dead are buried facing the east, from which it was prophesied that a good bahana (white man) would come, in Oraibi the dead are buried facing Grand Canyon in the west, from which the Hopis are said to have emerged, and to which their spirit counterparts are supposed to return. Diversity in creation myths also reflects heterogeneous cultural sources. One myth heard on Third Mesa depicts Huruing Wuhti (Hard Substances Woman) as the main deity of creation, while another heard on First Mesa names Gogyeng Sowuhti (Spider Old Woman) and her grandchildren, the Warrior Brothers, as the deities responsible for earthly and cosmological creation deeds. Still another story is told by the First Mesa Reed Clan, which claims to have been created at a spring near Mishongnovi rather than having emerged from the underworld with other Hopis.

Traditionally, a group that founded a village became its hereditary leader. Thus, Oraibi was first settled by members of the Bear Clan, with the result that it had Bear Clan chiefs until its disintegration early in the twentieth century. Walpi also was a Bear Clan settlement until the Bear Clan died out, after which it was headed—in trust, one might say—by a member of the Horn Clan. Awatovi was a Bow Clan village, and Moencopi, though a satellite of Oraibi, has Corn Clan leadership. Until recent times, the Hopi villages did not regard themselves as parts of a tribal whole, but as separate entities, virtually as village-states. Although the kikmongwi, or village chief, had considerable moral

[5]Ruth Underhill, *Pueblo Crafts*, pp. 24–29.
[6]Ruth DeEtte Simpson, *The Hopi Indians*, pp. 81–82.

authority in the community, his authority derived from his membership in the paramount clan. Every clan had a particular responsibility to fulfill, whether purely ceremonial or, for example, leadership in war. Decisions involving war or village defense usually were in the hands of a designated warrior clan or society at whose head was the kaletakmongwi, or war chief. According to Hopi recollections, it was the war chief of Walpi, rather than the village chief, who decided that the village would participate with Oraibi in the sacking of Awatovi.[7] Responsibilities in the field of ceremonial life fell to leaders of the various kiva societies, principally but not exclusively the four most important fraternities—Kwakwanteu (One Horn), Aalteu (Two Horn), Wuwuchimteu, and Tataukyameu ("The Singers"). Inasmuch as life in the villages was largely regulated by the ceremonial calendar, the moral if not political authority of the kiva society leaders was considerable. Each clan had authority over its own lands and fields, which it had acquired as assignments by the paramount clan or in some other fashion.[8]

In brief, the village was a complex of authorities and responsibilities that sometimes were in conflict but usually in harmony. It had no simple, orderly, schematized political structure, but depended on a balance of forces to keep it functioning. Some observers have characterized the traditional social situation as "organized anarchy." When all went well, it worked, but when the stresses became too great, the village fell apart and perished. The Hopis' concept of themselves and their villages as a single society came only with the U.S. Government's Indian Reorganization Act of 1934 and the consequent election of a tribal council. However, to this day there are Hopis who reject the "reorganization" on principle, with the result that some of the villages are split between progressives and traditionalists.[9]

[7]See text 15, "The Destruction of Awatovi."

[8]Yava, *Big Falling Snow,* pp. 95–96, describes how the chief of the Walpi Reed Clan refused permission for an archaeological restoration of Awatovi, whose lands had come under the authority of his clan at the time of Awatovi's destruction.

[9]In 1968, during the collection of the Hopi texts in this book, the author was told by a traditionalist in Moencopi that he could work with either the traditionalists or the progressives, but not both. "If you are going to the progressives for help," he said, "then I can't do anything for you."

The Hopi system of landholding and farming has been described in detail by numerous investigators, but for the purposes
of this brief introduction, there is probably no better summary
than that provided by the 1894 Hopi petition to Washington
which, among other things, protested against the Government's
attempt to redivide clan lands.[10] Explaining how the Hopi land
system worked, the petition stated:

During the last two years strangers have looked over our land with
spy-glasses and made marks upon it, and we know but little of what
this means. As we believe that you have no wish to disturb our possessions, we want to tell you something about this Hopi land.

None of us ever asked that it should be measured into separate
lots, and given to individuals for this would cause confusion.

The family, the dwelling house and the field are inseparable, because the woman is the heart of these, and they rest with her. Among
us the family traces its kin from the mother, hence all its possessions
are hers. The man builds the house but the woman is the owner, because she repairs and preserves it; the man cultivates the field, but he
renders its harvest into the woman's keeping, because upon her it rests
to prepare the food, and the surplus of stores for barter depends upon
her thrift.

A man plants the fields of his wife, and the fields assigned to the
children she bears, and informally he calls them his, although in fact
they are not. Even of the field which he inherits from his mother, its
harvest he may dispose of at will, but the field itself he may not. He
may permit his son to occupy it and gather its produce, but at the father's death the son may not own it, for then it passes to the father's
sister's son, or nearest mother's kin, and thus our fields and houses
always remain with our mother's family.

According to the number of children a woman has, fields for them
are assigned to her, from some of the land of her family group, and
her husband takes care of them. Hence our fields are numerous but

[10]This document, in the collection of the National Archives, is dated March
27 and 28, 1894 and is addressed to "the Washington Chiefs." It is signed by
123 clan and village leaders from all three mesas. It expresses concern not only
for the government's attempt to reallocate clan lands but also for the lack of
clear-cut Hopi boundaries that would keep out the expanding Navajos. It is
generally accepted that the petition was drafted by Thomas Keam, the trader
after whom Keam's Canyon is named.

small, and several belonging to the same family may be close together, or they may be miles apart, because arable localities are not continuous. There are other reasons for the irregularity in size and situation of our family lands, as interrupted sequence of inheritance caused by extinction of families, but chiefly owing to the following condition, and to which we especially invite your attention.

In the Spring and early Summer there usually comes from the Southwest a succession of gales, oftentimes strong enough to blow away the sandy soil from the face of some of our fields, and to expose the underlying clay, which is hard, and sour, and barren; as the sand is the only fertile land, when it moves, the planters must follow it, and other fields must be provided in place of those which have been devastated. Sometimes generations pass away and these barren spots remain, while in other instances, after a few years, the winds have again restored the desirable sand upon them. In such event its fertility is disclosed by the nature of the grass and shrubs that grow upon it. If these are promising, a number of us unite to clear off the land and make it again fit for planting, when it may be given back to its former owner, or if a long time has elapsed, to other heirs, or it may be given to some person of the same family group more in need of a planting place.

These limited changes in land holding are effected by mutual discussion and concession among the elders, and among all the thinking men and women of the family groups interested. In effect, the same system of holding, and the same method of planting, obtain among the Tewa, and all the Hopi villages, and under them we provide ourselves with food in abundance. . . .

The Texts

The texts in this collection include myths, legends, and clan chronicles; stories of migrations and events behind the abandonment of villages; tales of adventure, personal exploits, human endurance, and macabre happenings; and comments on or explanations of traditions, beliefs, and history. They come from tape recordings made in or near the Hopi villages at various times during the years 1968–76, and again in 1981, and have been transcribed as literally as possible, though with occasional minor rephrasing and editing for readability. Tenses and genders sometimes have been altered to avoid confusion. Any other alterations by the editor appear within brackets, and footnotes are employed for general observations that might be of value to readers.

This is not, of course, the first collection of its kind to appear in print. A distinguished collection of Hopi narrations, *The Traditions of the Hopi*, was published by H. R. Voth in 1905.[11] Some of the narrations given here deal with traditions or recollections told by Voth's informants, and comparison of the variants will be of special interest to students of the Hopi scene. A number of the texts, however, are, to my knowledge, in print for the first time. One of my primary informants was Albert Yava, of Tewa Village, but only a few of his texts are included for the reason that most of what he had to tell forms the substance of another book, *Big Falling Snow: The Life, Times and Recollections of a Tewa-Hopi Indian* (1978).

Many Hopis know something of Voth's work, not only his *Traditions* but other writings as well. More than a few of my informants and narrators contended that Voth frequently misunderstood what was told to him, or that he was told things known to his informants to be untrue, or that he obtained information from unknowledgeable persons. Voth was a Mennonite missionary, and some persons expressed the conviction that no "true Hopi" would give a missionary anything but the most superficial kind of information. Others condemned him for his rude intrusions into Hopi ceremonial life, as well as for his publicizing of kiva secrets. And at least one person believed that Voth's knowledge of the Hopi language was rudimentary, and that he therefore could not have understood everything that was told to him.

Some of the criticisms of Voth and his writings appear to contain elements of truth. By all reliable accounts, he was unpleasantly aggressive in his intrusions into kiva ceremonies, and he did not indicate to the Hopis that he planned to publish his discoveries. His translations on occasion indicate misunderstanding, and some of his texts suggest that he either had a poor informant or that this informant willfully distorted information.[12]

---

[11]See also Ekkehart Malotki, *Hopitutuwutsi*; H.G. Lockett, "The Unwritten Literature of the Hopi"; and W. D. Wallis, "Folk Tales from Shumopovi, Second Mesa," *Journal of American Folk-Lore*, Vol. 49, 1936.

[12]See text 39, "Comments on Voth." In his book *Big Falling Snow*, p. 107, Albert Yava says: "That missionary Voth who set down all the stories he heard over there in Oraibi translated masauwu as 'skeleton.' I think that the man

Despite all this, *The Traditions of the Hopi* remains a notable collection of Hopi oral literature and an invaluable basic reference. It gives us a good picture of what the oral literature was like some seventy-five years ago, just before the breakup of Oraibi, which damaged that village's ceremonial life beyond repair. Voth's *Traditions* has to be a point of reference for any collection published since his time. One must refer back to Voth to help answer such questions as: To what extent, and in what form, have Hopi oral traditions survived in the face of the white social intrusions since the turn of the century? To what degree have they been modified by contact with white religious proselytizers, or affected by new technological knowledge, or even by anthropological knowledge and a more objective view of who the Hopis are and where they came from? And what themes in the Hopi oral literature have the more enduring content?

Some of the material included in this present collection of texts has been drawn on for an earlier book of narratives, *The Fourth World of the Hopis* (1971), but none of those narratives was rendered literally, and many of them were composites combining information or details provided by a number of persons. The texts given herein are those of individual informants or narrators, unadulterated by the views of other Hopis, and, in the literary sense, unmanipulated for effect. Each informant tells only what he himself recalls, knows, or believes.

Certain brief texts taken alone may seem trivial, but I am convinced that each one of them contributes something worthwhile to the total picture of the Hopi narrative tradition or to an understanding of Hopi thoughts on the past and the present.

Some Shared Traditions

Numerous elements in Hopi traditions, myths, and beliefs echo themes familiar to other Indian cultures in the Americas. The Eastern Pueblos, the Navajos, and others, as well as the

---

who translated for him probably didn't know English too well. A masauwu isn't a skeleton, but the breath or spirit of a person who has died. Masauwu as a proper name means the Death Personage who owned all the land in this Fourth World when the people emerged from down below."

Hopis, believe that their peoples passed through a series of worlds before arriving in the present world. Counterparts of the Hopi Pokangs, the Warrior Brothers, are found elsewhere in North, Middle, and South America. The tradition of some Hopi clans that Huruing Wuhti, Hard Substances Woman, created humans and animals out of cuticle rubbed from her body is paralleled in other Southwestern cultures. The belief that the first humans had to struggle against primeval monsters or giants for survival, and the myth of destruction by flood (central to the Hopi story of Palatkwapi) are likewise widely shared, as is the conceit that spirits of the dead eat only the odors of food and throw the food itself away. So, also, is the concept of Coyote as trickster, buffoon, and culture hero.[13]

Sharings of this kind may be quite ancient, since those wandering groups that eventually became Hopis had contacts with Indians of the Great Plains to the north and east, with cultures far to the south in what is now Mexico, with the Eastern Pueblos, and probably with groups west of the Colorado River in what is now California. Ingathering clans that came to rest on the Hopi mesas are described in Hopi traditions as speaking languages (in addition to those of the Eastern Pueblos) such as Shoshonian, Athabascan, Piman, and Yuman. Although there were stretches of time during which the Hopi mesa villages were relatively isolated, there probably was never a period when the process of cultural exchange was not at work. This does not mean that Hopis were merely part of a generalized Indian culture. Some aspects of Hopi beliefs and traditions are uniquely their own, created out of their specialized experiences.

European Cultural Intrusions

While the Eastern Pueblos had to live under Spanish and Catholic domination almost continuously following Spain's conquest of the Rio Grande region, except for a brief respite following the Pueblo Revolt of 1680, the Hopis were too remote from the center of colonial rule to receive much attention. Catholic

[13]Stith Thompson, *The Folktale*, pp. 303–18.

missions were eventually established in the major Hopi villages, but they were destroyed during the Pueblo Revolt, and except for one unsuccessful attempt at the end of the century, no
effort was undertaken to reestablish them. When Hopis of several villages went to war against Awatovi in the year 1700 or
thereabouts, they killed or scattered a population said to have
been significantly converted to Catholicism, a situation they
equated with corruption and evil. After that event (which has
continued to haunt Hopis who regard themselves as the Peaceful People), there was no further direct Catholic influence in the
Hopi villages. However, there was continuing contact with the
Eastern Pueblos, who were absorbing elements of Spanish and
Catholic belief.[14]

It is difficult to assess what non-Indian concepts might have
entered Hopi life during the period of the Catholic missions, or
from contact with the Eastern Pueblos. The concept of Maski,
the Land of the Dead, certainly seems to echo Christian teachings about limbo and hell. But if the fiery pit does in fact derive
from Christian theology, the theme has been so thoroughly
"Hopi-ized" that no one can make the assertion with authority.

Contacts with the "Anglos" from the east came in the mid-
nineteenth century, following the Treaty of Guadalupe Hidalgo
of 1848, by which Mexico ceded to the United States those southwestern territories comprising what are now New Mexico, Arizona, Nevada, California, and Utah. Missionary efforts to wean
the Hopis away from their traditional religion came soon thereafter. A century of proselytizing efforts has certainly contributed
to the fading of old Hopi traditions, and elderly Hopis speak
often of the decay of the ancient ways. Yet though numbers of
Hopis have fallen away from religious traditions of the past, the
traditions themselves survive in the kiva societies and in the
clans, weakened, no doubt, but persistent. One might reasonably expect that elements of the new religions on the Hopi mesas

---

[14]For a good account of the Pueblo Revolt and the subsequent sacking of
Awatovi, see Montgomery, Smith, and Brew, *Franciscan Awatovi*, pp. 18 ff. An
interesting account of the Awatovi affair in the oral tradition is to be found in
Yava, *Big Falling Snow* pp. 88–96. A Reed Clan version is given in text 15 of this
collection, "The Destruction of Awatovi."

would infiltrate the old beliefs. It is hard to know the extent to which this has occurred. But wherever old traditions are still reflected in narrations of clan or village experiences, Christian influences are not readily evident. It would be incautious to ascribe Christian origins to certain elements of Hopi tradition that seem as if they *might* be non-Indian intrusions.

For example, there is the Hopi belief, based on ancient prophecy, that a good bahana, or white man, was to come from the east, bringing harmony, moral leadership, and well-being to the Hopi people. Hopis generally say that the prophecy was made at the time of the emergence from the Third World. Some non-Hopis have grasped at this tradition as a non-Indian intrusion, an idea introduced by missionaries to enhance their proselytizing opportunities. But elderly Hopis born before the first Mennonite mission was established in Oraibi reject this supposition. They insist that the tradition was passed on to them by preceding generations.

Analogies with Indian traditions known farther south dispel the supposition of a missionary intrusion in regard to the coming of the good bahana. The classification of the Hopi language as Uto-Aztecan signals something to us about ancient Hopi connections to the cultures of Mexico. And we know that Toltec mythology speaks of a bearded, light-skinned king-deity by the name of Quetzalcoatl who sailed away eastward, promising that he would return at some future time.[15] This is not an isolated parallel with Middle American traditions. We also have Quetzalcoatl as an Aztec plumed serpent god to compare with the Hopi Water Clan's Paleuleukang, a horned serpent god.

Although European-Christian elements and motifs do not appear to have been substantially absorbed into Hopi traditions as revealed in narratives, they do seem to have penetrated into the thinking of some narrators. As a result, uncertainty is sometimes expressed about the meaning of a story, even about the "facts" asserted by the story. The village of Oraibi had a well-established Mennonite mission by the early years of the twentieth century, and Moencopi, a satellite village of Oraibi, had a

---

[15]See notes on Quetzalcoatl by George M. Foster in *Dictionary of Folklore, Mythology, and Legend*, p. 915.

Mormon mission until, under pressure from the government, the Mormons abandoned their holdings around Tuba City. It is not surprising, therefore, that doctrines of these cults influenced Hopi concepts. One elderly informant in Moencopi identified the place of Hopi origins as Jerusalem, from where, "somehow," the people got to North America. Before reaching the Hopi mesas, they had to contend with such enemies as Chinese, Mongolians, and Navajos. In Oraibi, another informant, an elderly man, expressed some doubt about the emergence myth, especially the climbing of the bamboo to reach the upper world, adding his belief that the Hopis "might have come from Mother Earth in Jerusalem." In speaking of the prophecy that all Hopis would be reunited when the migrations were completed, he said, "Maybe some of them will go to heaven and some of them will go to hell." Another elder of Oraibi rationalized that the emergence story was for children, to hold them until such time as they would be initiated into a kiva society, when they would be given a more sophisticated explanation of Hopi beginnings.

There is also apparent among some narrators an awareness that science and new knowledge have overrun old beliefs, that myths and legends must be explained by reference to facts and events known to the white man. An informant in Oraibi perceived a pumpkin filled with ashes, used in the Masauwu ceremony, as a symbol and prophecy of the nuclear bomb. In Walpi, a narrator noted that astronauts had just landed on the moon and wondered if that might not be the destination of another Hopi migration—in effect, the Fifth World.

Narratives as Property and History

Although many of the stories coming from the Hopi mesas are, one might say, in the public domain, the closer narratives get to mysteries of the kivas or the religious aspects of clan experiences, the more inhibitions are placed on them. This applies to the telling of stories not only to outsiders, but within the villages themselves. Certain stories or accounts or explanations are, in effect, properties of particular clans or fraternities. Asked to speak of details of his clan's origins, a Hopi might respond that he had been warned never to talk about such things. Or he might say that he first must consult with his "uncle" (a clan senior or a ceremonial sponsor), who would advise him whether he could say anything. On occasion, a Hopi would indicate that a particular story belonged to a different clan and that he didn't have the right to tell it. In part, this reluctance or inhibition reflects a sense of propriety as well as an awareness that the true facts about a particular tradition are known only to the authorized custodians of that tradition. It would be presumptuous for a member of the Tobacco Clan, for example, to try to explain the meanings and symbolism of a Snake Clan ritual. To know about the Water Clan, one must go to the Water Clan, and to know about the Bear Clan, one must go to the Bear Clan. Thus each clan is shown respect, its knowledge and status defined, as well as its rights.

While many stories are of the entertainment variety, some of them are ingredients of clan chronicles or doctrines, and though they contain what we usually define as myth or legend, they are seen as history. And because this "history" is not written, but preserved orally through stories, songs, and ritual dramas, great attention must be paid to their accuracy. Therefore, clan (or kiva society) authority is of great importance. A responsible person will not chance mutilating facts. And if he is knowledgeable, he will tend toward literalness in story narration. He will be attentive to what kind of a tree grew in a certain place, or to what direction a man took in departing from a village, or to what kind of a prayer feather was made, not because that detail is meaningful to the outcome of his narrative, but because that is the way the story was told to him, the way it really happened.

One story in this collection, "The Village at Lamehva," was narrated only after permission was given by the clan chief concerned. Another, an account of the destruction of Awatovi, was told by the chief of the Walpi clan that was directly involved in that event. He stressed that only his clan knew all the details of the destruction, and that people of other clans and villages had badly mangled the story.

Still, it is generally acknowledged that different clans may be authorities on different aspects of a particular happening. So, while the Reed Clan in Walpi may be the authority on the attack against Awatovi, the Tobacco Clan, which lived in Awatovi at the time the attack came, may have other knowledge of the event.

It should be added that among many Hopis there is now a special reluctance to give stories—particularly if they concern ceremonial life or religious matters—to outsiders. Early in the century, Hopis were much more open in speaking to students of their culture than they are at present. Current attitudes reflect strong feelings that knowledge gatherers of the past have unscrupulously exposed kiva secrets in books, photographs, and museum displays, both breaching confidence and vitiating the strength that derives from secrecy. A particular ceremony or a particular story may be regarded as property. Thus some Hopis have complained that the Navajos not only stole their land and livestock, "they stole our ceremonies too." They perceive no flattery or compliment in imitation. Hopi traditions are regarded as belonging to the communities in the same sense that village sites do. While white visitors are welcomed to kachina dances, they are prohibited from bringing cameras and tape recorders into the villages.

There are some Hopis who do not feel this rigid possessiveness about traditions and narratives, but who nevertheless are inhibited by the thought that the white man cannot possibly understand such things because of his general ignorance about the Hopi culture. An outsider watching a kachina dance may take in visually everything that is done, but the complex of symbolic meanings eludes him—the designs of the masks, the paraphernalia of the costumes, the words of the songs, the colors used to paint a dance staff. They all refer to something behind the dance itself. One informant said with conviction, "A white man will never . . . understand a Hopi. He can live his whole life in the village and not understand us. You have to be born a Hopi and raised a Hopi to understand how we think. Almost everything we do is a religious act, from the time we get up to the time we go to sleep. How can the white man ever understand that?"

Recurring Themes in Hopi Narrations

Flight from Evil

The themes of dissension, flight from evil, and search for harmony are first sounded in the emergence myth. The people are motivated to leave the Third World because witchcraft—

medicine used for evil purposes—is making life unbearable. When the people have found a way of climbing up to the Fourth World, Spider Old Woman warns them that they must be sure to leave all the "evil ones" behind, lest they contaminate the new land above. When the emergence is completed, however, it is discovered that a witch or sorcerer has arrived in the upper world, undetected until too late. From that time onward, the people are to be plagued by confrontations with evil in various forms, including dissension and the loss of respect for the wisdom of elders. The theme reappears in numerous clan stories and tales recounting the corruption that caused the fall and abandonment of villages.

Palatkwa (or Palatkwapi), the ancient legendary village in the south claimed by the Water, Tobacco, Sand, Rabbit, and other clans, repeats the experience of the Third World: people become careless in their ways, lose respect for the kikmongwi or chief, fail to care properly for their fields, gamble and frolic instead of working, violate propriety in sexual relationships, and harass the elderly instead of taking care of them. Seeing that everything is hopeless, the kikmongwi, by the use of mysterious and powerful medicine, causes the destruction of the village and forces the survivors to begin a new migration to a place where they can begin life anew with a more sober awareness that people must lead decent lives. (See text 6, "The Palatkwapi Story, I," and text 8, "The Palatkwapi Story, III.")

Again, in "Destruction by Fire" (text 19), the morals of the people of Pivanhonkapi degenerate—women are raped, the chief's wife is seduced, and the people prefer gambling in the kiva to caring for their fields and families. In desperation, the chief sends for persons with powerful medicine and has them destroy his village. Thus the people of Pivanhonkapi are forced out into the wilderness to wander and leave evil and corruption behind.

Awatovi, another village where morals deteriorate to a point where the kikmongwi can no longer cope or command respect, suffers a similar fate. The evils that infect Awatovi are the usual ones, but there is a new element as well. Many Awatovis have converted to Catholicism, and the village is split into two factions. From the Hopi point of view, the apostasy of the Catholic converts is the focus of the infection because it rejects the wisdom and teachings of the elders, disparages traditions, and flouts the very scheme of life. So the chief goes to Oraibi and Walpi and asks the authorities there to destroy Awatovi, which they do. (See text 15, "The Destruction of Awatovi.")

The theme of a chief having his village destroyed because of its corruption was sufficiently familiar in the oral literature for one of Voth's informants to have said: "This is the way chiefs often punished their children (people) when they became 'bewitched.' That is one reason why there are so very many ruins all over the country. Many people were killed in that way because their chiefs became angry and invited some chief or inhabitant from other villages to destroy their people" (*The Traditions of the Hopi*, p.256).

A variant of this widespread theme is that friction between two villages causes one of them to abandon its site and go elsewhere so as to leave dissension behind. We see the people of Sikyatki moving away because of difficulties with the Walpis (text 11, "The Dispersal from Sikyatki, I"); the Lamehva people moving away from their village because of trouble with Kaiotakwi (text 16, "The Village at Lamehva"); the Payupki people leaving because of trouble with neighboring Tsikuvi (text 20, "The Races at Tsikuvi"); and the people abandoning Huckovi because of difficulties with the neighboring village of Pivanhonkapi (text 18, "The Spruce Tree Ceremony at Pivanhonkapi"). Frictions between clans within the same village also launch people into new migrations, as in the story of how the Snake Clan departed from Tokonave to begin its journey to the Hopi mesas. (See "Tokonave: The Snake and Horn People," in Courlander, *The Fourth World of the Hopis*, pp.82 ff.) The best-known historic instance of clan frictions breaking up a village is the Oraibi split of 1906. Confrontation between the Bear Clan on one side and, on the other, the Coyote and Fire clans over the question of relationships with the whites and the government resulted in an unhealable breach and the rapid decay of the village and its religious organizations. (See text 40, "The Split at Oraibi.")

How many of the old, now extinct, villages really parted from one another because of social stresses, and how many were abandoned or destroyed because of corruption, we shall probably never know. In oral literature, we often encounter "explanations" devised long after facts have been obscured by time and distance. It may be that the theme of escape from corruption and dissension was drawn on by narrators to fill voids in knowledge, or to make moral points. Yet because it is encountered so frequently, we have to regard it as having major importance in traditional Hopi thinking.

Hard Work in a Hard Land

In Hopi tradition, hard work in an inhospitable environment is both a virtue and a fulfillment of prophecy, and the motif comes to the surface now and again in clan stories, histories, tales of personal adventure, and even animal tales. The prophecy dates back to the emergence from the Third World and the division of the corn among the tribes. (See text 1, "The Four Worlds and the Emergence," and text 2, "Emergence: Choosing the Corn.") Each tribe received a different variety of corn and a corresponding group personality and a destiny. The Hopis received the short blue ear, the symbol of a hardworking life. The Navajos received a large ear, and consequently did not have to work so hard to survive, while the Hopis had to become devoted farmers and grow more corn ears to keep themselves alive. But hard work in a hard desert environment was not only destiny, it was also virtue. Clan stories sometimes tell of the search for a rugged land of cliffs, buttes, and sparse water that other peoples would not covet. Not only would such a place be secure against human predators, it would keep alive the work ethic and prevent the moral deterioration that comes with easy living.

Some accounts of the destruction of Palatkwapi, for example, say that life became too easy for the people, and that life became corrupt. (See texts 6, 7, 8, and 9.) Likewise, clan stories explaining the abandonment of Kawestima—the complex of cliff dwellings in the area of Kayenta, Arizona—say that water was too abundant there and crops too bountiful, for which reason the chiefs ordained that the people must move to a less favored region so that their religious values could be preserved. The various wandering clans that gathered in what is now Hopi country, it is explained, believed that the rocky land with much sand

and little water was a place where the people could live righteous lives.

The mythology of the destined hard life, often reflected in narrations, was the basis on which conservative Hopis refused for a long while to accept offerings from the white man, such as drilled wells and running water, that would make for easier living. They feared what convenience and plenty might do to the human spirit and —even more important—to the delicate balance of social forces. Long after standpipes were available in some of the villages, many of the older people still descended to the springs and carried water home on their backs.

The "work ethic" as we generally understand this term is frequently stressed in Hopi narrations. Again and again we hear of the young girl working at her grinding stones. If a young man comes to get acquainted with her in the evening, after the field work is done, he usually finds her in the grinding room kneeling over her work, and there she may continue her labor even after others have gone to sleep. If her family accepts a young man's marriage proposal, she works for days grinding corn to be taken to (among others) the young man's mother. Acceptance of the corn gift signals approval by the young man's family. In time of hardship it is proper to work without complaining. Even at such times (as in text 58, "The Girl and the Kachina"), a person should never stop giving thanks to the Creator (or other deities) for what one has, and for the gift of life.

New and sometimes disturbing elements have intruded into the traditional Hopi view of life, but work, the challenge of a hard environment, endurance, and gratitude for one's existence remain implicit elements in many Hopi narratives.

Running, Racing, and Gambling

Running, racing, and gambling contests of various kinds appear not only in stories of individual adventure and achievement but also in myth-legends, clan and village "histories," and tales of awe and wonder. Fleetness of foot and endurance are regarded as supreme psycho-physical accomplishments. We hear again and again of races between villages and of individual running feats, not only in the old stories but in recollections of more recent times. In Oraibi there are older people who recall challenges by footracers of Walpi, and in Walpi there are stories of challenges from Oraibi. People speak of how only a few generations ago the men and boys of Oraibi would gather early in the morning to run in a group to Moencopi (some fifty miles away), cultivate their gardens there, and then return running to Oraibi. In Walpi there are recollections of Hopi mail carriers who ran mail from Keam's Canyon to Holbrook, about seventy miles, in a single day.

Such stories and the exaggerations they may have undergone in the telling reflect the traditional value placed on footracing, not only as social competition but also as an expression of community (and religious) vitality. The so-called kachina races, in which young men attired in kachina costumes challenge the young men of neighboring villages, are believed to bring a blessing or good medicine to the people. In the kachina races of earlier years, religious connections were more visible than now. The personators of the kachinas prayed and purified their thoughts in the kivas before the races took place. Festive and secular as the races might seem, they carried the meaning of good fortune, rain, and fertility. The racing that takes place each year in the Horn and Flute rites is strictly ceremonial.

In the old stories about clans and villages, racing usually takes place as a result of invitation or challenge. Though the races begin in a social atmosphere, in the end they may prove to have important, even grave, consequences. In many tales, the races escalate from tests of speed and strength to competitions between medicine and counter-medicine, witchcraft and counter-witchcraft, drawing on the dynamic forces of nature that reside in animals or inanimate objects. In "The Races at Tsikuvi" (text 20), for example, both sides invoke the intervention of magical elements, and the consequences of the races are so serious that the people of Payupki are forced to abandon their village. Even where witchcraft is not introduced, as in "The Dispersal from Sikyatki, I" (text 11), the contest may be laden with serious implications. The Sikyatki race ends with death and the scattering of the people of the village.

One recurring motif is that of a father or chief instructing a son or nephew to condition himself to become an excellent runner, with the purpose (usually unrevealed) of preparing the young man for a test or an ordeal to come. Thus, in "The Palatkwapi Story, III" (text 8), the young man practices running as a prelude to a series of ominous events that end in his death and in the destruction of Palatkwapi by earthquake and flood. Again, in "The Boy Who Crossed the Great Water" (text 54), a young man practices running in preparation for a long journey in which his speed and endurance will be crucial to his survival. In this instance, his father also instructs him how to train himself for arrow shooting and playing stick ball, two other activities on which his survival will depend.

Another recurring motif is that of boys racing against girls or competing against them in the game of shinny. In some of these competitions, the girls contrive to win by raising their skirts and tucking them into their belts. The sight of the girls' thighs (and possibly more) so distracts the boys that they cannot keep their minds on the game, as in "The Boy Who Crossed the Great Water."

Other forms of gambling contests, frequently for crucial stakes, also appear in Hopi narrations. In "The Boy and the Eagle" (text. 53), the young protagonist is forced to play for his life with Hasokata, North Wind Old Man. In this case, the game is totolospi, a reed- or stick-throwing game scored by combinations of odds and evens. The boy loses, and he is put on a shelf to die in the bitter cold wind. However, Spider Old Woman sends a party of kachinas to Hasokata's kiva, and they have another contest with Hasokata with the boy's life as the prize. The kachinas plant corn and other crops on the kiva floor and sing and dance to make them grow, while Hasokata sends down freezing winds to counteract the kachinas' medicine. The kachinas win, and the boy's life is saved. A variant narration has the contestants playing the ball-and-cup game. In another story, "The Races at Tsikuvi" (text 20), there is a gambling contest between Payupki archers and a Spaniard with a musket, the crucial stakes in this event being cattle.

The outcome of a historical event in this century—the breakup of Oraibi in 1906—also hung on a contest, a "push-of-war" between those who favored cooperation with the whites and those who opposed cooperation. The Friendlies won, and the

Hostiles departed from Oraibi and built new villages at Bakavi and Hotevilla.

In three stories in this collection, the winner (or winners) of a race take the women of the defeated village as prizes. (See "The Races at Tsikuvi," text 20, "The Boy Who Crossed the Great Water," text 54, and "The Dispersal from Sikyatki, III," text 13.) It is difficult not to see in this element of the racing theme a metaphoric allusion to a former practice of taking women from villages or tribes defeated in battle. Older Hopis acknowledge this to have been a practice in "early" days and suggest that this is how certain clans came to be represented among the present-day Hopi villages. This is supported by nearly all accounts of the destruction of Awatovi ("The Destruction of Awatovi," text 15), in which many young women and girls were captured and divided between two (in some versions, among three) Hopi villages.

Indeed, it is interesting to speculate on the element of allusion in the recurring motif of gambling contests with grave consequences. It is possible that such contests, though they are no more than contests in the mind of the narrator, are distilled symbols of violence that does not correspond to the "Hopi Way." In "The Dispersal from Sikyatki, III," the disguise is carried to the point where birds, not humans, are the protagonists of the struggle.

As to the reliance on gambling to resolve dilemmas and stalemates, we may also speculate on its function as a derivative of divination, as a mechanism of establishing order, and even justice, out of chaos and chance.

Transformations: Man-to-Animal, Animal-to-Man

Hopi lore is full of transformations of humans into animals and animals into humans. A person enters a kiva belonging to bears, snakes, antelopes, or coyotes and sees these creatures remove their pelts and hang them on the wall. With their skins thus removed, they become humans, though obviously humans of special endowments. In "The Village at Lamehva" (text 16), dogs remove their pelts and take on human form. In "Honwaima and the Bear People" (text 57), it is bears who perform this act, and in "The Antelope Boy" (text 56), antelopes. Whenever Hopi narratives refer to "antelope people," "swallow people," "snake people," and so on, they are speaking of persons or groups of persons who spend part of their time in one form, part in another. Such beings frequently are possessors of special knowledge or medicine, such as the art of healing. In one version of the Palatkwapi story, a young man who is killed and buried in the plaza becomes transformed into a deity, the One-Horned Water Serpent. In a story in this collection ("A Wife Who Joined a Secret Society," text 55), a woman is turned into a mule as punishment. In some tales, people are punished by being turned into coyotes or other less than noble creatures such as beetles.

While there is mystery and wonder in tales featuring such transformations, there is little surprise or disbelief because Hopis, like many other Indian groups, see the dividing line between various living forms as tenuous. As one informant stated, "Animals do not look like people, but they think like people do, and they are really people under their pelts."

Animals as Messengers or Agents

In numerous stories, birds or four-footed creatures serve as messengers, advisors, servants, guards, or scouts for village chiefs, medicine men, or other important personages. Thus, in "The Boy Who Crossed the Great Water" (text 54), an eagle serves as lookout for the chief of the distant village where the boy is forced to compete for his life. The eagle reports to the chief in detail as the boy approaches. Later in the story, when the boy is being pursued, his father sends for bird messengers of his own, an owl and a crow, and instructs them to do certain things to slow down the pursuers.

In "The Races at Tsikuvi" (text 20), Spider Old Woman calls on her servant, a hawk, to knock down a footracer who has turned himself into a dove. In "The Village at Lamehva" (text 16), a snake, a deer, a bear, and a mole—servants of the chief of the dog people—guard the trail to the dog people's kiva.

The animal-messenger or servant is credible in traditional Hopi belief to the extent that animals and humans are thought of as closely related. Believability is heightened by the roles of animals in myths and myth-legends. Choronologically, we have our first animal messengers in the emergence story, widely regarded as literally true. Whereas Noah's messenger, the dove, could convey his message only by carrying a fragment of an olive branch, Hopi animal messengers speak, think, and usually behave like humans. And they bring to their work certain aptitudes, sometimes related to medicine or magic, that humans do not possess.

Journeys to Distant Lands

Quests and journeys to far-off lands are featured in numerous Hopi tales, both in the legends that are regarded as "history" and in tales of human accomplishment. In the legend of the Snake Clan's beginnings and its migration from the north, a young man travels in a hollow log down the Colorado River to the sea, where he discovers the snake rituals that are preserved to this day. (See Yava, *Big Falling Snow,* pp.55–59.) Again, in the origin story of the Reed Clan (text 16, "The Village at Lamehva"), a young man makes a long journey through dangerous country to a place called Suchaptekwi, where he obtains his village's first hunting dog. In "The Boy Who Crossed the Great Water" (text 54), a young man makes a long trip to bring back wives for unmarried men in his village. In one narrative of adventure and exploits, a boy is carried away to a far-off place in the sky called Tokpela (Endless Space) by an eagle, and his journey is in reverse, back to his home village. (See text 53, "The Boy and the Eagle.") "The Land of the Dead" (text 24) tells of a young man who performs the incredible feat of going to the place where the spirits of the dead reside and returning again to the land of the living. (See also the version in Yava, *Big Falling Snow,* pp. 99–104.)

The Number Four

The number four runs through Hopi oral literature as it does through Hopi life. There are four sacred directions. Events occur in sequences of four or multiples of four. When the force of medicine is set into motion, its consequences become fully evident on the fourth day. A migration may take four years, or a clan arrives at its destination after four stops (though sometimes the arrival is calculated as the fourth stop).

Thus in the emergence myth, four birds are sent from the lower world to investigate the world above. The people plant four different things to grow up and serve them as a means of exit from the lower world, and only the fourth (a bamboo) is successful. The land into which they finally emerge is the fourth world. The people then chant the sun into the sky, and it is on the fourth chant that they are successful.

The legends and clan histories also depend heavily on the number four. For example, in the Palatkwapi story (texts 6, 7, 8, and 9), a young man practices for four days to become a fleet runner. He comes running to the village four times as an omen. He wears four masks, one on top of the other. He is captured, killed, and buried in the plaza, and on the fourth day following, Palatkwapi is destroyed by earthquake and flood.

Even in what might be described as "secular" stories (though Hopi tales are not easily classified in this manner), the number four appears in almost every context. It measures days, years, a series of efforts or events, whatever requires measurement. In rituals, the number four is sacred. In workaday life, it is always significant, sometimes mysterious or ominous.

Miniature Magic

In numerous Hopi narrations, miniature objects have the force and power of larger counterparts. A pebble has the weight of a boulder; a tiny feather has the warmth of a blanket or the strength of a tree branch; a spark has the heat of a fire; a drop of water quenches thirst and a single grain of corn staves off starvation; and a human is able to pass through the small hole of a ground spider.

A number of these mini-magical motifs occur in various versions of "The Boy and the Eagle" (text 53). In this tale, the protagonist is carried away from his home on the back of an eagle and deposited at the very top of a spire of rock in a world in the sky, called Tokpela. A tiny bird brings him a seed of some kind to assuage his hunger, and a taste of water from its mouth. Then it pulls out its feathers and places them in cracks in the rock wall, in the fashion of a mountain climber's metal spikes, and carries the boy down to safety. At a certain place, he is invited by Spider Grandmother to enter her underground kiva. The entrance is only the small hole of a ground spider, but the boy nevertheless enters. Later he is captured by North Wind Old Man, stripped of his clothing, and forced to lie in the frigid cold. When Spider Grandmother finds him freezing to death, she places a turkey feather on him and he is warmed by it. Finally she lowers him from Tokpela to the world of people on a spider web.

Recurring Characters

Gogyeng Sowuhti—variously translated by Hopis as Spider Old Woman, Spider Grandmother, Spider Lady, or simply Grandmother or Grandma—appears frequently in Hopi myths and legends, adventure stories, clan "histories," and Coyote tales, so often, in fact, that she might almost be regarded as a theme as well as an actor. She has two forms, that of a small spider and that of an aged, or ageless, grandmother. As a spider she lives below the surface of the ground in a small chamber likened to a kiva, from which she emerges through a hole compared to the sipapuni through which the people passed when they emerged from the underworld. In both forms, Gogyeng Sowuhti has ceremonial, medicinal, and perhaps social significance. As an old grandmother, she personifies goodness, justice, kindness, and permissiveness of human frailties. In one village or another, or in the desert wilderness, she endlessly comes to the aid of people in need or danger. Wherever humans feel helpless in the face of great odds or cruel injustice, Gogyeng Sowuhti may suddenly appear and help them with advice or the employment of medicine.

In both personifications, she represents the inner force of things, benevolence, and the spirit and the vital nature of the earth. She herself is living medicine, as Indians use that word. She calls forth the "breath" that resides in wild creatures and inanimate substances and conquers evils that have been turned loose through sorcery or malevolent thoughts of humans, witches, or monsters. In non-Indian terms, she is the magician par excellence whose role is to counteract what is malevolent and purify what is contaminated. No situation is too large for her to cope with or too small to claim her attention.

In "The Village at Lamehva" (text 16), she creates and peoples an entire village because her grandsons, the Warrior Brothers, are lonesome. In one version of the Awatovi story (text 15), she finds a young woman who has been kidnaped and punishes the sorcerer who has abducted her. In the creation myth (text 1), she guides the people up from the underworld and sends them on their migrations. In a story explaining how the Second Mesa village of Payupki was vacated, she helps the people win crucial footraces against a neighboring village and later assists them in an equally crucial contest with a Spaniard (text 20). Again, in a story about a great prairie fire created by sorcerers, she saves the village of Oraibi by weaving a magical web across the fire's path (text 19).

While Spider Grandmother's medicine is powerful, its nature is not different from that of human medicine men and women. It is distinguished mainly by her knowledge of what lies beyond the awareness of humans, and because it is always used with compassion and in the cause of justice. The myth of the emergence from the underworld usually tells that a sorcerer or witch came up unnoticed with the people. In some variants, Spider Grandmother advises the "wise men"—that is, the medicine men—how to loft the sun and moon into the sky, while in others, it is the witch or sorcerer who advises them (text 1). The achievement is the same in each case. The Hopi term powaka, which Hopis translate as "witch" or "sorcerer," means one who has enough knowledge of medicine to perform what non-Indians would call "magical" acts, and of itself it does not signify a doer of evil. One narrator spoke of Spider Grandmother as "kind of a witch." Another referred to the deity Alosoka by saying, "Now, there's another devilish thing." Another said of Masauwu, "He is a powerful one, can do all kinds of witchlike things." To the Hopi, therefore, the word witch does not necessarily have an opprobrious meaning. In the text cited above, the sorcerer is called "the evil one," a term possibly borrowed from Biblical literature. But the narrator quotes him as saying that "the evil one has a part to play in the world. You have to have the good and the evil."

Some accounts of the emergence and dispersal of the people from the sipapuni say that the sorcerer went south with the bahanas, or white people, accounting for the present advanced technological knowledge of whites. Another says that while the Hopis originally possessed the knowledge of witchcraft, they gave it to the whites to get rid of it. These and other explanations tend to equate witchcraft and sorcery with the terms medicine or knowledge (of how to put unseen natural forces into motion). So while Spider Grandmother performs "witchlike" acts, those acts are benevolent and sometimes on a grand scale. Moreover, she is seen by some Hopis as the archetype of the good grandmother, or the clan mother, tolerant and loving of young children, wise, to whom a person in difficulty may go for help.

Closely identified with Spider Grandmother are the Warrior Brothers, Pokanghoya and Palengahoya, usually depicted as carefree boys who live with Spider Grandmother. They hunt for her, gather wood, and do other familiar chores, but spend long hours of the day running about or playing nahoydadatsia, a form of shinny, with sticks and a buckskin ball stuffed with deer hair. In their childish personations, they are mischief-makers and pranksters, often teasing Spider Grandmother and subjecting her to anxiety and fright. But in the myths and myth-legends, the Brothers are revealed as culture heroes who perform great deeds of creation, such as turning primeval mud into mountains and buttes, and warrior feats such as destroying the earth monsters. (As mentioned previously, in their role as culture heroes, they resemble the Warrior Twins or Brothers of other Indian cultures. Among the Maya, for example, the brothers Hun-Apu and Xbalanque are the destroyers of Vukub-Cakix, the great earth giant.[16]) Pokanghoya and Palengahoya also intervene at times to protect migrating Hopi clans or the Hopi villages from human enemies.[17] They are often described as carrying thunder and lightning in their hands, natural forces symbolized in ceremonies and pictographs by bullroarers and lightning frames. In Walpi, the Warrior Brothers are claimed by the Reed Clan and the Warrior Society

[16]This story, originally narrated in *Popol Vuh* (Collection of Written Leaves), appears in Lewis Spence, *Myths of Mexico and Peru*.

[17]See Voth, *The Traditions of the Hopi*, pp. 56 ff. Here the Warrior Brothers defend the people against the Apaches.

as tutelary deities, while in Oraibi, they are claimed by the Sun Clan.

Other traditional personages who appear from time to time in Hopi narrations include Muyingwa, deity of fertility; Huruing Wuhti, deity of hard substances such as coral, turquoise, rock crystals, etc.; Masauwu, deity of fire and death; Tawa, the sun god; kachinas from San Francisco Peaks, or, alternately, from Navajo Mountain or the Land of the Cloud People; Hasokata, North Old Man, owner of the north wind who invites passers-by to gamble for their lives; and Goat Man, who captures and seduces young girls.

Although Coyote is featured in a cycle of tales in which he appears as a trickster and buffoon, he (or she) also performs solid good deeds as a minor figure in a number of narratives. In "The Antelope Boy" (text 56), for example, a female coyote saves a newborn baby from starvation by taking it to the Antelope People, and in "The Destruction of Awatovi" (text 15), Coyote helps to find a woman abducted by an evil sorcerer. In some creation stories, Coyote is present in the upper world at the time of the emergence, and one brief tale (text 64) tells how he placed the stars in the sky.

Humor in Hopi Narrations

Only those who have sat in the kivas night after night in the winter months listening to stories of all kinds can say with certainty how large a role humor plays in Hopi narrations. Others must assess the element of humor on the basis of existing collections of Hopi tales and on stories told by Hopi friends and informants.

The myths and myth-legends are generally serious and solemn, containing as they do the substance of religious beliefs and histories of the clans. Adventure stories—tales of personal exploits and accomplishments—likewise have little in them that outsiders, at least, will recognize as humorous. Narrations of this type strive to create awe and wonder, sometimes a mood of anxiety and fear or terror, and humor could only break the spell.

It is in the animal stories, frequently featuring Coyote, and the tales about the Warrior Brothers and Spider Grandmother that humor comes to the surface. Often it is a cruel humor involving abusing, maiming, or killing, but, in this respect, it is not greatly different from popular genres of tales told in Europe, Africa, and Afro-America. Just as the mischief-makers in the folklore of those regions are allowed to perform cruel, antisocial acts denied to real people, so the Warrior Brothers and animals in the Coyote cycle make people laugh by doing indecent things, by rolling Spider Grandmother down a hill for a game (or by killing her), or by causing a mother coyote to cook and eat her own young. Indeed, many of these themes are found in almost identical form in the folklore of a great part of the world.

Sexual explicitness that appears in some stories does not seem to have special humorous or titillating intent. It is usually nothing more or less than straightforward narration of events in which all details are faithfully recorded. Awareness of the white man's sensitivity to sexual and defecatory processes may cause a narrator to bowdlerize passages that a Hopi would take for granted.[18] Clown acts that take place on certain ceremonial occasions have been similarly affected. Whereas these comic scenes at one time contained some naked performers, and, on occasion, simulated copulation or sexual allusions, such things have been toned down or eliminated because they offended the white man's sensitivities. The most offended of all, of course, were the missionaries.

---

[18]A Hopi tale taken down by Malotki (a variant of a story in this collection) contains a description of a sorcerers' gathering in which the following appears: "It was obviously the sorcerer's intention to be the first to rape the girl. . . . When the old man got ready to climb on top of her, the [Warrior Brothers] let something loose into the kiva. . . . Thereupon the people in the kiva noticed that a fly had come in and said, 'Wait a minute, it looks as if something has come in.' They struck at it and killed it. Then the old man went back to the girl again. He climbed back on her and yelled, 'Now let me tear her hymen!' He was just at the point of penetrating her when [Spider Grandmother] released another animal. The very moment that the chief pushed forward, something snatched the girl from underneath him. So the poor old wizard poked his penis into the ground." (Malotki, *Hopitutuwutsi*, p. 85). My own version, "A Wife Who Joined a Secret Society"(text 55), contains nothing as explicit, possibly because it was narrated by a woman.

But the clown performances continue to entertain spectators by their accent on the ridiculous, on mimicry, on vaudeville-type dialogues, and on a great deal of slapstick. Very little of this type of humor is to be found in the oral literature available in published form, though it may be present in some of the wintertime storytelling sessions in homes and kivas.

The Hopis themselves, as a general rule, have a consciousness of humor in life quite comparable to our own, and it may be expressed slyly, guardedly, or robustly, though in some instances outsiders may miss the point because they lack the Hopi frame of reference.

1
MYTHS
AND
LEGENDS

—1—

*The Four Worlds
and the Emergence*[1]

From what I learned from the old-timers about the underworld and how the people emerged into this last world, they
weren't people in the First World, they were what you might call
just creatures, bugs. Finally some good spirit turned them into
different forms.[2] Said, "You can't live down here as bugs and
things like that. Go to the next world after I turn you into something else." So he [she] turned them into some other forms, not
really human yet, and led them into the Second World. They
were still animal-like, like wildcats or mountain lions, had tails.
But the ones that were going to become human beings, their
tails were just short. The ones that were going to be animals had
[longer] tails.

And when things got bad down there [in the Second World],
they began to eat each other. The good spirit said, "This won't
do. I'll take you to another world, the Third World." So they
emerged from that animal world to the Third World where they
really became human-like. They didn't have any language. They
conversed by making sounds like animals. They were living there
for a long while. Then it became worse again. "Well, I think I'll
take you to the next world. But there's somebody living there.
You'll have to ask permission. If he accepts you, you can go. I
have a way of [getting you to] the Second, the Third, and the

---

[1]A portion of this text, edited by the narrator, appears in Yava, *Big Falling
Snow,* but there are details here which are not included in that publication.

[2]Later, the narrator identifies the good spirit as Spider Old Woman.

3

Fourth World. But if you want to go up there you will have to ask permission."

The way it is told by the old people, the Third World was below the Fourth, down in the ground, and the Second below the Third, and the First below the Second. But I wouldn't say that meant down in the center of the earth, but it's just a way of describing a manner of existing. This good spirit that brought them up from one place to another called herself Mother Spider. She was the one that did it, according to Hopi tradition. When they were about to come to the last world she said, "This spirit up above is a pure spirit. Now you'll be going into the stage when you know bad from good. In order to be accepted, you've got to leave your bad medicine behind, do away with it. I see a lot of you here doing evil things. If you're going to be accepted, leave your [evil medicine] here when you come up to the other world where you are going to live if you are accepted." The spirit she was talking about was Masauwu. Fire Clan was the one that named him. Fire Clan became the Fire Clan when they identified with Masauwu, but how they came together they don't tell us. When they emerged to the Fourth World, the Fire Clan laid claim to Masauwu as their relation. But Masauwu didn't really accept them.[3]

The people who wanted to escape from the Third World decided to send a scout up to see what it was like up there and make contact with Masauwu. They chose a swift bird, the swallow. But he tired before he reached the sky and had to come back. After that they sent a dove, then a hawk. The hawk found a small opening and went through, but he came back without seeing Masauwu. Finally they sent a catbird. He was the one that found Masauwu. Masauwu asked him, "Why are you here?" The catbird said, "The world below is infested with evil. The people want to come up here to live. They want to build their houses here, and plant their corn." Masauwu said, "Well, you

---

[3]The narrator refers here to the Bear Clan tradition that the Fire Clan refused to lead the Hopis on their migrations in the Fourth World. The Bear Clan accepted the responsibility and was the first to reach Hopi country where Masauwu was living, with the result that it was given the land around Shongopovi.

see how it is in this world. There isn't any light, just greyness. I have to use fire to warm my crops and make them grow. However, I have relatives down in the Third World. I gave them the secret of fire. Let them lead the people up here, and I will give them land and a place to settle. Let them come."

After the catbird returned to the Third World and reported that Masauwu would receive them, the people asked, "Now, how will we ever get up there?" So Spider Old Woman called on the chipmunk to plant a sunflower seed. It began to grow. It went up and almost reached the sky, but the weight of the blossom made the stem bend over. Spider Old Woman then asked the chipmunk to plant a spruce tree, but when the spruce finished growing it wasn't tall enough. The chipmunk planted a pine, but the pine also was too short. The fourth thing the chipmunk planted was a bamboo. It grew up and up. It pierced the sky.

Spider Old Woman said, "My children, now we have a road to the upper world. When we reach there your lives will be different. Up there you will be able to distinguish evil from good. Sorcerers cannot come with us, or they will contaminate the Fourth World. So be careful. If you see an evil person going up, turn him back."

The people started to climb up inside the bamboo stalk. The mockingbird took the lead. He went ahead of the people, and every time he came to a joint in the bamboo he said, "Pashumayani! Pashumayani! Pashumayani! Pash! Pash! Pash!—Be careful! Be careful!" How they got through the bamboo joints I don't know, because it was never explained in the stories. The people kept going. They traveled in groups. Down below, the people chose who they wanted to travel with, and when they'd get to a certain joint in the bamboo, the mockingbird would look down and ask, "Is everybody coming?" "Not all of them. They're still coming." "Well, we're about in the middle. Is everybody prepared to come up?" "No, there are still some at the bottom. They're waiting for others to move up." The mockingbird moved to the next joint, said, "We'd better hurry on up. I'm going to ask again. Is everybody prepared to come?" "There's just a handful left down below."

The mockingbird said, "Be sure to leave the evil ones down

there." "Who are the evil ones?" "Oh, you all know who they are. We had plenty of evil down there. We don't want it up here in this world." People said, "Who are the evil ones?" The mockingbird said, "You know who they are." "We don't. How can we tell if we leave the evil ones behind?" Mockingbird said, "Well, he'll be along. If you see the mark on his face, that's the evil one." "What kind of a mark has he got?" "Oh, he's got a long nose, and the tip of his nose is always dark." They looked at one another and said, "Now, who in the world is that evil one?" They couldn't determine who the evil one was. "Well, we haven't seen anybody with that kind of nose. Everyone's got the same kind of nose we've got." They couldn't determine who was the evil one.

So they moved to the next joint. They had one more joint to go. "Now has everybody started up?" "Yes." The mockingbird said, "Whoever comes out [of the bamboo] last, close it up." The mockingbird came out first. He sat there near the opening, saying, "Pashumayani! Pashumayani! Take it slow, take it easy!" Then when about half of the people had come up, he started directing everybody where to sit. "Go to the left of the reed [bamboo], and the next group go to the right, and the next group in between over here, and the next group in between over there."[4] The people kept coming. "Now how many more?" "We're the last ones." "All right, close up [the end of the bamboo]. Here is some cotton I brought." They stuffed up the end of the bamboo with cotton. "Well, did we leave the evil one down there?"

They looked at one another. Then this fellow that represents evil laughed. "Haah! You can't get along without the evil one. He has a part to play in this world. You have to have the good and the evil, so I came up." "So you are here?" "Yes." "We didn't want you up here." "Why?" "Because you're always doing something evil that we don't like." "Yes, I know that. But somebody's got to warn you early in the morning when daybreak is coming."[5]

---

[4]Indicating the four sacred corners or directions.

[5]There is an implication here of the common identity of "evil," "sorcery," "knowledge," and "medicine." In the white man's frame of reference, *evil one* suggests Satan, and the term may actually be an intrusion, as is the word *witch*. As is seen in the deeds of the "evil one," his actions are of great benefit to the

"How will you let us know?" "Soon as you see the white streak in the place where the light is going to be from, I'll give you a cry that [day is here]." "What kind of day?" The evil one said, "We're in a kind of [half] light now, but there'll be daylight to come. There are a lot of wise men here. Let's first fix up the old sky. Anybody got a buckskin with no holes in it?" Somebody said, "Here's one." "Where'd you get a buckskin with no holes?" "I didn't have to shoot this deer. I just outran him." "Well, spread it out, spread it out." The people said, "What are we supposed to do now?" "These wise men will know. I'm the evil one. You don't want me to come around, yet I'm teaching you people how to go about it."

He said, "Now, you people are talking about light. [We are going to] put this buckskin way over on this side [of the sky]. And another buckskin over there on the other side. There's going to be two phases in this world, light and dark. Right now we can see a little bit, but the new light is going to be beautiful. There'll be one light for the day and another light for the night." So they covered one buckskin with yellow pollen. And the other they covered with a half-mixed pollen. The evil one said, "Now these two [buckskins] are going to be our main [sources of] light. They will play the biggest part. One is called tawa, the sun. The other is called muyao, the moon."[6]

"We've got to have some other things, too," the evil one said, "things that will shine in the night sky. Who's got some yelaha [graphite]?" Somebody said, "Oh, I have some." "Let me see it. Oh, that's too dark. I have some that's white." He took out his yelaha and began to fix up those things that would become stars. He said, "Oh, you are wise people, but not wise enough." He took his pouch of yelaha and scattered the contents [into the sky]. They began to shine and sparkle. "That's the way it's going to be." People were afraid, they bent their heads, saying, "You evil

people. Other versions of the emergence myth attribute his beneficent creations to Spider Old Woman or human medicine men. For comparisons, see H. R. Voth, *The Traditions of the Hopi*, pp. 13–15, 20.

[6]The narrator neglects to tell how the buckskins were lofted into the sky.

one, you evil one." He said, "Oh, that's not evil. I want the whole sky to be lighted at night, so that no matter where you are you'll be guided by these lights. In the daytime the sun will give you light. With the moon and stars in the night you'll be able to travel." One wise man said, "Good." Somebody said, "So you're in favor of the evil one?" The wise man said. "Well, there's some good about that evil one. I think he did the right thing." The evil one said, "This is the way it's going to be. So let us chant." They started to chant.

At about the fourth chant they began to see a streak, a light streak [on the horizon]. "One more will do it. Just keep it up. Nobody fall asleep. Everybody stay awake. Now it's coming." Everybody looked to the east, saw the rays of the sun shooting up. Heh! They began to see things. They hadn't known they were in such a beautiful world. They looked around. There were lots of trees, lots of grass, lots of flowers. The evil one said, "You see now the beautiful world you were brought to. That other one, the moon, will come at night. But now we've got to get together and see how we are going to live. Let the mockingbird tell us who is going to lead us." The mockingbird said, "It's up to you wise men to decide about that. Would the Fire Clan lead?" But the man who was head of the Fire Clan didn't say anything. He just shook his head. So one big husky man got up. He said, "Well, if you people [the Fire Clan] don't want to lead, I'll take the lead." All right. They had an emblem already, made out of feathers, turquoise, and other stones. Whoever was going to be the leader was supposed to use the emblem as a token of authority. They had brought it out with them from the underworld. The man who took the emblem said, "Before we go on, we want to distinguish ourselves as clans, like we did before in the old days down below, when we identified with this group or that one. Now in this lighted world we want to know each other, which group we belong to. I'll choose the bear again for my clan.[7] I'll take the responsibility for leading the people, since the Fire Clan leader doesn't want to. He's the one that came up into this world

[7]Other accounts, including one given by this narrator, say that the clans took their names in the course of their migrations, not at the place of emergence.

first, and he's the one who should be in authority. I don't see why he doesn't want the responsibility." The Fire Clan leader said, "It's too great a thing for me to control the people." "Well, I'll take it," the Bear Clan man said.

The mockingbird had a big job. As the people came up in groups he told them where to station themselves around the si-papuni and he told them what language they were going to speak from that time on. He told the men to sit in a big circle, and in the middle he put out a lot of different kinds of corn. White corn, yellow corn, speckled corn, red speckled, blue speckled, grey speckled, every kind of corn. And in amongst all the corn there was a short stubby blue ear. The mockingbird said, "Now, all these different kinds of corn mean something. This yellow corn means enjoying everything in life. If you have that corn you'll be prosperous. But you'll have a short life. This short blue ear means a lasting life, a long life. People won't die young, they'll grow old. But they'll have to work hard. It will be a rugged life for them." The mockingbird explained about every different kind of corn and what it meant, and he told the tribes to choose the one they wanted. The men in the council were thinking about which ones they were going to choose. There was one tall, slender man sitting there, and he didn't think very long. He was the Navajo. He reached out and took the yellow ear, the one that meant a short life but an enjoyable one. He said, "I don't know why it takes you people so long to decide. I'll take this yellow one. Even if my life won't be long it'll be enjoyable. I'll enjoy women, I'll enjoy riches, I'll enjoy everything." (It seems to be true that the Navajos don't live to be very old. They die younger than Hopis).

Well, then all the other people around the circle began grabbing the corn ears. The Comanches got the red corn. The Sioux got the white corn. The Utes got the flint corn with the hard kernels. (Those different tribes are using the same corn today.) Every tribe got one particular kind of corn. But the leader of the bunch that were going to be Hopis, he was slow. He kept on sitting there, thinking about which corn would be the best for him. The corn disappeared pretty fast, until there was only one ear left, the short stubby blue one. So finally he took that one. He said, "That's the way it's going to be. I'm going to have to work hard, but I'll have a long life."

The people were getting ready to disperse, to go on their migrations, but they discovered that a child had died, the son of one of the chiefs. The people were all mourning, wondering why the child had died. The evil one said, "Say, don't cry about this. Come over here and look down [through the sipapuni]." They did that, they looked down into the Third World, and they saw the boy walking and running around down there. The evil one said, "You see, he's alive." The people said, "If he's alive, then why did we have to send him back there?" The evil one said, "It wouldn't be good to have [the spirits of] the dead among you living people. When your stalks [i.e., bodies] are old and not useful anymore, you'll go on living down there. Your stalk will remain here, and your iksi [breath] will go below and go on living."

After that, the people started on their migrations, saying that some day they would all come together again.[8]

Nuvayoiyava (Albert Yava)
Tewa Village, August 1969

———2———

Emergence:
Choosing the Corn

When we people were down below somewhere [in the Third World] there wasn't enough light down there. We were doing our farming and everything all right, but that place wasn't so well lighted. When the sun came up, it was dim. Dim light we had there. We had discussions about that, and there were white

---

[8]Hopi tradition says that groups yet to become Hopi clans went out in different directions, with the prophecy that when their migrations were completed they would be reunited. Other Indian tribes also dispersed from the sipapuni, with the exception of some groups that claimed independent creation. Various Oraibi accounts of the emergence say that whites were one of the tribes. The whites are said to have gone south into what is now Mexico, from where the Spanish intruders came in the colonial period.

men as well as us in the meetings. We knew there was light up here, a bright sun, and we knew there was someone living in this place. So the people wanted to leave that place below and come to a better land. You know there is always a witch doctor around, a sorcerer. There always has to be one among the people, or maybe two or three or four. Those witch doctors we had were trying very hard to get us up from below, just like those people with rockets have been trying to get to the moon.

Well, they fixed something up for us, made some bamboo grow up very tall. They planted the bamboo so it would come through the sipapuni. The people got ready. What we had to eat in those times was corn, and so the women got real busy making somiviki for us to take along on our journey. And we got out of the underworld on the bamboo and came up here. We came out of the lower place through an opening like the entrance to a kiva, where the bamboo was sticking out. Like I said, we knew that there was somebody up here. Masauwu was living in this place. Before we came out, the people were worried about what the bright sun would be like. They made pahos for the sun and left them for him [at shrines], so that the sun wouldn't be too hot and burn them. Well, they got a message from the god up here, the sun,[1] and he said it would be all right for us to come. So we came into this world through the sipapuni. I don't know where the sipapuni is.[2] Maybe across the ocean, in Belgium or Asia. I know that's where Christ was born. It's somewhere around there, but that was before Christ was born.

Well, when we came out into the daylight we looked at one another. Some of the people were black, some were dusky, some people had white skins. All different kinds. When the people were all together there at the sipapuni, the witch doctors laid out a circle of corn in all directions. Many kinds of corn, white ears, yellow ears. Some of those ears were real good ones, some were pretty small and poor, didn't have many seeds on them. The witch doctors told the people to choose what kind of food they were going to eat in this place. All the chiefs were sitting around, white, Indian, and black. And the chiefs chose their corn

[1]The sun god, Tawa.
[2]Some Oraibis believe that the sipapuni is in Salt Canyon. First Mesa Hopis generally believe the location is lost to memory.

and grabbed for it. But the Hopi chief was slow, and there wasn't much left. All there was left for him to choose was that poor short corn. That's what he picked up. The Paiutes and Navajos had good corn, big ears. So we Hopis have that small, short corn today, and the Paiutes and Navajos have those good ears.[3]

After that the tribes separated. When the whites left, they promised the Hopis that they would meet them again some time. One of those white men was one of the witches that came up from below. Those whites knew a lot of things, how to travel, how to turn their bodies into coyotes or anything they wanted. Also, they could build anything. But they say that Hopis were like that too in those times. The Hopis really had a head on them, just like the whites do today. They could make anything, even like airplanes. They had all the knowledge of how to do things, of how to construct whatever they needed in this world. But the Hopis decided that they didn't want it. They gave it up. They got together all their witch outfit [paraphernalia for performing sorcery] and gave it to the white men.[4]

Pautiwa (Ned Zeena)
Walpi, August 1969

———3———

Reflections on the Emergence

I'll tell you one thing, I don't hardly believe [that the people climbed up from the Third World in a bamboo]. I know that story a little bit, but I'm not interested in that. They can't do any-

---

[3]For a comparison with this scene, see Voth, *The Traditions of the Hopi*, p. 21.

[4]The terms *witch* and *medicine man* are frequently used interchangeably by Hopis, and both terms can have benign as well as malignant meanings, due in part to the inadequacies of translation into English. *Witch* is used by Don Tala-yesva in his book *Sun Chief* to refer to practitioners of bad magic. Some accounts of the emergence say that miracles were performed for the benefit of the people by Spider Old Woman, while others say these acts were performed by an "evil one" or sorcerer. See Yava, *Big Falling Snow*, pp. 40–41.

thing [like that] unless they've got two horns.[1] Maybe the Two Horn people had some power to plant that—first they planted that spruce, but when they came up to the top it bent down. Then the second time they planted a bamboo, and that is the one they [climbed]. How in the world could they climb on that small stalk? That's one thing I don't believe. I think we might have come from Mother Earth in Jerusalem somewhere. I think we must have come from across the ocean. They say they made a ship out of that moose [?] skin.

When the people came up from the underworld [according to the story], the daughter of one of the leaders died, because of bad people [sorcerers]. She [the sorcerer] told them, "Look down [through the sipapuni], there she is playing with other children." That's what she told them. They were going to kill her, but they believed [what she said]—that when a person finishes with this world he goes down there and lives with those people. But I don't know, they might have fled from something that was real bad in the underworld and come up to the upper world where it would be safer for them. That's what I think. See, my own idea. They had some kind of a power, maybe they were what Hopis call two-heart people, powaka. I[2] couldn't invent anything [as a way of fleeing] from the underworld. How could I come up to this upper world?

They said first that they heard footsteps in the upper world. How could they hear that far away? Up to the upper world? How could they hear a footstep? I believe we were the Lost Tribe, like the white people were telling us. We are living peaceably now, but a long time ago we were [the Lost Tribe]. They say that a bunch of those people disappeared and haven't been found. Maybe they're at Old Oraibi now. Those people roamed all through the wilderness clear up to Canada and [down to] Mexico.

Masauwu was the one that was making the footsteps in the upper world. He lived in different places [in the upper world]. Each [village?] had their own place where their Masauwu was. There was supposed to be quite a number of them. There couldn't be [just] one Masauwu.

---

[1]That is, unless they belong to the Two Horn Fraternity.
[2]Meaning ordinary persons like himself.

He owns the fire. Fire Clan and Masauwu, that's one clan. Then the Juniper and the Sagebrush clans, and Coyote. [They are affiliated.] And I think that [group] includes the War Twins [clans?][3] because they are the warriors.[4] Those people, those clans, are the ones that are supposed to be the warriors to protect the people if they are attacked. Those Twins are the head gods of the Fire Clan. My wife belongs to the Masauwu Clan.

Chuka (Don C. Talayesva)
Oraibi, July 1970

———4———

Origins

My uncle has been telling that story about where we come from ever since I was a kid. Most of that story I can't tell you. My uncle said, "Keep it to yourself." But I can tell you a little part. In the beginning, he told me, we started from Jerusalem. He was an old man, but he still knew about that Jerusalem. I don't know where that is. Well, that's the place where we're from. And then somehow we got up to the north of this country. They'd been traveling a long ways. There were people somewhere in that other country, they had hair just up here, long braids. They must be Chinese. There were some people somewhere [over

[3]One does not often hear of these clans. Fewkes, in his article "Tusayan Migration Traditions," lists a Pokanghoya Clan and a Palengahoya Clan in the same group as the Reed Clan, which on First Mesa claims the Warrior Brothers as its tutelary deities.

[4]That is, the Fire and Coyote clans and their affiliates have the responsibility of defending the village. The narrator refers to Oraibi. In the First Mesa villages, the Reed Clan claims the Warrior Brothers and is, or was, responsible for the defense of the villages

there] in Mongolia. There were Navajos. Russia and Germany. That's all he mentioned. But they were enemies. They didn't care who you were, they'd kill you and eat you. That's the place where we are from. And my uncle said we were over at Mesa Verde, and we left there in 1600.[1] Then we located at Oraibi in 1150.[2] That was before Columbus discovered America, 1492. I'm Bamboo Clan, and Bow and Arrow. We were the first to come. Other clans came afterward.[3] All these ruins around here belong to the Hopis. They'd been traveling all over looking for somebody, or somebody's footprint. That's when we learned nobody was here, just the animals, no human beings. We were the first to come here, so they told me.

Louis Numkena, Sr.
Moencopi, August 1968

———5———

*Beginnings of
the Bear Clan*

It was the time when people had no clans. Nobody belonged to any clans. They roamed around in the wilderness. Well, the first ones came to a dead bear. And they saw that this bear must have been a powerful one and a good healer. So they named their clan after the bear. That was the first bunch. The second bunch came [to that place]. The bear was getting rotten, but the skin was still good, and they cut it and made a rope [strap] out of it.

[1]That is, his group, the Bamboo Clan.
[2]Narrator meant to indicate that Hopis in general, not his group, settled at Oraibi at this time.
[3]To Hopi country.

That rope came from the same bear.[1] Then the next bunch came and there was grease in the head around the eye [sockets]. They became Grease Cavity Clan. Then next came the Bone Clan.[2] The next one that came to the same place [saw that] a gopher had built a home there,[3] and became Gopher Clan. Another group came and saw that in the eye socket of the bear the spider had made a web, and they called themselves the Spider Clan.[4] Everything had to do with that dead animal. All the groups were related because of that. I've heard that in Walpi the Spruce Clan is mixed [affiliated] with the Bear Clan.[5] They all scattered but were supposed to come back together again. We'll come back together when we are finished with this world. Maybe some of them will go to heaven and some of them will go to hell.[6]

Chuka (Don C. Talayesva)
Oraibi, July 1970

—————6—————

The Palatkwapi Story, I

A Walpi Tobacco Clan Version

We Tobacco Clan people used to live near Phoenix some-where, over at Superstitious Mountain, that's what we were told.

[1]The narrator forgot to mention that this group became the Strap Clan.

[2]This clan is not mentioned on First Mesa. Presumably it named itself after the bones of the bear.

[3]Under the skeleton of the bear.

[4]The narrator mentioned this later. It has been interpolated.

[5]On First Mesa, the Bluebird Clan also is affiliated with the Bear. The name was adopted because a bluebird was seen at the same site.

[6]For another account of the Bear Clan naming, see Yava, *Big Falling Snow*, pp. 50–51. Also, Voth, *Traditions of the Hopi*, p. 37.

Tobacco Clan, Frog Clan,[1] and Sand Clan, we were all together at that place. I forget what Superstitious Mountain was called in the Hopi language. There was a village there on a kind of a mesa. I think it was a big village. The people were living there for a long time. Everything was okay. Then the young folks began to not mind their parents. They didn't want to do the things they were supposed to do. They didn't want to follow their religion. The old folks were trying their best to talk to the young ones about the right way of living, but the kids didn't pay any attention to them. They just wanted to go ahead and do whatever they wanted. Everything got bad. The young men started to go around and get the young womenfolks and rape them. They did everything. All kinds of bad things were going on.

The village chief didn't know what to do. He was a Frog Clan man, the clan chief. So he went to the Sand Clan chief and the Rabbit Clan chief—the Tobacco and Rabbit clans were sort of together then, and the Rabbit Clan chief was the same as the Tobacco Clan chief—to talk about it and see what could be done. Now, there was a boy in the village, a young man maybe sixteen or seventeen years old who was living according to his religion. He wasn't going around doing bad things. He was helping his family. His name was Chung'eu, Smoke Pipe. The chiefs knew about him and talked about him. Well, it was very bad, all those younger generation were going crazy, doing crazy things. That's the way they were.

So one of the chiefs said they should send for Suyoko [Soyoko], that giant man who comes around in the village and tells people how to behave. This one's name was Tsaveyo. He's the one with the big mouth [i.e., jaws], black face, and eyes sticking out. They wanted to call him to come and give the people advice about their religion. They called Chung'eu over and told him that he would be the Tsaveyo. They told everything to him. At first he didn't want to do it. He was afraid. But they had a meeting for four nights [to talk about it]. Finally he said he would do it. So they had it announced to the people that someone was coming to talk to them about how they'd been acting.

[1]Implying all the clans of the Water Clan group.

They took this boy Chung'eu in the kiva, and they had him there four days and four nights, talking to him, telling him what to say to the people. He got everything in his head. On the fourth day they were getting him ready. He brought his mask into the kiva. They started dressing him, putting his costume on him. Then they took him out somewhere below [the village] to wait. When the time came the chakmongwi, the village cryer, went up on top of the roof and started announcing that someone was coming on the road trail to see the people. He was coming, all right. That Tsaveyo was a husky man. He had that stone axe in one hand and a spear on the other side. Feathers around his head. He had those shells on all around him, and every step he made, it gave off sounds. He was acting like he was pretty mad. He looked pretty awful. Well, all the people were around the edge of the mesa looking down below and seeing that something was coming. He was carrying a big basket.

When he came up to the mesa [top], the chiefs went over there to meet him. They put down a prayer stick for him to go over it. They welcomed him, and asked him why he had come. He told the chiefs that he had come to talk to the people, they weren't behaving and minding their religion, and that's what he was there about. The chiefs took him over to the plaza and he started talking to the people. He had a big voice. Well, some of these kids, when he said something they'd just laugh. They didn't seem to mind [object to] him. He got through speaking about everything. Spent the whole day talking. I guess about half of the people got ashamed of what they'd been doing. They wanted to stop [their bad actions] and be with their religion again. But the other half of the people didn't care. When it was all over, they sent the Tsaveyo back home.

The village quieted down for a while, maybe a year. Everything was all right. Then it started again, and now the bad ones really made trouble. They [some men] went and raped the chief's wife. That was the end. The chief got real mad. So he got together with the Smoke chief [Tobacco Clan chief] and the Sand Clan chief, he gathered them up and they had a talk. He said he was really angry about what happened [to his wife], what they'd done to him. The village chief had a young daughter two or three years old named Kachinmana. He was so angry that he wanted to give that kid away to someone. And he wanted all the people to get out from there [the village]. The chiefs wanted to call someone else [another monster]. This one was the big water snake. That's the one they were asking for to come. The village chief wanted to give his daughter away to the snake.

They set a date when they wanted that to happen. They wanted that snake to come right out of the sipapuni that was in the plaza. They wanted him to come out right there. So they announced what was going to happen. Well, everybody was just laughing, they didn't believe it was going to happen. Before the fourth day came the buildings were cracking up. An earthquake was shaking things, and parts of the mesa were falling off. Then people began to get scared. The Tobacco Chief wanted to leave the place with some of the persons who were behaving well, who still believed in their religion. So they were getting ready, picking out things to take along, like their tipuni [tiponi, sacred clan symbol] and all such things. The Tobacco Clan was ready to go. They were the ones that left the place first. They went off a little way. They wanted to watch what was going to happen. So they just camped down below the mesa. Next was the Sand Clan. The Sand Clan chief wanted to go too. He took half of his people, and they went down the mesa in a different direction from the Tobacco Clan. And the Frog Clan was the only one left in the village. It was the Frog Clan that had the power to call the water snake. They were the ones who were responsible for everything that was happening.

The village chief was going to leave the little girl in the plaza for the water snake. They took the little girl, the daughter of the chief, down to the spring and dressed her, down by the water hole. They used the moss from the water hole to make black marks on her. They painted her legs black halfway; also they painted her cheeks halfway across and put a feather in her hair. They put an ova, a bridal shawl, around her. Then they took her to the plaza of the village and left her there. There were people in the houses, bad people who didn't go with the Tobacco and Sand Clan chiefs. They still didn't believe what was going to happen. This was on the fourth day, and around twelve o'clock the whole place began to shake again. This time it was bad. The bad people had to come out of their houses because now they were really scared. They didn't know which way to go and so they gathered in the plaza. And they saw the little girl sitting there, dressed that way. Then the houses began to fall down and water started coming out of the kiva. Everything got flooded, the plaza and the rest of the village. Pretty soon that big water snake—they call him Paleuleukang—came out of the sipapuni. Put his head high up in the air so he could look around and see everything. He had a big horn on the back of his head. And those people there in the plaza were really scared, because the village was getting flooded and all their houses were falling down.

Well, the water snake saw everything. He saw the little girl sitting there. She didn't seem to be afraid of him. So he picked her up and went down with her through the sipapuni, took her into his kiva down below. After that, the village chief and the Frog Clan went out of the village. They were the last ones to go. But they made the bad people stay behind. The last thing that happened was that the whole plaza caved in, sank into the ground. That village was completely gone.

That's when all those clans started north. They all lived together at Homolovi for a while—that's down near Winslow—and after a while, I don't know how many years, they came up this way. Frog and Sand clans came here to First Mesa, but we Tobacco and Rabbit clans joined that village over on Antelope Mesa, Awatovi it was called. We stayed over there for a long time. We only came over here when Awatovi was destroyed. At that time the village of Sikyatki was still alive over there. Walpi was up here, the people had moved up from the old village down below. That's when the Tobacco Clan came to this mesa.

Postscript to the Narration: I'm a Tobacco Clan person. I became a Tobacco Chief at one time, around 1932. I was chief till my uncle took me out. So I can tell you something about the Tobacco Clan coming here. When Awatovi was destroyed, the Tobacco Clan leader over there took all the sacred tiponi and things and brought them here.[2] He went clear up to the end of the mesa there, where the Snake Rock is, the Masauwu shrine,

[2]The narrator here refers not only to Tobacco Clan paraphernalia, but to the altars and other sacred objects of the Two Horn, the Wuwuchim, and the Tataukyam kiva societies. Those three fraternities are widely recognized as having originated at Awatovi.

brought all the sacred things from the Awatovi kivas. All the sacred things that we have now are from Awatovi. We still use them there. The other villages just copied these things. But the original ones, we still have them in Walpi. The other villages copied these ceremonies too.

Pautiwa (Ned Zeena)
Walpi, August 1969

—————7—————

The Palatkwapi Story, II

An Oraibi Coyote Clan Version

According to the story, there was a big disaster at Palatkwapi, a flood which destroyed almost the whole village, and most of the people deserted the place. The whole court [plaza] was covered with water. And there was one man who wanted to come down [from his housetop], but the water was too deep. Another man came to the foot of the ladder to help him, and they saw a water snake right in the middle of the pahoki, the shrine, sort of standing up. And the two men were afraid. They said, "Look what's over there!" They said, "I don't know what all that means. He's a water snake." But the court was enclosed [on three sides] and they had to pass by the water snake to get out. They were walking in the water and they kept watching the water snake. He was a big one. While they were passing the water snake he spoke to them.

He said, "Where are you men going?" They told him they were going to follow their people who were going up north. There was another group going down south, the water snake told them, and in that direction it was all desert and no place where you could rest. "Take a little piece [of my skin] from my neck," the water snake said. The snake had furry skin, and the fur around his neck was beautiful. They were looking at it and asking, "How are we going to take it off?" He said, "You have a knife." They said, "Yes, we have a knife." It was a stone knife, a flint knife. They said, "What are we going to do?" He said, "Just walk over here. Don't be afraid. I'm your uncle." That's what the snake told them, "I'm your uncle, so just come up and take part of my neck [skin] up here." They said, "Okay, we'll take some of the skin off." They took a little part of the skin. He said, "Don't be afraid, take as much as you can. It's just part of the food, made out of [corn] mush."[1]

So they took off a big piece of the skin, with meat, scalped him. He said, "That will fix you up. You carry this along, and in case you have a drought, or if you have some ceremony, remember me on this. When you make a paho, take two or three hairs off and use them in the paho, and I will send the rain up there." So that's what happened and they started off.[2] After a long walk they found their people who'd gone on ahead.

Most of the houses in the village were down. Everything was destroyed. But there were two places, two houses that were still standing, and there was a man living in each house. One was a blind man and one was a cripple who couldn't walk. One morning the crippled man and the blind man were calling on each other [for help]. "Oh, I didn't know you were still here. I'm here too." They began to talk about how they were going to get out of the village and go north. The blind man said, "Well, you're able to see, but can't walk. I can't see but you can see. I could carry you on my back, and we can start in the morning." So they agreed to do this.

All the next day they went north. Finally toward evening the crippled man saw a deer. The blind man was pretty able-bodied, and all that day the crippled man had been guiding him, "Go this way, go that way." And now the crippled man saw a deer close to the mountain. He told the blind man to stop. He had a quiver on his back, and a bow. He said, "You can stop here and I'll try to kill the deer." He got the deer. The blind man

---

[1]This appears to refer to the idea that "corn is our body, corn is life."

[2]This portion was originally told later. The narrator asked that it be positioned at the beginning.

said, "What shall I do?" And the crippled man said, "I'll direct you. Walk ahead, I'll tell you where to go." And going that way, they got to the carcass of the deer. This was in the evening. After they'd butchered the deer they got some wood. And they were very happy about successfully hunting. The blind man said, "This is a very handy way of hunting game." And of course they were happy to still be alive, so they could follow the people going north. When they were ready to roast [the meat], they said, "We'll first roast the head because it isn't [too] big, and all day tomorrow we can dry the meat, we can put it out and let it sun-dry." So they both agreed and built a fire. The blind man ran around doing things and the crippled man just sat there giving directions. They started the fire with flint, and when they got the fire going they put the deer's head on the fire to cook.

That meat must have smelled very nice, very sweet. They were sitting around talking about how far they might have to go to find the people, said, "We've got enough meat here to take care of us." The lame man said, "How are we going to carry all this meat with us? You have to carry me and I'm heavy." The blind man said, "Well, we can just dry this meat up and stack it up, and I can carry the meat and yourself." But while they were talking, something appeared a little ways off, and it circled them. The crippled man said, "There's something coming. It's some-thing like a bogey man. Something that's got big googly eyes, a big mouth with [large] teeth."[3] He had his bow and arrows. He said, "What shall we do?" "I don't know what we'll do." The crippled man was ready to shoot. The thing kept circling around. The lame man was watching, holding his bow and arrow, watch-ing the fierce-looking thing. And all at once he shot the arrow. He didn't hit the monster, but he hit the deer's head that was on the fire. And it blew up [with a loud noise]. It was [like] light-ning. The crippled man jumped up. And the other man's eyes were opened, he could see. They were so excited they didn't know what to do. The lame man was running around saying, "I'm not going to sit down. If I do I might go back [lame]." And the blind man was saying, "What's this all about? Look at these stars. I'm not going to go to sleep, I'm going to stay right here

[3]A Soyoko monster of some kind.

[looking]." All night they were doing that till the morning. The bogey man went away somewhere.

They finally got their deer meat prepared [and dried] in the sun. They were resting there all day. They also had the skin. Some day they were going to take the fur off of it. The next day, when the meat was all dried up, they got ready to go. They cut around the edge of the skin to make string, and they tied the meat up. Then they started off. They traveled pretty slow through the mountains. But one time they traveled all night and they caught up somewhere with the main group that was going north. They saw a bunch of people ahead of them. Now they were both walking, both men were whole again, carrying the meat on their backs. The people were very surprised. They wondered how the lame man could walk and the blind man could see. So those two men told their story.

The people in the group were of different clans. Of course they all traveled on foot, because they didn't yet have burros or anything like that. Womenfolks were carrying cooking vessels and menfolks were carrying the rations. And the children, everybody had to help. Right there where the lame man and blind man caught up with them, they made a little shrine. Of course they always carried little feathers along, and so they left prayer feathers [on the shrine]. In several days they were coming to the San Francisco Mountains [Nuvatikyao]. They left shrines wherever they stopped. At last they came to the big peak where Flagstaff is. It was a high mountain.

There are volcanoes up there. My grandmother says that during her childhood one of those volcanoes was in action, erupting. It's the one they call Sunset Mountain, Sunset Crater.[4] Now, when those people from Palatkwapi arrived there, they settled all around that place. They settled several places. I know there are a lot of ruins around there. They made a nice home there. During the winter, they went down in the canyons and trapped some animals. But on account of the volcanic eruptions they were

---

[4]The San Francisco Mountains are of volcanic origin, and there are numerous craters in the region of Flagstaff. However, the last eruption of Sunset Crater is believed to have occurred in A.D. 1064. People then living in the area undoubtedly passed down the story of the event, and Hopi memory sometimes plays false as to when it actually happened.

afraid. And they left again. They started to follow the Little Colorado River [eastward]. They came to a place where Winslow is now. The place they settled was called Homolovi. And then some of them went from there in different directions. I believe it was the Sun Clan that settled at Homolovi.

At that time this land around here was full of vegetation. The clans that reached Homolovi divided up, made an agreement. "We'll circle around, and if we find a good place, we'll stay, but then we'll go on looking some more." One thing they never forgot is that they were looking for a promised land. They always remembered that they were looking for a land where they could find good things. They could have fruit and good water, all good things. So some of the clans went south and some went along the Little Colorado River. Most people went north. Someone discovered that there was a village up here at Oraibi, and they went back and told the other people.

Those two men who had been crippled and blind were with the Sun Clan, because those people thought these men had something to do with the Warriors, Palengahoya and Pokanghoya. One of the Sun Clan people said he'd go and find out about those people living at Oraibi. They were living in the cliffs at that time.[5] Also some Reed Clan people went to investigate. And they found that the people living around Oraibi were sort of pioneers, and that they spoke a language something like the language the Palatkwapi people spoke. The Reed Clan people said to them, "Well, we'd like to come and live with you." And the Oraibi people said, yes, okay. But they had four years to wait, because the Hopis always counted in fours. In four years the Reed Clan came again, and the Oraibis said, "Well, I'll probably recognize you pretty soon. What clan do you belong to?" "I'm Reed Clan." "What kind of [ceremonial] duty do you have?"[6] They told him. (Each clan has different important things that they do.) They said, "We are the clan that owns the kachinas. We can prophesy how well the people will [fare] each summer, according to the kachinas." The Oraibis said, "Well, I guess that will be all right." But they took another four days to answer no or yes.

So the Reed Clan waited near Oraibi for another four days.

---

[5]Old cave dwelling sites are to be found within a few miles of Oraibi.
[6]Each clan had to have something of ceremonial value to contribute.

But while they were camping out there they carried out some ceremonies. It was during winter, and snow was on the ground. But in the place where the Reed Clan was camping, flowers were growing in the ground. The Oraibi chief said, "Well, these people have something." In four days he went to the Reed Clan and said, "You're welcome." So they began to move up. Here they came, but they came dressed up like kachinas. And like in the midwinter Bean Ceremony, they carried lots of green things [that they'd grown down there].

The Sun Clan came next. They told the Oraibis, "We belong to the sun and control the [summer] heat and all that. We get the plants growing." The Oraibis said they could come, so finally the Sun Clan went up and joined the village.

Now, some of the people in this migration [from Homolovi] didn't go toward Oraibi. They came to a place below First Mesa where there was a good spring, a wonderful artesian spring. This was Sikyatki, but there wasn't any village there then, just a spring. These people had a piece of the water snake's skin with them. What happened, when those two men left Palatkwapi with the skin they got from the water snake's neck, after they caught up with the others they divided the skin among all the clans, so each clan had a small piece. Where Walpi is today, at that time there were only a few people living up on top.[7] The clans that settled at Sikyatki were the Coyote Clan and the Fox Clan.[8] and there was one other that I don't remember.[9] Three clans. There were about a hundred people. They made a village there, copied after their old village at Palatkwapi. They made a court and houses like they were in the old village, and shrines too. And they stayed there many years.

> Homer Cooyama
> Kikeuchmovi, July 1970

[7]During the time of Sikyatki's existence, the people who later founded Walpi were living on a lower shelf of the mesa in the village of Keuchaptevela.

[8]Hopis on First Mesa say that the Coyote and Fox clans had no part in the Palatkwa story but came from the Rio Grande pueblos. However, all agree that Sikyatki was a Coyote Clan village.

[9]The Fire Clan, also called Masauwu or Ghost Clan, affiliated with the Coyote Clan, is generally believed to have shared the original settlement.

————8————

The Palatkwapi Story, III

An Oraibi Sun Clan Version

I understand that the Sun Clan came from the underworld, down in the Salt Canyon where the sipapu [sipapuni] is. After they got out from that place, the Spider Woman divided them up into certain groups, and each one took its particular kind of corn. Then they started out in every direction. [Some of them got to Palatkwa.] I don't know what state that Palatkwa was in. It's down south. Called Red Mother Earth, that's what it said in a book. I don't know, I just been figuring that we might not be Hopis, we might have been Papago Indians, because they come from the south where Palatkwapi is. Well, we Sun Clan are from there, and different clans that made settlements at First Mesa and Mishongnovi. But I'm talking about my group.

In the old times [at Palatkwa], people were living happily, peaceably, helping each other. When there was some kind of work to do for somebody, they'd all unite. Then, in so many years, they were getting to be bad. They went into the kiva and danced there and gambled there and a lot of them made private business there among those others. It was getting to be bad. And they took all the kind-hearted good women, and it didn't sound very good. And one of the chiefs had a wife, they took her too. He was thinking about what he could do to quiet them down, make them behave. So he studied that for a while, then he found a way to do [something] with the people.

He had a nephew. He called him to come to his house. He talked to him about those things that had to be done. He didn't tell him the whole story, what he'd been thinking. "Now you run. Four mornings you run and practice up. Then when you think you are swift enough, I'll tell you what is next." So the nephew practiced up every morning, ran about five or eight miles, came back and took a bath when he came to the spring. On the fourth day, in the evening, his uncle called him again.

"Now," he said, "you are going out to hunt deer. You go to them and chase them. You'll have a bow and arrows. You'll have a sharp knife. Put it in your belt, wear it peacfully." It was a knife case, you might say. "Then that old deer, he won't be able to run the whole day. If he gets tired he'll break off from the bunch. Chase that old deer, and when you catch him, cut off the horn[s], not the antlers, but the [two] small horn[s] on each side. Cut them off, bring them to me."

So the young man went out and chased the deer. A little after noontime the old deer broke off from the bunch, he was getting tired. He went on for a while, until the young man caught him by the horns and knocked him down. And he cut off the short horn[s]. And the deer began to cry like a Hopi. "Poor thing, me! Is this the problem [thing] you are going to do?" But the boy didn't answer him. He didn't know the purpose of cutting off the horn[s].[1] He brought the horn[s] to his uncle, and they laid them by the fire and they prayed and smoked.

Then the uncle said, "Now, I'm going to make the masks for you. You will wear them and go to their kivas where they're having a good time every night. Like a ghost." So he made four masks. That first night he dressed the nephew up, painting his face with a red line across the center of the nose, and putting beads close around his neck. Then about midnight he put four masks on him. Told him to go out someplace and then come down to the village. He was supposed to go on top of a house three or four stories high and grind corn[2] and that would notify them, to let them know what you are. So the first night he went up to the top house and ground corn and sang some kind of a

---

[1]Different renditions of the Palatkwapi myth-legend explain the need for the horns, or sometimes a single horn, in different ways. In most, the small or spike horn eventually becomes a distinguishing anatomical feature of the horned water snake, Paleuleukang. In others, the uncle furrows the ground with the points of the horns as a way of stimulating the earthquake and flood that destroy the village. For an explanation of the horns as earthquake medicine, see Yava, *Big Falling Snow*, p. 66.

[2]That is, go through the motions of grinding corn, or grind on a mata without corn. This motif figures in a number of stories and is intended to have ominous implications.

song. When he finished, he came down and went away in the same direction from which he'd come.

And there was one man in the village, a quiet, nice fellow, was sitting at the mouth of the kiva and he saw that ghost. He told the other people that he'd seen something. They acted kind of brave and said they were going to catch him. "We're going to catch him and hang him." That's what most of them said. "We can hang him in the plaza and the next day we can see if he's a ghost or a human being."

A section of this narration dealing with the capture of the young man, his execution, the destruction of the village by earthquake and flood, and the exodus has been lost. There follows the part of the story dealing with the migration northward from Homolovi, on the Little Colorado River near present-day Winslow:

[While the people were at Homolovi] they saw the children coming, the two children who were carrying the flesh from the water snake's neck. When the children arrived, their parents were glad and wept over them. Then they quieted down and departed from that place and went [northward] through these Hopi buttes. The last Hopi buttes out that way, they passed there and went a couple of miles and then they made a settlement there.

One of those groups of people belonged to the Cistern Clan,[3] and also [there was] the Corn Clan. They were chiefs of the Lakone Ceremony [Lalakontu, a women's society]. They were going to try to bring luck. So they had a ceremony there and made a paho and used a tiny piece of the [water snake's] flesh. They put it in a dish and used it for painting the prayer stick. Then they deposited the prayer stick. And the earth began to shake again. It rained pretty hard. They believed they'd put too much flesh on the paho. They thought they'd have to be very careful. Thereafter when they were going to use the flesh again they'd cut out a tiny piece, using a small measurement.

From there they went on through these buttes till they came to Kwatufteika, Eagle Mesa Point. They made a settlement there.

[3]The Water or Rain Cloud Clan and its affiliates.

And from there the clans began to separate. Those that had the Paleuleukang flesh [the Water Clan group] went to First Mesa and some to Mishongnovi. Our people [the Sun Clan] weren't sure which way they were going to go. So they sent a messenger over to Awatovi to ask if it would be all right for them to come and live there. They knew there was a village there because in the morning they could see smoke over there, and they could also see smoke at Shimopavi [Shongopovi]. When the messenger arrived he asked if the people could stay in Awatovi. But the chief said, "Well, but there's no place for you to stay. We're all filled up." No success. The messenger came back and repeated what he'd been told. Then they saw that smoke rising from Shimopavi in the afternoon. And they sent another messenger over there.

He went to Shimopavi and asked the chief if they could be accepted there. He said, "All right, if you're not powakas [sorcerers or witches]. Maybe some day we'll want to get help from you. Good hospitality." So the messenger went back and told what the chief had said. Four days afterward, that same night a lady gave birth to a baby, and that is how the Sun Clan people got divided. Early in the morning the first bunch left [the encampment] and went up to the village. They got to Shimopavi just as the sun was rising, showing his forehead. And so they were called Kala, Forehead Clan. That's how they got that name.

The second group that was delayed by the lady who had a baby, that's my group, the Sun Clan. They arrived there at noontime when the sun was in the sky. We were the last people that assembled there from wandering around the wilderness. At that time, Shimopavi was down below the mesa. My uncle told me that we brought different kinds of carved stone animals. Horses and sheep[4] were ours; they didn't belong to any other clan, only to us. So we were living there, but there were too many attacks from hostile people, so we moved up to the top of the mesa, where Shimopavi is now. We went up there before the Spanish came.

[4]Horses and sheep were not present among the Hopis until the arrival of the Spanish. The Sun Clan's claim to own, or be supreme over, horses and sheep therefore must have come later.

That's the story of our Sun Clan. There are several clans that are joined to the Sun Clan—the Moon Clan, and the Eagle Clan, and the Grey Hawk Clan, and the Turkey. They're all compounded as one clan. The Sun [mask] has eagle feathers coming out all around. Our god, Tawa, the Sun, we believe him to be the head god of all the other clans. We were told that all human beings, and domesticated animals, and wild animals are our children, because our head god is the Sun. The Sun is the one that gives us life. So when anyone comes into my house I greet them kindly because they are my children. I never tell them, "Go away." I give them good hospitality, feed them. That's the way that when I'm dead my name will be getting bigger all the time.

We had a [Sun Clan] uncle, Lenachi, he was the one that was supposed to know how to bring rain. He married among the Hopis in Oraibi and lived with his wife there. She belonged to the Bamboo Clan. One of his sisters was a widow in Shimopavi. She couldn't make a living because there was nobody to take care of her or do anything for her. So every year in harvest time he went to Oraibi and helped the people so they would give him some corn for her, this yellow corn, and he'd carry it on his back to Shimopavi. But then he was getting old, getting no good. He told her, "Now, I'm getting old and weak. I think it's better for you to marry someone here, so that will stop the work of carrying corn to our place [Shimopavi]." It seems she didn't listen to him at first, but finally she married a man [and stayed in Oraibi]. I don't know what clan he belonged to.

But that woman was our grandmother. She had five children born. That was a time when the Navajos were making war on the Hopis. When those five children were grown up [and had children of their own?], the Navajos killed every one of them. That's what I know.

There's another Sun Clan on Third Mesa, but they belong to a different group. I don't know where they came from. They were not in our group. Those Sun Clan people live in Hotevilla. They don't seem to care for us. They say we belong to the Forehead Clan. But we are not Forehead Clan, we are Sun Clan.

Chuka (Don C. Talayesva)
Oraibi, July 1970

————9————

The Palatkwapi Story, IV

A Walpi Water Clan Version

The following is an excerpt from a long Palatkwapi narration by Albert Yava, the complete text of which appears in his book of recollections, Big Falling Snow. *The segment given here describes the destruction of Palatkwapi, which is missing from the preceding account given by Don Talayesva. Yava heard this account from his father, Sitaiema, of the Water Clan.*

The Kikmongwi said, "I have prepared four masks and other medicine for you. Tomorrow go to the mountain out there. Put this medicine in your mouth." It was fire, so that when the young man breathed, flames would come out. Then the chief said, "Put on this mask." It was a Kiwan Kachina mask. "Now, on top of that one, place this mask." It was the mask of the Auheulani Kachina who appears in Soyalana, the winter solstice ceremony. "On top of that one, put on this mask." It was a Talavai Kachina, the one who who comes to distribute beans at dawn on the last day of the Powamu festival. "On top of all of these masks," the kikmongwi said, "put this one on." It was a Masauwu mask with red hair and a spotted face. The kikmongwi said, "When darkness falls, come running into the village and circle it four times. Then go to the highest roof, sing the song I am going to give you, and grind the grinding stones together as if you were grinding corn."

The young man did as he was instructed. When the time came, he put the fire in his mouth and put the four masks over his face, the Masauwu mask on top. There is a great deal of symbolic meaning in these four masks. For one thing, they represent the four seasons. And the Masauwu mask on top, the fierce-looking one, represents death. It also represented the chief. And in addition to that, it was an omen of the chief's intentions. So there were several layers of meaning in the Masauwu mask alone, and the three other masks had additional meanings. The young man began running from the mountain where he was staying, and as he approached the village it was getting dark and most of the people were already in their houses. But one man was lying on the roof of one of the houses. The chief's nephew was breathing fire, and the man saw the flame approaching. He saw the chief's nephew go around the village four times and then climb to the roof of the highest house. There the young man, wearing all the masks and breathing flame, ground with the grinding stones and chanted this song:

Tu-ta-heh! Tu-ta-heh! Tu-ta voe-na heh! Tu-ta voe-na heh! Heh heh heh!

The man who was watching him went to the kiva roof and tapped on it. He called down, "You men in the kiva! There's a strange thing going on up here! Something moves around the village breathing fire, and now it is up above grinding with grinding stones and singing!" Someone answered, "Oh, is it you? You are always telling stories like that." The man said, "No, it is something ominous." They called back, "Do not disturb us. It's just your imagination again."

The following night the chief's nephew came again, running around the village four times and then going to the highest roof, where he chanted his song and ground with the grinding stones. That same man saw him, and he went to the kiva again and called down that a strange event was taking place. This time one person came up, and he saw the kikmongwi's nephew on the roof breathing fire and grinding the mealing stones together. He called into the kiva opening, saying, "Yes, it's true. There's some kind of a person or spirit breathing fire on the roof." There was laughing down below, and someone answered. "It's a ridiculous story. You two men are just alike."

On the third night the two men watched together, and this time when they called into the kiva, everybody came up. They saw the fearsome figure running and breathing fire. They saw him grinding. They heard him singing. They were worried. They wondered what it meant. Because everything came in fours, they expected that he would come the next night, and they made plans to capture the strange personage. So the next night while the kikmongwi's nephew was up on the roof grinding and singing, they blocked all the passageways in the village so that he could not get out. When he was through with his song, he came down, but he could not find a way out of the village. They chased him one way and another until, finally, they caught him. They took him into the kiva, and in the light from the fire they saw the Masauwu mask. It was a terrifying sight.

They removed the Masauwu mask and laid it aside. They took off the Talavai mask and set it down. They took off the Auheulani mask, then the beautiful Kiwan mask, and at last the face of the kikmongwi's nephew was revealed. They said to him, "It appears that you are a bad omen. What is it? What is the meaning of the running, the breathing of fire, the masks?" But the young man could not answer these questions. He said, "I don't know the meaning. I merely did what I was instructed to do." They asked him, "Who was it that instructed you?" He answered, "My uncle, the kikmongwi." They asked, "Why did he instruct you to do these things?" The young man said, "Because someone seduced his wife, the mother of the village." Now the people began to see how serious the matter was. They began to understand the meaning of the masks. They saw that the Masauwu mask was bringing a message to them. Still, they did not understand everything. They said to one another, "This young man meant to harm us. He must be killed."

The young man said, "I hope you will not kill me, because I was doing only what I was instructed to do by the kikmongwi." They said, "Yes, we are going to kill you. That is the only thing we can do to deal with this bad omen." The young man said, "Well, if that is how it is going to be, then this is what you are supposed to do. Bury me in the village plaza and leave my arm sticking out of the grave. This is the way it has to be done." So they killed him immediately and buried him in the plaza with one arm protruding from the earth. His thumb was folded over, so four fingers were pointed upward. Now, the next day when the people came into the plaza they saw that one of the four fingers was folded over and only three were still pointed up-

ward. They wondered about it. The next morning, they saw that
the middle finger was folded down, and only two fingers were
straight. The third morning only one finger was still pointing
upward. The people didn't understand the meaning of it, but
they were uneasy. On the fourth morning all four fingers were
folded down, and the people began to understand that something awesome was about to happen.

Then the earth began to shake and the rain began to fall.
Water came out of the cracks in the rocks. In the houses, water
spurted out of the fireplaces. (In those days the fireplaces were
in the corners of the rooms.) Where there was supposed to be
fire, water was pouring out. The houses became flooded, and
the people ran outside to keep from drowning. But the water
was rising outside also. A large pond formed in the plaza where
the young man had been buried. And from that pond Paleuleukang, the great water serpent, started to emerge. His head with
the single horn came out, then his body. He raised his head high
above the plaza, surveying the village.

Nuvayoiyava (Albert Yava)
Tewa Village, July 1970

————10————

Some Hopi Beliefs

As a whole, Hopis are a peaceful people. That has to do
with their religion. If a man doesn't have a religion he's merely
like a wild animal, ready to chew you up. No matter what clan a
man is from, he is still a Hopi and practices Hopi religion. It's a
religion combined with the different [kiva] societies. That's what
makes the Hopi outstanding. Because of all the different societies, they have different kivas named after these societies. They
had fourteen kivas up there [in Oraibi]. Maybe one kiva belongs
to three different clans, the next one two. There's hardly any one

clan that has a kiva to itself. There's always some combination [of clans]. So if anyone wants to tell a story, he lets those associated clans know about it. They let each other know that they are sincere about it. That way they can get along. They all have some covenant, you might say, to get along good, because Hopis are peaceful, they don't want to fight even in that one kiva. Outsiders don't know what Hopi means, they can't translate it, but we ourselves know it means Peaceful in our language.

When the Spaniards came in here one time looking for the Seven Cities of Cibola, they found Oraibi already existing. And they happened to meet a lot of children, because children are apt to run up to you; they are curious. In those days, the children's noses were running, and that's why the Spanish called them Moqui, Noses Running.[1] But in the Hopi language Moqui means dead. The Hopis didn't mind being called "dead," because it meant to them that they were all on an even spiritual plane, but when they heard that it meant "running noses" they didn't like it. White people called Indians savages, but the Indians would never call themselves savages, because they were civilized. Even though they never had education in school, they had minds that knew the difference between good and evil.

As to where these people around here came from, you see this mark sometimes: ∼∼∼. That means water. And sometimes you mark this way: ∼∼∼◉. They came across water, they made a circle and wound off again. Several years they occupied that land. They mentioned two peaks. The Bow Clan spoke of a place where they settled that had two peaks, meaning two witnesses. They said they came between two peaks, representing an island that was not destroyed by the flood. The flood left that place for them to stay. The two peaks are spoken of as a reminder of what happened. The two peaks are two witnesses of what took place here. They testify to the truth of it. From that place, they moved all along the coast, and finally they came to the south. But before that there was a water crossing from someplace. Hopis still believe there is something beyond. There is to be another world to come

[1]Spanish moquear = to blow the nose. Moquita = snivel.

to. Everything the Hopis do expresses this belief. Making pahos and rituals, everything relates to their belief that when they leave this world they are going somewhere. There was a promised land, and everybody was always looking for that place. When the Badger Clan first arrived and wanted to come into Old Oraibi, they camped down below for four years. The Oraibis always noticed that that place [where the Badger Clan was staying] always had flowers growing all around, even in the winter. For that reason the kikmongwi went down and said it was all right for them to come in. When they came into the village they came in a bean procession [carrying newly grown bean plants], in the middle of winter. That's what they were looking for, a paradise or a place where they would always have plenty to eat.

Those people who got here, the flood had destroyed most of them but a few had survived. They were the remnant of something big. That's always the way, that some survive, except for the ones that were destroyed, no more to be remembered. But these Hopi people know that they came from across the ocean and migrated here. And they never forget their religion.

That story about the Hopis coming out of the underworld, that's the way we tell it to our children. When the white people came around, we didn't tell them about the water voyage either, it's a kind of secret. We don't tell the children, just give them the underworld story. The ones that arrived from the water crossing, they didn't go far, just circled around, never went beyond the Mississippi River, that's what they say. All the Hopis have the same religion, looking for that promised land. They all remember and stick together, even though some of the things they say and do come from their imagination, like altars and similar things.

About the underworld, they claim that long years back this earth was flat. And they noticed that the rivers flowed without filling up. Where was this water going? They decided that maybe there was some land under there, down below, and the water was going down there, the underworld. That is what we debated in the kiva. Some say, "Well, where is the sun coming from? Is it just one sun that goes down and comes back? It must be that the sun goes around, so that it is always giving the people light."

They talked that way in the kivas. We kids listened to the discussions. And it seemed to us that people must be living in the
next [lower] world too. When this destruction[2] took place down
below, they claim that this evil [one][3] took advantage. This evil
[one] impersonated a human being. Therefore he was punished.
That punishment is not so clear, I know. But they debate that in
the kivas of the One Horned Lodge and the Two Horn Lodge.

One Horned Lodge is the one that has the authority and
privilege to anoint the chief. The Two Horned, according to that
lodge, is the one that has experience, the one that asks leniency
when people get in bad, they don't want to punish them. They
say, "Well, poor fellow," and so on. The Two Horn is the experienced one. He has bumped against One Horn sometime [in the
past], something he wasn't strong enough for, and his horn was
split. He had one horn before, but after that he had two horns,
one split into two. So those two, the One Horn and Two Horn,
are the ones that are going to be there at the last day of judgment, when you leave this world. According to the deeds a person does in this world, a [dead spirit] goes westward. If you have
done good deeds, you travel on much faster. You'll be stationed
at one point, and the next year you move. And those people
that have done bad deeds may be staying there two, three, four
years. You'll see them on both sides of the road. People who've
done good deeds will say, "Oh, you're still here." The Two
Horned Lodge, when they come to the last judgment, will say,
"Well, this man has done bad deeds, but he's reconciled back to
his people. He says, 'My people, I've done wrong.' " So the One
Horn and the Two Horn fight for this man.

Homer Cooyama
Kikeuchmovi, July 1970

[2]The idea of "destruction" of the Third World, from which people are said
to have emerged, appears to be an interpolation of the Palatkwa destruction
theme.
[3]A tangential and somewhat confusing reference to the deity Masauwu.
Some traditions say he was thrown into the fiery pit in the afterworld and that
he came out badly burned and disfigured. See text 23, "The Deity Masauwu."

———11———

The Dispersal from Sikyatki, I

A Walpi-Hano Version

The Coyotes and the affiliated Fire Clan were the ones that settled at Sikyatki, a large village at the base of First Mesa, on the east side, about a mile north of Walpi. There's nothing but ruins there now, but you can still see it was an extensive settlement. Sikyatki was on some high knolls close to the cliffside, and down below you can see the fields, thirteen of them marked off by lines of stones. There is some dispute over whether those fields were laid out by the Sikyatkis or whether they were laid out later, after the village was gone.

If you are coming from the east on the blacktop road, just before you get to Polacca, you will notice twin mounds on top of the mesa. There was a village up there called Kukeuchomo. Directly below, close to the mesa wall, is where Sikyatki was. We were told by our old people that Kukeuchomo and Sikyatki were related villages. Kukeuchomo was a kind of guard post for Sikyatki. Some of the houses were facing east and some were facing west, and from up there the people could see hostile forces coming from any direction. The Kukeuchomos seem to have been Coyotes and Fire Clan also, with some Corn Clan people mixed in. Of course, Sikyatki must have contained a number of clans, but it was the Coyote and Fire groups that established it, and they were the ruling clans. There was another small settlement up on top of the cliff called Terkinovi. It was a Bear Clan village that might have been there before Sikyatki came into being. They had terraced gardens on the west side of the mesa. It may be that those Bear Clan people eventually moved to Keuchaptevela.

But Sikyatki was the main settlement over there. It was there long before the Spanish ever arrived in this country. The Spanish explorers and the Catholic missionaries who came here in the early days never mentioned Sikyatki in their historical writings, though they mentioned all the other main Hopi villages.

So I think Sikyatki was already gone by that time. There are quite a few different stories about Sikyatki and how it came to an end, but some of them are just not true, and some are silly.

There were quite a few anthropologists around here in the 1890s and the early 1900s. They got information from different people that Sikyatki was destroyed by the Keuchaptevela people. That story is false. Whoever told it that way had got Sikyatki mixed up with Awatovi. There's always this kind of confusion, with people telling things they really don't know or understand. Awatovi was destroyed, but Sikyatki wasn't destroyed by anybody, just the elements. It was abandoned. Those houses stood there a long time. It was the abandonment that dispersed the Coyote Clan to the other villages.[1] I think some of the wrong stories about Sikyatki were cooked up over in Oraibi, where the people are too far away to know what really happened over there. I will give you the Sikyatki story as it was passed down to us First Mesa people, who were the ones immediately involved. I believe this version is nearer the truth than any of the others, though there may be details here and there that were added by an imaginative person somewhere along the line.

The way the story goes—I'm going to tell it briefly because it could be quite long—the people were living down in Keuchaptevela, on the shelf. They hadn't yet moved to the top of the mesa. There was a lot of visiting back and forth with Sikyatki. Young men in Sikyatki who were looking for wives or girl friends would come to Keuchaptevela in the evening and watch the girls and try to get acquainted. There was one beautiful girl in Keuchaptevela who was the daughter of the chakmongwi, the village crier. A number of Sikyatki boys were attracted to her, but she wasn't interested in any of them.

One particular Sikyatki boy was so taken with her that he couldn't leave her alone. He kept following her. As the custom was, he went to that little window or porthole that opened from the girl's corn-grinding room and tried to talk to her while she

---

[1]Jesse Fewkes, in his "Archeological Expedition to Arizona in 1895," p. 635, says: "There appears to be no good evidence that Sikyatki was destroyed by fire, nor would it seem that it was gradually abandoned."

was working there, but she didn't give him any encouragement. He said he wanted to court her, but she said, "No, I'm not ready to become a woman. I have an old father and mother to take care of. They need me. So I don't want to be courted." The boy persisted, wouldn't go away, so at last she hung her winnowing basket over the little window and cut him off.

Well, that young man wouldn't let things lie. He came back the next evening and the evening after that. Finally the girl became exasperated and threw a handful of ground corn through the window into his face. He was angry and went back to Sikyatki. He spoke to some of his friends about the girl. He said, "The chakmongwi's daughter over in Keuchaptevela doesn't want to have anything to do with us. I think we ought to see to it that nobody else gets her." They understood what he was hinting at. They said, "No, we aren't going to do anything like that. It doesn't matter to us. There are other girls. If you do anything foolish, it will make trouble between the villages. You'd better forget about her."

But the boy refused to let himself get turned back. The next evening, he took his bow and some arrows and returned to Keuchaptevela. He went to the window of the girl's grinding room. He saw her working grinding corn. He put an arrow in his bow and shot her. She fell dead against the wall. After that he ran back to Sikyatki. The girl's father and mother didn't hear the sound of grinding. When they called to her, there wasn't any answer. So they went to the grinding room and found her lying dead with an arrow in her back. They cried out, and the girl's brother came. He saw his sister lying dead. He examined the arrow. On the shaft where the feathers were attached, there was a pointed mark. Every village had a different way of marking its arrows. When the boy saw the markings, he said, "That arrow comes from Sikyatki."

Word traveled around that the crier chief's daughter had been killed. People were disturbed, but nothing happened out in the open. The father of the girl told his son, "I want you to practice running. I want you to run toward Star Butte every morning. Run as hard as you can. In time you will be able to get to the butte and back before the sun comes up. Then I will know you are ready."[2] So the young man went running every morning until he was able to get to Star Butte and back before the sun rose. Then his father said, "Good, I think you are swift enough now. Listen to me carefully. I will announce that in four days our Racer Kachinas are going to Sikyatki. You will go as a Haircutter Kachina. Take some baked corn, some red and yellow piki, and other things like that as prizes. When all the prizes have been given out and the races are coming to an end, then you will carry out the instructions that I will give you."

The day of the races came. The young men in Keuchaptevela who were going to compete put on their kachina costumes and ran to Sikyatki. The races began. The Racer Kachinas ran against whatever young men challenged them. The son of the Keuchaptevela crier chief won many races. Whenever he beat a Sikyatki runner he took tribute the way Haircutter Kachinas do, by cutting off a handful of the loser's hair with his flint knife. When it was getting late, he ran his last race. He caught his opponent just as they were coming into the plaza, and cut off some of his hair.

Then he turned and climbed the ladder to the roof of the house belonging to the crier chief of Sikyatki. Arriving on the roof, he saw a group of girls standing there. He saw the daughter of the Sikyatki crier chief. He ran to where she was standing. He threw her down and cut off her head. Holding the head by the hair, he jumped to the ground on the far side of the houses. The Sikyatki people were stunned. When they realized what had happened, the young men began to pursue the Haircutter Kachina up the stairway to the top of the cliff and across the sandhill on the west side. When he came within sight of Keuchaptevela, he turned and waved the head at his pursuers. That was a challenge, you might say a taunt, for them to come after him. But they didn't dare to follow him.

So now the feelings between the two villages became very hard. Both villages understood that there couldn't be any peace between them. The chief of Keuchaptevela told the chief of Sikyatki, "Now it is even. You people killed our daughter, and in return we killed your daughter. How the matter will go from here

[2]This motif also appears in the Palatkwapi legend.

will be up to you. If you want war, we will give you war. But if you don't want war, the best thing is for you to move away."

The leaders in Sikyatki thought about it for a while, then they decided to abandon their village. They packed up what they could carry and went away. The Coyote people went out into the valley, and there they broke up into groups. One group went to Oraibi and was accepted there. Some went to the Second Mesa villages. And one group went back to Jemez in New Mexico, the place they had come from in the beginning. After a little time had passed, some of the Coyotes drifted back here and were accepted in Keuchaptevela. Sikyatki was a ghost village. No one was supposed to go over there. The Keuchaptevela leaders said that the walls of Sikyatki were doomed to fall down and return to the earth. There was a prophecy—I don't know where it started— that one day the cliff would collapse and cover Sikyatki. Nowadays people think there was something to it because the cliff edge up there at Kukeuchomo broke off, taking part of a kiva with it and fell into the Sikyatki spring. That spring is pretty choked up now. People sometimes ask, "How in the world could those old-timers know that the mesa wall would collapse on Sikyatki?"

Nuvayoiyava (Albert Yava)
Tewa Village, August 1969

The Falling Walls

Another narrator had the following to add to the account given above:

After the people left Sikyatki, the cliff walls began to fall down into the village. There was a prophecy about that. Before they left, they took a hair out of the snake [skin] they had brought from Palatkwa. They said, "All this [village] is going to be destroyed. Nobody is to settle here. Nobody can live here anymore." They made a paho out of the snake hair and placed it there, and pretty soon the whole [cliff] began sinking. There was an old settlement on top of the cliff which Sikyatki used as a watchtower. Pieces of that village also fell off the cliff into Sikyatki.

The medicine they made out of the snake hair was powerful. It made the prophecy come true.[3]

Homer Cooyama
Kikeuchmovi, July 1970

————12————

The Dispersal from Sikyatki, II

An Oraibi Version

Some time after Sikyatki was settled by the Coyote Clan, about a hundred people were living there.[1] Sikyatki was copied after Palatkwa. There was a court, and the houses were built the same way. And they made a shrine, the same as at Palatkwa. They stayed there many many years and got acquainted with the people at Walpi.[2] There were just a few people there, Sikyatki already outnumbered them. Those Walpi people had to go down below the mesa to get their water, but the Sikyatki people were quite close to the water. They were pretty progressive. They had pretty girls, maidens, in each village. It happened that there was a very attractive maiden in Walpi. She was the daughter of the town crier [chakmongwi]. And in Sikyatki there was a young

[3]Other informants rejected the possibility that the Coyote and Fire clans owned a piece of the skin of the great water serpent of Palatkwa since neither of those clans came from that place. A portion of Paleuleukang's skin, the property of the Water Clan and its affiliated clans, is said to be kept in a secret place in Walpi and is reportedly used in certain Paleuleukang rituals. But Water Clan people point out that the Coyote Clan and its affiliates came from Jemez and had no part in the events at Palatkwapi.

[1]Jesse W. Fewkes, who made extensive excavations at Sikyatki, estimated that the population was between 300 and 500 ("Archeological Expedition to Arizona in 1895," p. 637).
[2]Old Walpi, that is to say Keuchaptevela.

man, the nephew of the chief [kikmongwi] down there. He decided he would go up and try to make the girl's acquaintance.

It used to be that during the ceremonials, the young maidens would come out to see the dances at noontime. The girls would come in one group, all dressed up, with that whirl hairdo [squash blossom] on both sides of their head. When the maidens came out that way, the young men kept their eyes on them and sort of picked out girls they would like to know better. This young man from Sikyatki, he saw the chakmongwi's daughter at a time like that and he didn't forget her. He went back and told his parents about her. Usually it was your parents who decided for you, whether you could marry with a certain person. They had to belong to different clans. This was very strict in those days, you couldn't marry with anyone closely related. The parents had to think about these things. A girl's parents had to figure out who a young man was, who his relations were. They might figure it this way: "His father is chief, or his uncle is the town crier." Or, "His people have a big field, they raise a lot of corn." A boy's parents would say, "If you can stand it when you get over there with those people,[3] you can be a good farmer. You know how to weave." They'd talk about all kinds of things like this.

Well, the young man, the nephew of the chief, said, "I'd like to talk to that young maiden." He went up there to Walpi one time. It was during the night. And there was a little hole there in the wall of the grinding room where the girl was working, grinding corn. That air hole in the wall, that was where the young men would go to speak with girls they wanted to get acquainted with. This young man went there and talked to the girl. They asked each other a lot of questions: "Can you do this?" and "Can you do that?" He went there and talked to the girl several times. Other young men also were going there to talk to the girl, because she was very attractive.

There was another young man in Sikyatki who was also attracted to the girl. You might say he had an ugly disposition. He was full of jealousy for the nephew of the chief. One night he went up there. He was fooling around and it was late. He went to

---

[3]A boy would go to live in the village, sometimes the house, of the bride.

the girl's grinding-room wall, and he was talking to her through the air hole. But she'd already made a choice, the chief's nephew from Sikyatki. This other man, he was the type to do mischief. And when the girl indicated she didn't want him, he took aim with his bow and arrow [through the air vent] and killed her. Then he went back to his village. The girl's parents were very sad. All through the winter they mourned for her. They wondered who could have committed this act. They went around everywhere trying to find out who the person was.

There was a young man in Walpi, a cousin of the dead girl. He was the son of the chief of that village.[4] He wanted to find the murderer. He went to Oraibi trying to get information, but he didn't get anything. One day he was resting in the shade and something came to his mind. It seemed to him that the girl's murderer must have come from Sikyatki because it was so close. And after that, he studied those people down in Sikyatki. He'd go down and visit them sometimes and look around.

One night he made a visit down in Sikyatki.[5] There was one young man down there that he suspected, a person with a mean disposition, but he wasn't sure. There was moonlight. He came to the village. He heard some people talking up on the rooftops. (In warm weather, the people often slept on top of their houses.) He crept up silently to the second floor. He saw three young men lying there, close together. They were conversing. That man with the mean disposition was lying in the middle. He was laughing. He was saying, "It's a long time now, since last winter. I don't think anybody will find out what happened, how that girl got killed." Those other two boys asked him, "How did you do it?" And he told them that he'd gone up to Walpi several times, but the girl didn't like him so he decided to kill her. "How did you kill her?" He told them all about it. The young man from Walpi drew out his arrow, walked over and killed him right there. Later he told everyone about it, and he had two witnesses who had heard everything.

Right then there developed enmity between the villages. The

[4]Apparently the narrator realized at this point that the avenger of the girl had to come from Walpi rather than Sikyatki. The nephew of the Sikyatki chief is dropped from the narration.
[5]This paragraph is transposed from a later explanation.

two village chiefs were not getting along. The seasons seemed to change. They had water there in Sikyatki, but the rocks fell into it from the cliffside, ruined the spring. The weather seemed to change. The surroundings didn't look like they used to. They danced and danced [for rain], but there wasn't much spirit in it. So the Sikyatki people decided to move on to another place. They heard that the Oraibi people needed some of their things [ceremonies]. The Oraibi dancers didn't have any coyote skins on their backs. Coyotes are very brave, and the coyote skins represented bravery. So when things got very bad in Sikyatki, the people left and went different ways, but some of them went to Oraibi, where they were accepted because they had things the Oraibis needed.

The same narrator also gave another account of Walpi's revenge against Sikyatki, as follows:

The young man [son of the Walpi chief] said, "I'm going to make it even. There's going to be some kind of a dance, a Nuvakchina, a Snow Kachina Dance, over there, a seven day dance. I have a clue [that the murderer came from Sikyatki]." The chief and the town crier agreed, and they made some prayer feathers. They said, "Now it's up to you, if you are willing to take care of this matter." This young man went down to Sikyatki and studied it. And all that time he was practicing running. He went across the gap [a break in the mesa top] up on the mesa and looked down on Sikyatki. He practiced running day and night. He went down to the village and practiced running, coming back on that long, sandy hill. In seven days, he was pretty much of a runner. And all this time he was figuring what he was going to do. He had already made a mask, fixed it so it would be very tight on his face, instead of loose. It was a Homsuna [Hair Cutter] mask, means a mask that can see everything, black, had an eye made of corn kernels, a little short mouth, and a little ear.

It was noontime. The events were going on in Sikyatki. At noontime something was always going on. Noontime means the middle. A young man "goes up the middle" and he's supposed to be matured. And from there after he's married, it's supposed to be a different life. At noontime when they're going to have that noon dance, they bring gifts, and all the people are supposed to be dressed up. So when that was going on, the young man watched from up on top [of the mesa] and saw that the fourth dance was going on. When a particular dance is taking place, they dance in three spots, over here, over there, then the next location. Only three positions, they don't want to go to four. When this noon dance was going on, they danced the first round, then the second round, then started for the third position. That's when the young man from Walpi came down. He could tell because of the pause in the song, knew they were moving to the third place.

All the people in the plaza were watching, and he came in. They had three clowns entertaining them, and when the young man came in wearing that mask, the people thought he was coming to entertain them. Everybody wondered where he came from and what he was going to do. Nobody knew. The clowns didn't know either, because they hadn't planned this, he wasn't on their program of entertainment. This Homsuna Kachina was unknown to them. He was running, and while he was running, he kept his eyes on the young maidens up there on the rooftops. He wanted to find the daughter of the chief. And he spotted her. So he ran up there where the girls were standing. The girls ran into the upper house, and he followed them. The girls were sort of piled up in a corner. He grabbed hold of the girl who was the chief's daughter. He caught hold of her hair and took her scalp. Then he went out and carried it around so the people could see.

Then all the young men started to chase him. And when they got to the sand dunes up there on top of the mesa they hadn't caught him. He was still waving the scalp. There's always a limit, a place with a certain mark, and they couldn't follow him past that mark. They tried to shoot him with arrows from there, but they couldn't hit him. So he was free. When he passed the mark he took his mask off, waved it in a circle. The people couldn't do anything more and they had to go back. The dance didn't go on, they stopped everything. That's what happened. The girl in Walpi was dead, but the daughter of the Sikyatki chief was alive, just scalped.

Homer Cooyama
Kikeuchmovi, July 1970

————13————

The Dispersal from Sikyatki, III

Bird Race Version, from Oraibi

Those people at Sikyatki came from Jemez, according to what I was told, and most of them were of the Coyote Clan. They didn't do any weaving, but they did a lot of farming. They made their living from that. The Navajos called them Maidesh, Maideshkishi, that's what they called the people from Jemez. They were Coyote Clan, and [later] they branched out from there to the different Hopi villages. They were mean people.

I know a story about Sikyatki. It may be a fairy story or it may be a true story. There was a man from Muchovi [a now extinct village near Keam's Canyon] up on top of the mesa cutting cedar trees. He was going to cut the wood and dry it so he could use it for fuel. He was also herding some sheep.[1] And he heard a chopping noise, somebody cutting with an axe. He went to find out about it. He saw a man there. He said "Does this wood belong to you?" "Yeah." "Did you chop this wood down to make fuel?" "No." "This wood is mine." They started to make an argument. That other man was from Sikyatki. The story of the argument spread.

The man from Muchovi told the story to the members of his kiva. Next morning while they were in the kiva they heard the sound of a rattle coming.[2] The man came to the top of the kiva. They welcomed him. "Come in, sit down," that's what they told him. He said, "Yesterday one of our boys had trouble with one of yours. It was pretty hard to settle that trouble. I was sent here to notify you that four days from now our villages are going to have a race. The winner will take the loser's life. Whoever loses will be killed." He told the Muchovi people they had better get their best cattle in and kill them and eat them, because it would be

[1]During Sikyatki's time the Hopis did not yet have livestock.
[2]The messenger either carried a hand rattle or wore rattles on his legs.

their last chance to eat [something good] before they themselves would be killed. The Muchovi men hung their heads down[3] for a while, and then the Sikyatki man went back to his village.

Now, there was one boy enrolled in the Muchovi kiva—this might be a fairy story—who was a swallow boy.[4] [They decided that] he was the one to run the race for their village. The kiva chief sent for him to come down and smoke with them. They told him that he would run in the race against the Sikyatki runner. When they were through talking, the boy went back to the big hole in the cliff wall where he lived.[5] This boy had one grandmother.[6] When he got home his grandmother said, "I've been waiting for you. The news that I hear is not good, it's awful, and you are the one chosen to run the race. Sit down and eat. You'll have to have partners to go with you on your race." So he had his early meal, and she told him, "You go up to Keam's Canyon, on that south wall there are some swallows living. Select some of them that look like you for partners. Their feathers on the outside should look like yours, so you all look like the same bird." So he went up there and found the swallows, but when they saw him they became frightened and flew into their holes. There was one big hole and the swallow boy went inside and found an old man sitting by the fireplace. The old man said, "At last you've come to visit us." The old man knew who he was. "Well, sit down and we'll smoke." (They always do this when someone comes to another person's kiva, especially if it is a far place. They do this to pray for good things. They always use that mountain tobacco, Indian tobacco.)

When they finished smoking, the old man asked what he could do for him. Then the boy told about the troublesome thing that had come on his village because of the argument over chopping wood. The old man told the ladies [lady swallows], "Set

[3]Indicating dejection, and also meditation.
[4]It is not clear in this rendition whether the boy always has the form of a swallow, or whether he has both human and swallow forms. One variant narrative says the boy belonged to the Swallow Clan, and that his people could make him assume the form of a swallow.
[5]That is, he lived in a cliff wall like other swallows.
[6]The narrator specified later that she was Spider Grandmother.

the table so we can eat." So they sat down and ate. After that, the old man chose a couple of boys [swallows] to be the ones to go with the Muchovi swallow boy. "You birds look about the same as him. Now, you [all] go up to Acoma, where Mt. Taylor is, there are swallow people living up there too. You get one of those birds too, so there will be four." So they flew to Acoma, and on the way they practiced racing. When they reached Acoma, the swallow people already knew they were coming. When they got to Acoma from Keam's Canyon, the people there gave them a good breakfast. They said, "Well, we knew you were coming. But we had to think about how good [i.e., how swift] our racers are, so we might win the race. But we're going to win, we're going to win. We're going to get rid of them, those Sikyatki people." So one swallow was chosen, a girl.

Then from there the four of them went back to Keam's Canyon, and they had supper. The old man said to the swallow boy, "Your swallow brothers will remain here tonight. Go home to Muchovi. On the third day you come again." So he returned with a peaceful heart. When the people saw him coming they told him to go to the kiva and tell the news. So he went to the kiva and they smoked and he told what the swallows were going to do for him. They began to feel pretty good then. They'd been worrying about it because the Muchovi people didn't run very much, and the Sikyatki people were good runners, nobody had ever beaten them.

On the third day they made their prayer offerings, deposited their prayer feathers in the four directions to ask for help so they could win the race. They stayed up all night praying in the kiva, doing all they could so that they could be freed from those Sikyatki people. The next day, the fourth day, that same man came again from Sikyatki. "Now I've come to let you know it's time to put on your good clothing and wash your hair. And after you've had your breakfast, go over there where the race is going to take place." So they did that, and when they got to the place where the race was going to start, the Sikyatki people were there already. The Sikyatki chief made a line along the ground with cornmeal and put prayer feathers, eagle plume feathers, along the ground to show their runner which way to go. He made a speech. "Over yonder south of Old Walpi [Keuchaptevela] is our runner, a chicken hawk." He addressed the chicken hawk, "Come over to us now, we're going to have a race. We've made prayers for you and I think you've received them already. So please help us and come now for the race." In a little while they saw the chicken hawk flying toward them, and when he got there he landed in the place where the prayer feathers were. "Now," the Sikyatki chief said, "it's time for you Muchovi people to call someone to race for you."

Then the Muchovi chief put down the prayer feathers and the sacred cornmeal, and he sprinkled the meal out in this direction, east. "My good runner, please come here right away, we are waiting for you." Everybody was looking up on the mesa, but the swallow came flying in just above the ground. Instead of seeing the bird down below, they were looking up above. They didn't see him land on the place where they made a path for him. The swallow said, "I'm already here!" He was there where they made the path, fluttering his wings.

The Sikyatki chief said, "All right, now we're going to start." He gave the number four times: "One, two, three, four, go!" The birds took off. They were going to fly to the San Francisco Peak and come back. They had to circle the peak. They were going at a high speed. When the swallow was all in, another swallow was waiting for him, flying overhead. "It's your turn," and the second swallow would take his place. The swallows took turns flying to the San Francisco Peak, and coming back it was the same way. In the afternoon the people saw the chicken hawk coming. The Sikyatki people called out, "There comes our bird!" But while they were watching him, the swallow had arrived already. He was just sitting there waiting.

The Sikyatki people had stuck two long knives in the ground before the race started. They were going to use those knives to kill the Muchovi people if their chicken hawk won. The losers were supposed to be killed. But the chicken hawk had lost. He was sitting on the ground panting, he was all wet, sweating, couldn't catch a good breath. "All right," the Sikyatki chief said, "you can do as you please with me." The Muchovi chief said, "Now we are the boss, my children. We will take all the Sikyatki females. Take them home. If a woman is carrying a baby, look at the baby and see if it is a female. If it is a girl baby, take it home, so we can increase." So the Muchovi people did that. But before they took them away, the Muchovi chief went over and took the knife out of the ground and cut the throat of the chicken hawk. The Muchovi people didn't kill any people from Sikyatki. They told the Sikyatki men to go home and live peaceably. The Sikyatki men went away, some crying, some making angry sounds.[7]

That's the way the story was told to me. Those Sikyatki men didn't stay very long in their village. They scattered from that place and made their homes in different villages where they had clan relatives.

> Chuka (Don C. Talayesva)
> Oraibi, July 1970

————14————

*How the Coyote Clan
Went to Oraibi*

When the people of Sikyatki abandoned their village, there were two main clans there, Coyote and Fox. But the Coyote Clan was not yet called by that name, they were called Laangnyam. They started off from Sikyatki and they went south around Castle Butte. They stopped at a certain place, and in a year's time they moved on. While they were on this journey, sometimes people would go back to Sikyatki and get things they needed, vessels and foodstuffs. They'd take a short cut, of course, for the people were moving around in a kind of circle. These people had already finished their migration [from the sipapuni], and so they didn't travel far from where they were. They heard that Oraibi was getting big, and they were planning to join that village.

So these people were traveling along. There was a young

---

[7]The theme of a village losing all its women as the result of a gambling contest is found also in "The Races at Tsikuvi," text 20.

couple with small children. One of them was a little girl who was crying all the time, and they tried to please her by giving her Hopi dolls, but it didn't work. They couldn't get the girl to stop crying. As they went along on the journey they could hear the coyotes. Early in the morning a man went out for firewood. He discovered a [coyote] hole, and there were three little coyotes inside, just born. He took one of them that had pretty fur and carried it to the camp. "Look what I found." Everybody was excited. That little girl that was always crying saw it. She ran up. She loved it. After that, she was happy to have the little coyote to play with. She didn't cry any more.

From there, the people went on toward Oraibi. They camped [below the village] four nights and four days. On the fourth day they went up and asked the Oraibis if they could live in the village, if they could be accepted there. The Oraibis asked them what they could do, and who they were. They told them they were the Fox Clan and the Laangnyam. They said that this plant that gave them their name was useful food, and the straw was good for sweeping with. Then they said they, the Laangnyam, were taking the name Coyote for their clan because a coyote puppy had made the little girl happy. "We know." they said, "that the coyote is very brave, and we think that we also should be brave." Now, that Oraibi society lacked something to represent bravery,[1] something like the Warrior Brothers. The Fox and the Coyote clans explained all the ways they could help the people of Oraibi, and at last the Oraibis received them.

That's how the Coyote Clan came to Oraibi. After that during the ceremonies the Coyotes represented the brave ones who did risky things. And that's when they began to use fox tails in the kachina costumes.

Later on, some of the Coyote Clan people went from there to live in other villages.

Homer Cooyama
Kikeuchmovi, July 1970

[1]That is, it lacked rituals or "medicine" that could give force to bravery. "Oraibi society" seems to refer to a particular kiva fraternity. The Sun Clan had already brought the Warrior Brothers to Oraibi.

—————15—————

The Destruction of Awatovi

A Walpi Reed Clan Version

There was a man married with a girl up there, in Awatovi. They raised everything—corn, melons—everything. They grew flowers. Then, in four years, there were some mean guys up there, they tried to take away his wife. The man's name was Sikyachiti, Yellow Bird. For four years he'd been living good, and after that they tried to take away his wife. [One day] about noon-time she went to get water [at the spring]. And there was a man there, dressed up in kachina clothes, a nice looking man. He met her. He had little bells on. She met him there. The lady put water in her jugs. He asked her to give him water. She said, "Get it yourself." [He said,] "No, give it to me." He wasn't a kachina, just a man dressed in kachina clothes to make the woman love him. That's the way some of the men did. They called him a tuskyata. Then she did it, she gave water to the man. He was drinking and the girl was watching him. Then the man tried to do something with that lady. Then he told her, "Let's go this way." And he took her and she left her water right there, and he took her a little ways from there and held her and tried to love her. [She said,] "No, I don't want it." He took her from there and kept walking, and they were on the other side of the mesa where the rocks are. He said, "I have a house right here." There was a hole in the rocks and a stepladder going down into it [a cave]. He said, "Come in," and he put the lady down in there. "This is the way [it will be] till you want it." Then he put a big rock on the top to cover the hole, and went back to the village.

The girl's husband and mother were looking for her. They couldn't find her. They all just got sick [with worry]. They were lonesome for her. The father went out to work his field, but he worried about her and went home. The girl's husband, Yellow Bird, always went out looking. One time he was [resting] under the shade and he saw somebody coming. It was a coyote. The young man told the coyote, "Sit down." The coyote said, "I'm sure sorry you're lonesome and sick. I might be able to find her for you." "When?" "Four nights from now." "You got to do it for me." "Yes, wait [to hear from] me." The boy went back to Awatovi to take care of his son, and they talked about what the coyote said. The coyote went home. He had a grandmother, and he told her about the lady they were looking for. She said, "Okay, let's go."

They went the other side of Zuni, at Springerville, where the salt is. They didn't get that far the first day, took them two days. And when they got there they met them, Grandma [Gogyeng So-wuhti, Spider Grandmother] and the two little boys [the Warrior Brothers]. Spider Grandmother asked them what they wanted, and the coyote grandma said they wanted to find the kidnaped lady; her husband was very sick and all her people were sick, almost dead [from worry]. This Gogyeng Sowuhti did a lot of work like this, finding people that were missing. She was a povoslowa. She had some kind of glass thing and she'd look at it and it would tell where someone was at. Not ordinary glass, some special kind of glass. Gogyeng Sowuhti found out from the glass where the man had hidden the woman. "You found it?" She said, "Yes sir," and she told them.

Then the coyote and coyote grandma came back home. And they told Yellow Bird to be out there at night, and they told him where. "But there might be some of those bad guys over there. Don't do anything with those guys. Those are mean guys." That night the coyote looked for the lady after sundown, and his grandma was with him. They brought some medicine from Gogyeng Sowuhti. They had the glass from Spider Grandmother. They came to the spring, Yachakpa. The grandma said, "The lady filled her jugs here, and the mean guy took her from here to his house. He took her from here, made the lady go with him." They saw everything in the glass. "Then they went up this way, over on this side of the mesa. And they stayed right there." They ran and came to a little flat place. "Right here!"

That coyote [grandma] dressed up like [i.e., turned herself into] a bear. She was growling, digging the dirt and big rocks away and uncovered the opening of the cave. The lady was right there, and the bad guy was in there too. They took the lady out.

Poor thing, she almost passed out now. The bad guy who was there dressed up as [i.e., turned into] some kind of animal and started to fight, but the bear was bigger and heavier, and it hit him and knocked him down. "Well, let's go, I knocked him down." They carried the lady back to her house, and all her people were waiting for her. Everybody was crying about her. "Poor thing."

This is the kind of thing those mean guys in Awatovi were doing. In Hopi we call those mean guys kwitamuh. Coyote grandma talked to them, said they had to listen to her. When they were sitting there at the fire at night and they heard the coyote calling from outside, they were supposed to listen. "I'm a coyote," she said, "listen to me." And [she made it happen that] for four years those people didn't have any crops, and they got real hungry, and they stopped doing those mean things for a while. Then after four years they began to have crops again.[1] And then those bad guys started doing those things again.

They started taking the ladies into the kiva and having a good time with them, every night, all night. Then they took the wife of the chakmongwi[2] in there. Oh, they had a good time with all the ladies, sometimes on top of them, the ladies and the girls. They didn't listen to the old-timers. The chakmongwi was mad, he was thinking about it. At that time there was already a village up here at Walpi. So he went to Walpi, where that big rock is standing up[3] at the far end of the village. Went up that way and talked to the Walpi chakmongwi. "What did you come over here for?" "They're not doing right up there at Awatovi. Everybody's gone crazy. Running all over with the ladies. Even my wife. And they did it to my wife. I'm sure mad. Somebody's got to help me to make them stop." "What do you want me to do?" "I want you to make war on those bad people." "I can't do that. That's not my position [responsibility]. I can't do that to anyone, because I have to take care of my own

---

[1] It is indicated or implied in several places in the narrative that the coyote grandma is another Gogyeng Sowuti, or Spider Grandmother, with supernatural powers.

[2] The chakmongwi is the crier chief. Throughout the narration, the narrator said chakmongwi rather than kikmongwi, meaning village chief.

[3] Known as Snake Rock.

people. I don't want to do that." That's what the Walpi chakmongwi said. "Why don't you go and try Oraibi?"

Well, the Awatovi chakmongwi went home. About evening
his wife was dressing up, bathing and all those things. She said,
"Why don't you go with us, have fun, be happy?" He couldn't
say anything. But after one day he walked to Oraibi. He talked
to the chakmongwi. He said the same thing that he said in Walpi.
"Can't you help me? They're doing all those crazy things up
there, and my wife is with them. My partner's wife too. They
took all of them." "Well, okay," Oraibi said. The Awatovi chakmongwi said, "Then if we have a war up there, and you clean
us up, you can have the land." The Oraibi chakmongwi considered everything. He said, "I'm ready to go. That land can go to
the First Mesa village [Walpi]. If I go over there to help you, I just
want to take some people, some women. Let's go over to First
Mesa and talk to them. They have a war chief there. We'll talk to
him. If they go to war against Awatovi, let them have the land."

So they went to Walpi, straight up to the end where the
highest houses were, where the war chief [kalatakmongwi or
kalehtakmongwi] was living. Somebody called, "Come in." They
went in. He gave them a smoke. The two men told him why they
had come. "I just came to see you, you are the war chief. Can
you go up to my village, Awatovi, to punish my people for doing
all those bad things?" "Okay, I'll do it. It's my work, I'm a war
chief." The war chief was in charge of the clan that was supposed
to guard the village. The Oraibi man said, "See, I told you he
would help." The Awatovi man said, "Thanks for helping me. If
you do that, you can take my land." The Oraibis would go to
capture some people. The war chief took the two men to see the
chakmongwi, and they smoked. The chakmongwi asked why
they had come. The war chief said, "I just wanted you to know
that we are going to Awatovi to clean those people up." "Okay,
you want to do it?" "Yes." "Well, okay, you already promised.
You've got to go. It's your decision. You are the war chief."

They told the people up there, and from then on all the men
began to make arrows. The Awatovi chakmongwi said, "All right,
in four days be ready. Come up to the top of the mesa on this
side where the rock is and wait there for me. Then I'll get up on
top of the house and shake some kind of a blanket. That's when

you start coming in. Go to the kivas and take those ladders out and throw fire and hot chilis down inside. That will take care of them." "Okay, we'll do that." "Then you'll have all my land." "Okay, we're both coming." The Oraibi chakmongwi went home and told his people to make arrows.

On the fourth day, the Oraibis and the Walpis met and went together to Awatovi. They got up there [to a hiding place] in the afternoon, and the Awatovis didn't know it. Then some of the good people of Awatovi brought them food there. Some of the people of Awatovi were good. Then the men from Oraibi and Walpi started to practice what they were going to do; they were practicing all night. Just about sunrise the Awatovi chakmongwi got up there on the house and waved the blanket for them to come. So they ran into the village and caught people and threw them down in the kivas. Even the chakmongwi's wife, they caught her and threw her down. They took the ladders out. And when they had a lot of people down there they threw burning bark and wood down, and then they threw the chilis in there. It makes you cough and kills you.

The people they didn't kill, women and children, they brought them this way, over to Yachakpa, that spring. They waited for some of their warriors that were missing. When those men came they said they'd also killed the Awatovi chakmongwi. Then they kept going. And in the rocks over on this side they caught some Awatovi men and killed them. They cut off all the heads and put them together. The Hopis call that place Maskoteu [Skull Mound]. It's near Five Houses, over on this side. Then they were coming up this way. Where those green trees are over there near the Polacca Wash, where that sandy hill is sticking up, they killed some others and threw them into the wash. That's why they call that place Masturki, Place of the Dead People. Then they came up this way. Where my fields are on the other side by those hills, they stopped again. They killed some more men, ladies, and children and put the bodies all together and said, "Well, what is growing on this hill now?" So they called that place Maschumo, Dead Persons' Hill."

After that they divided the captives. They brought the Smoke Clan people [Pipnyamrieu] to Walpi. The chief of Oraibi took a lot of those girls and ladies. Then they brought six more men and ladies up here. Then the Oraibis took more ladies. They wanted to raise more kids over there. Then over on Second Mesa, Mishongnovi, they took six girls and six boys. Told them, "Don't think about going back to Tallahogan [Awatovi or Awatovi Mesa]. You've lost all that. Don't talk about it any more. If you go back to Awatovi you'll all die." It's really true about that. You shouldn't go back to your ruin, that's the Hopi law.

Narrator's commentary on the story: Those Second Mesa people try to tell you everything that happened, but they didn't go on that war party to Awatovi and they don't know the real facts.[4] They weren't there. Now, I'm Reed Clan, and it was my clan that was involved. I'm the war chief in Walpi now. I learned this story from my old uncle. He was war chief before me, and he had to tell me everything about it, the true story. That Tallahogan area now belongs to the Reed Clan, because we were the ones that fought up there, and the chief of Awatovi gave it to us. The Snake Clan chief knows this story too, but no one else. All the old people who knew the story are gone. My uncle never told me that it was the Catholic business in Awatovi that made Walpi and Oraibi go over there. But what it was, that kind of church, the Catholic Church, made the people crazy, that's why it happened.

There were other villages on that mesa, five villages over on the other side. Kawaika was one. Then another one, Meusiptanga, near where that trading post is. Another one was Chakpahu. Those people were all Pueblos and they went back east.

This year we're going to have the Basket Dance, Owakulti, in Walpi. My clan brought all those Owakulti things [paraphernalia] back from Awatovi. That ceremony came from Awatovi. We're going to have it in October, and I have to be in charge. When some person wants that ceremony he lets me know. Then they can take the [ritual] things from my house. It was my clan, the Reed Clan, that brought them here.

Stuart Tuvengyamtiwa
Polacca, July 1970

---

[4]Some other accounts say that the Oraibis recruited men from Mishongnovi on their way to Awatovi.

———16———

The Village at Lamehva

How the Reed Clan Came to Walpi[1]

Spider Woman and her two grandchildren, Pokanghoya and Palengahoya, were living together. The grandchildren heard that their grandmother could create things, and they wanted her to make some people for them to talk to. Grandmother said that this was impossible to do. They said, "You're a liar, you're a liar, I bet you can do it. But you don't want to. We're so bored here and we want to talk to somebody." They were living up above Lamehva[2] a couple of miles.

These two boys went out of the house. They were really bored. Usually they did nothing but play ball.[3] They were wandering around, wandering around, pretty soon they went down to this well. They didn't know what to do, they were looking around to talk to somebody. They started playing with mud, making little houses, then they started making people. They were doing that all day, and then they went back to their grandmother. "Oh, we were looking for somebody to talk to but we couldn't find them." Grandmother said, "I told you there wasn't anybody to talk to." "So we went down to this well and just sat there and started playing with mud. We built some houses out of mud, and we made some people to live in those houses. We built all that and it was time to come home, so we're here."

Then the grandma laughed at them. "Well, you better stay here for four days, and don't go anyplace around there now, because you won't find anybody. Play around in the other direc-

---

[1]The story of the Reed Clan in Walpi is distinct from the Reed Clan story in the more western villages. Some Hopis speak of the Walpi Reed Clan and the Oraibi Reed clan as different clans with the same name.

[2]Lamehva is a walled-in spring at the foot of Second Mesa below Mishongnovi.

[3]Nahoydadatsia, a kind of shinny.

tion." So they did that. But they began wondering, "Why doesn't she want us to go down there?" But for three days they played over there in the other direction. On the fourth morning the grandmother told them, "You two guys better get up. Remember you built something down there. Get up and go and see what's up over there." So they got up, ate their breakfast, and then they started going. They played ball while they were going toward where they built the houses at Lamehva. Finally they got about fifty yards from the place, and they heard people talking, a lot of people talking. So they peeked out from behind a rock to see what was going on. They saw some people down there. They looked for a while, then they said, "Let's go down there. Hey, maybe that's the people that we made. It's the same houses that we built. Grandmother must have done this, brought everything to life. Let's go down and meet them."

So they went down there. Pretty soon the head [village] chief who was sitting on the roof hollered, "There's somebody coming, visitors coming. Kiavakovi, somebody coming. Welcome them." So people came over and welcomed these two little boys. "Feed them, feed them. Come in here and sit down. We never saw anybody else around here. You're the first ones to come. Sit down and make yourselves at home." So the people fed them piki and other Hopi food. Then the boys went to another place and were welcomed. They went through all those houses that they'd built, didn't miss a house, and everywhere they went the people gave them piki. The two boys were happy. They were talking to everybody. When they came out of the last house they started back home. When they arrived at their grandmother's they gave her the piki they'd brought. She asked them where they'd got that piki. They said, "Grandma, remember those houses we made down there? [The ones down there now] are exactly the same kind that we made. There are people living in them, and they gave us this food to bring you." Grandma accepted the food and was happy. She laughed. "Well, you finally found someone to talk to." "Yes, we're happy." Grandma said, "Those are the people you made and the houses you made. Those people are your children now, so behave and respect them. Treat them well and don't ever do anything that's bad to them." So the two boys used to go out and visit their people [when they wanted someone to talk to].

In about a year or two some other people moved up to those Corn Rocks, Kaiotakwi. They used to go hunting. And the people at Lamehva used to go hunting. But the people up above [at Kaiotakwi] usually killed more food than the Lamehva people. The Lamehva people had only a cat to help them hunt. The son of the Lamehva kikmongwi wanted to go out and find some kind of a hunting animal faster than a cat, an animal that could scent game, catch rabbits, and things like that. The boy's name was Sikyakokuh. He asked his father where dogs lived. His father told him that place was a long way off. But the boy sure wanted to go. "If we have a dog maybe we can hunt better than the people in Kaiotakwi and get more meat." "Well," the kikmongwi said, "when do you want to go?" "As quick as possible." So the kikmongwi brought together his fellow [ceremonial] chiefs, and they began to make pahos [prayer feathers or prayer sticks]. When they finished they sat down and smoked [and talked] all night. The boy's sisters made piki for him.

The next morning the boy wrapped everything in a pouch and took off. Started walking. And he passed where Polacca is now, but there wasn't any Polacca at that time, going towards the east. And finally out in the wilderness he met Spider Woman. She told him that she'd been waiting for him, that she was the one that had put it in his mind to come out there where she was, so that she could go along with him. "It's a dangerous place you are going to and there are a lot of guards there, so I have to go with you. I'll just climb up on your ear [in the form of a spider] and sit there.

He started on the journey. And at a certain place they met a snake. He was acting very angry, shaking his rattles. Spider Woman told the boy [whispering in his ear] to tell the snake to calm down. The boy told the snake to calm down. "I've got something for you here." He took one of the pahos out and gave it to the snake. The snake calmed down. He was very glad to receive the paho, because his own paho was old, and he was happy to have a new one. So he let them pass, and they went on. Then they met a bear. The same thing—the bear was angry, and the boy told him to calm down and gave him a paho. The bear was happy with that, and they went on again. And when they were among the pines, the boy met a deer, a buck. He was angry too. With all those guards, nobody could go where the boy was wanting to go. The boy gave the deer a prayer stick too. And then he told the deer he wanted his antlers. (Spider Woman had told the boy to ask for them.) The deer agreed to give them. Told the boy to take hold of the antlers and twist them off. "But when you're coming down from that place," the deer said, "be sure to leave them here on top of the trees." The boy twisted off the antlers and went on. Then they spotted this big mountain.

They had to climb that mountain. It was slippery like ice or glass, and that's why Spider Woman had told the boy to ask for the antlers. He used them like mountain climbers' staffs, they kept him from slipping. When the boy had almost reached the place up above, he heard a dog barking. He said, "What's that?" And Spider Grandmother told him that it was a dog, what they'd come for. The boy was really excited. He went on climbing till he reached the top of the mountain. And right on top there was a big puddle of water, and there was a little dog running around the edge of it, and a ladder was sticking up out of the middle of the water. When the dog saw them he ran, went down the ladder, carrying the news that somebody was coming. Told his uncle. And the uncle gave out the word that everybody should welcome the boy. The little dog returned, and the boy petted him. All those dogs knew that he was coming. The dog took him down to his uncle[4] They went down the ladder. Something was done by one of those dogs and the water disappeared. So the boy went down into the kiva below.

The uncle of the dogs greeted him. Said, "Boy, you are a brave man to come here. Nobody ever did that before. Where are you from?" "Well, I'm from way out west. I heard about you people and I sure wanted to have one of you. So I brought these for you." And he gave him all those prayer sticks. The uncle accepted them. "Thank you, thank you, I sure need these things. I appreciate that you brought them for me." The uncle started putting tobacco in his pipe. Then he sat down and gave the boy the pipe to start smoking. I forgot to say that when they were still coming to the mountain they met a mole, he was one of guards, and they gave him a prayer stick too. That mole didn't come with them but stayed in his own house and started digging. Dug a hole through the ground right under the dog peo-

[4]The word uncle is commonly used to mean a senior ceremonial leader, or a person's kiva teacher.

ple's kiva, right under where the boy was sitting. The dog people's uncle didn't think the boy could smoke that strong tobacco he gave him. (It was a kind of test.) But the boy just smoked and smoked. The mole had made an opening in the ground right under the boy and drew the smoke from [his anus] and let it out somewhere. When the uncle saw the boy smoking and smoking without it hurting him or making him dizzy, he was impressed. He finally asked the boy what he could do for him.

"Well," the boy told him, "we go out hunting for rabbits for meat. The people who live in the village above us, they have a hunter they call cat, and they catch a lot of game. I heard about you people up here, that you are faster and more experienced than the cat. I told my father I wanted to come here and find you." The uncle said, "Well, we know about it already." The uncle told him to rest for a while. He called on the ladies—they were in the back rooms—to come and feed the visitor. So they came from different directions, bringing piki, corn and melons and peaches, whatever things they raised. So the boy ate, and after he was finished they cleared up. And the man told this little dog [who had brought the boy into the kiva], "Better go get your [other] uncle, we'll hear what he says. If he says okay, then the boy can take one of you."

So this little dog started running and barking, he's a kind of errand dog. In a short time that guy came. Spider Woman whispered in the boy's ear that this guy was a mean one. "Soon as he comes in, give him this prayer feather, and get the pipe ready." The uncle came in. Said, "What you doing here? You must be a brave guy to come here." He talked mean. The boy said, "Well, we've got this for you," and he gave him a paho. After that the guy calmed down, and he offered the boy a smoke. The first uncle told the second one that the boy came for a dog, so he could hunt rabbits and other things, like be a watchdog. The boy told what he'd told before, that the other village had a cat.

This uncle was satisfied. He said, "Well, since you brought me this paho, I guess you can take one of our dogs, any one that you choose. But I'm not going to stay, I'm going up, I'm a busy man." So he took off again. This other uncle sent [the messenger dog] to go into the back room and tell all these dogs to dress up in their furs. So they put on their dog pelts, spotted ones and all kinds. Then they came out into the main part of the kiva and had a dance. They had a song to sing:

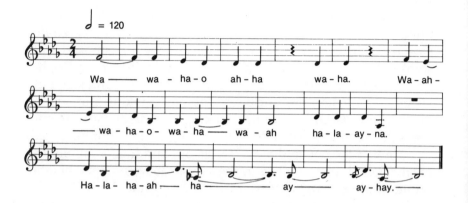

The words weren't human words, but dog words, just barking.

So they danced all night, till morning. Then the uncle said, "Now you [dogs] sit down. I don't know which one he will pick out to go with him and help him. Behave yourselves." They sat down. Then Spider Woman told the boy to take that spotted one. He was barely moving, the last one. The boy told the uncle that he would take the spotted one. "I think I'll take him, he's the fastest one." It was just a puppy, wiggling around. The uncle said, "Boy, you're a good guesser. That's a good dog. Since you chose him, take him." Spider Woman told the boy, "Go pick him up and feed him." The boy went over and picked him up. Put him in his lap and petted him. That night he went to sleep with the dog.

The next morning when he was getting ready to leave, the uncle told the dog to be a good dog and behave, to be a good watchdog and do everything for the people. "Help these people out. Don't do anything wrong. Don't bite people. If anything happens to you, if they kill you, you'll come right back home to us." Then he told the boy that if anyone did anything bad to the dog or killed him, that person's knees would be crippled. "If the dog should die, bury him properly and make some pahos for him. Four days after that, go and check his grave. He won't be there. He'll come right back here." The boy agreed. And that morning he left, carrying the little dog.

They went down [the mountain] and met this mole. I guess he got all smoked out. But he was happy. He welcomed the boy and sent him on his way. And where they met the buck, they put the antlers on the tree as the buck had told them. They went on and met that same bear. The bear was happy the boy had got the dog. They went on till they came to the place where the boy had met Spider Woman, and he left her there. When he got back to Lamehva his sisters were waiting for him. They'd been looking every day. They spotted him coming. "Here comes Sikyako-kuh! He's got something running behind him!" They called out the news to their mother. And everyone passed the word around that he was coming, and that there was something with him. They'd never seen a dog before. The father came, everybody gathered. And the two girls ran out to meet him. They picked up the little dog. It was cute. They carried him home. That night the village chiefs smoked, smoked. All the people were happy. Everybody wanted to see the little dog, treated him just like a baby. They washed his hair and gave him a name.[5] They called him Pintopakokeuji, Spotted Behind. That dog was running around and the two girls really liked him.

Well, everywhere the boy went he took this little dog to go hunting. [Sometimes] the little dog went by himself. Pretty soon he began growing up, growing up. Then he was a grown dog. Boy, if he spotted a rabbit it didn't take long to catch him. They came back to the village with loads of rabbits. The boy had a hunting party for the Lamehva people, the men, they went out hunting together. Oh, that dog was really killing rabbits right and left, killed rabbits for everybody. Then they came home. They had all the meat they wanted, and they were happy, and they were really nice to that dog.

I guess those people back at the dog kiva knew what was going to happen. This dog, Pintopakokeuji, went to the upper village, Kaiotakwi. The people up there were jealous. They heard about what the dog was doing for the lower village. Up there, though, they couldn't get enough meat for themselves. They got jealous and wondered what they were going to do. They tried several times to kill the dog. Finally these guys up there got some meat [from hunting], and they had it up on a roof. And the dog happened to come around. He was looking around and found the meat. He ate it and went home. Somebody was watching and saw that it was the dog who did it. He went down [to Lamehva] and told them the dog stole the meat. The boy said, "This

---

[5]Hair washing with yucca suds is part of the usual naming ceremony.

dog didn't go anyplace, it must be another dog." He didn't know that the dog had been away. (The dog did it when the people were asleep.)

After that, the dog began going to the upper village every night. Finally, the people up there decided to make a bait for him. They did that, and they watched for him at night, and then they grabbed him and hit him with clubs and killed him, and threw him off of a cliff. The boy started looking for his dog. Didn't know where he went. Finally he found him, dead. He started crying. Carried the dog back home. His sisters and everybody [in Lamehva] started crying. They didn't know what to do.

The boy told his father, "We have to make pahos. The people who did this will get lame. That's what they told me up there [at the dog kiva]. They told me to make prayer feathers and go way out and bury the dog, then to go back [in four days] to see if anything has bothered it." So [the father] made prayer feathers for the dog, and the boy picked up the dog and started going. And over where that church is, on that same side of the mesa, there was a big rock there, and the boy buried the dog under there. Put rocks around the grave and put the feathers in, and put down all the food that the sisters made. Then he started back. The people were all sad. Everybody just sat around doing nothing. They missed that dog.

Then after four days the boy went back to the grave. He looked in it. There was nothing there. I guess that dog woke up—his spirit or something—early in the morning. There were tracks, and the boy followed them. Followed the tracks for quite a ways. Couldn't believe that the dog went home, where he came from. The boy came back to the village, said that the dog already had gone home. That's what the dog's uncle had told him would happen. After that the Lamehva people were sad, and they had trouble with the people up there [at Kaiotakwi].

So they decided to get away from this place. They started planning, planning. Then they all dressed and formed a line. Then the two little girls, the sisters, and some brothers too, left that place[6] early in the morning in a fog. That fog came down and covered them. That's how they left, in the mist, going along

[6]The wording suggests that only the boy and his family departed from Lamehva, but the narrator later indicated that the entire village left.

the same trail that the dog had taken. And they traveled over to where we are now, the old village below Walpi, Keuchapteika [Keuchaptevela]. That's where they settled. It's all ruins now. From there the people came up to Walpi [later], to where that highest house is. That's where the old people say we were living [i.e., the Reed Clan from Lamehva]. And they told us that if there is trouble [in the village] and they start chasing people away, those people will go in certain directions to find their [former?] settlements again. It didn't happen yet. But they told us Reed Clan people that we're not going to move from here, because we already moved from Lamehva.[7] They told us that we didn't have any food or anything when we came here. Those other clans can go anywhere they want to go, but us Reed Clan aren't going anywhere. Going to stay right where we are now. Stay there.

On account of that dog, we are here. Because of the dog we were you might say kicked out of the other place. One of these dogs [living today] is ours, is us. That's the kind of dog we had at Lamehva. That's the story of my people, the Reed Clan, and we're living right up there [at Walpi] now. We're related to Sun and Eagle clans. The mountain that the boy went to for the dog is Suchaptekwi. They say it's over in New Mexico some place, maybe right around Albuquerque.

Kilaoka
Walpi, August 1969

————17————

The Reed Clan's Arrival

My clan was the first one on Walpi. We built the first house up there. We people came from Second Mesa, where the church is, down on this side. That's my ruin. The Pokanghoyas made us when they were little kids. Made us out of clay or adobe, all

[7]That is, the Reed Clan had completed its migrations.

kinds of us. "This will be father, this will be mother, this will be uncle, brother." The Pokangs did that. That's where we Reed Clan got started. Then we moved up here. We stayed up here with some kind of old man, a Masauwu. He slept there by that Snake Rock.[1] Some of those people [around Second Mesa] were doing things wrong, some of them were mean, bewitched. That's why we came here. Those Pokanghoyas looked for us about how many days, tracking, tracking, didn't even find us. So whose village was this? We were the first ones.

Later other people came and asked permission to enter. The Snake Chief came [and was allowed to come in]. He was under the Reed Clan. If that Snake Chief couldn't mind you, talked back to you, you went up to him and held his ear and shook it. Today the Walpi chief is Snake Clan.[2] He is under us. I told him many times, "Ned, I'm the authority, and if you don't do right I'll take your ear and shake it." He doesn't say anything. He knows we were first.

Stuart Tuvengyamtiwa
Polacca, July 1970

————18————

The Spruce Tree Ceremony
at Pivanhonkapi

How the Village of Huckovi Was Abandoned

Huckovi is west from Old Oraibi, on a high place on the mesa. The people were Hopis. They were driven out from that place by some kind of tuwapomovitay or tuwapontamachay.

---

[1]A tall, weathered rock at the edge of the Walpi plaza. It has a hollow on one side and is used as a shrine.

[2]Actually, the chief (Ned Nayatewa) belonged to the Horn Clan, though he held the position in trust for the Bear and Snake clans.

That's a woman that is supposed to own the wild animals, a spirit you might say. There was another village, Pivanhonkapi, about four miles west of Oraibi. The people over there were getting ready to put on a dance. There was a boy in the village [who was one of the dancers]. There was jealousy over the boy between two girls. He had a girlfriend in his own village. But there was that girl in Huckovi who wanted him. But he didn't trust her very much [i.e., he rejected her]. She got angry and wanted to do something bad to him.

For the dance, they put up spruce trees along the rim of the mesa, four trees. During the dance the kachinas were supposed to climb up the trees and sing their song and jump to the next tree. But [the girl in Huckovi] must have had some kind of power to do something mean. She broke one of the holes that the trees were set in, made a kind of a crack [in the rock]. The kachina who was supposed to go to that tree was the boy that she was jealous about. If he went up there, if he swung to another tree, the tree would come down, and he would fall. But the grande-madame, Spider Grandmother, saw what was going on and she fixed the broken rock with sweet cornmeal. She told the people about the break, and they all went to the place together, and she spit on the cornmeal and made it like cement and fixed everything.

So when the dancers were in the trees, nothing broke. Then the Kachina Mother told the dancers to perform their Spruce Tree Dance again, but they said no. So nothing happened, no trees fell down. At noontime the dancers returned to their kiva for lunch. One of the beams of the kiva was broken, but it hadn't parted yet. The girl in Huckovi had done that. They didn't notice it. So the two Warrior Twins[1] went up on the ridge of the mesa, a place called Apovanevi—the white people call it Mount Beautiful —to get chicken feathers.[2] And while they were doing that, the kiva beam broke and caved down and killed all the people that were in the kiva. It was pretty bad. All those dancers were dead. When evening time came, they were not happy in Pivanhonkapi. Over in Huckovi, they clapped their hands and thought they had

[1]The Warrior Brothers, Palengahoya and Pokanghoya, apparently were supposed to guard the village from danger during the ceremony.
[2]The feathers were for ritual use.

done good. That kachina boy who was wanted by the two girls was dead, of course.

During the night when it was getting dark one of the men of Pivanhonkapi was sitting on top of his house. He was looking around and he saw a walking fire coming right towards him, right towards where he was. It got nearer and nearer and then went down to the foot of the village, then went into the Pivanhonkapi plaza. There was a shrine in the plaza, and the [figure that was carrying the fire] sat on the shrine and sang a song, like this:

She sounded like a ghost:

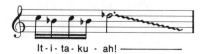

That's what she said. And all the dogs began to bark. Then she went on the housetop, said, "You come over here. Don't fear about me, you come over here, I'm the one that's going to help you people. There was an accident here a little while ago, and I want to do something that will please you." He went over, and she said, "Now, my boy, that was a sad thing that came upon you. I'll be on your side. I'm from the Little Colorado River. When I heard this news I wanted to come and help you. Those were pretty good people that you lost. I want to drive those Huckovi people from their village so you will get your liberty [from them]. All right. I want you to make four pieces of that soft parrot plume feathers. You turn that over to me, and when I get them from you I will help you."

So the man went to his place and fixed four pieces of parrot feathers for her and took them to her. She was well pleased. She said, "Now I want to go over to that place [Huckovi] and find out what kind of people they are, brave or not."

Next day when it was getting dark he saw that light again.

That ghost-like woman was singing that same song again, going toward Huckovi, that other village. She got to the foot of the mesa and climbed up into that village. Then she sent up to the tallest house and began to grind corn.[3] The song she sang:

Tu-ta-heh! Tu-ta-heh! Tu-ta voe-na heh!

Tu-ta voe-na heh! heh! Anh! ———

That's what she said. The people were beginning to tremble. They were shaking. Tutaheh, that was the name of the ghost woman, she pretended she was grinding corn with a mata and a grinder. Then she came down on the ladder and went away. But nobody put a hand on her, they were all afraid.

The next day she came again. This time they said, "We'll catch her, whoever she is. We're not afraid of her." On the trail that went to the bottom of the village, the men placed themselves there to catch her. When she came, the first man she came to got up and ran away, to the top of the mountain. All the men escaped and went up to the top of the mountain above the village. They never put their hands on her.

Then all the people began to move from that place. They selected whatever they were going to take along—grub and the blankets they were going to sleep with. Then the ghost woman drove them from the village down to the bottom and drove them out toward the west. They came to a certain place and they stopped [to sleep]. The next day she came back again and drove them some more, out to the Little Colorado River. Then she appeared to them just after sundown, came to them a little earlier. And they learned she lived at that place, the Little Colorado River. She made them cross the river and she left them there,

[3]That is, she went through the motions of grinding corn on a grinding stone. Comparable scenes are found in a number of stories. The grinding and the singing are intended to have ominous significance.

and from there they moved out to California. They say that those
people went to live near Riverside, you might say east, where
Redlands is. They made their home there. We call them Huc-
kovisinom, means Huckovi people. They call those people [in
California] Mission Indians. Some of their words are just like
our Hopi language. Over at the ruins of Pivanhonkapi you can
still see the holes in the rock where they put those trees for the
Spruce Tree Dance.

Chuka (Don C. Talayesva)
Oraibi, July 1970

———19———

Destruction by Fire

How the Village of Pivanhonkapi Perished

Pivanhonkapi, that village that had the spruce dance, they
say it was burned down in a big prairie fire that came from those
peaks in the south [San Francisco Mountains]. Oraibi was right
in the path of that fire too, but nothing there was touched by
fire. They say the flames went right around Oraibi. I heard that
some wizards, some two-heart people, had somthing to do with
it. They say there was a village of them out there somewhere, I
don't know where it was. But the main one responsible was the
chief of Pivanhonkapi.

Those people in his village were getting out of hand. They
didn't respect him and behave the way they were supposed to.
They used to go down in the kiva and do things there that they
weren't supposed to do. They got to gambling all the time, and
if a man didn't have anything else to bet he would bet his wife.
If the other person won he would take the woman. Maybe he
didn't keep her, just used her for betting, but if he wanted her
to stay with him he took her home with him. The women gambled too, forgot to grind their corn and make piki, just hung

around the kiva all the time. The chief kept telling the people they had to stop all this. He said he was the father of the village and they should listen to him. But instead of getting better, things got worse. Even the chief's wife was down there gambling. And it got so bad that men were taking other men's wives and women were taking other women's husbands. The men were not taking care of their fields either. Then one time the chief heard that his wife was playing around with the crier chief, and the crier chief took her and used her like she was his own wife. After that she went back to the kiva and gambled some more.[1]

Then the village chief said, "Well, now, there is no other way. This village of mine will have to come to an end." But he didn't know how to do it, so he sent his nephew with a message to the chief of the witches, the two-heart people[2]—they had a village a few miles north—to come and see him. That man came, and he sat down in the chief's kiva and they smoked together four times. Then the chief said, "Well, my village has got to be destroyed. The people are no good any more. They are doing bad things. They do not listen to me." Then he said, "I want you to see that Pivahonkapi is no more." The witch said, "Well, I can do that." The chief said, "I don't want anything to be left of this village." The witch chief said, "Yes, I can do that." The chief [of Pivanhonkapi] told him, "When we are gone, you can have our fields." The witch said, "Your fields are too far away, we don't want to walk so far to take care of them." The chief said, "Well, we have plenty of good peach trees out there, take them." The witch chief said, "Yes, that will be all right. Now you have to tell me how you want it to be done, by water, by wind, by shaking the earth, or by fire." And the Pivanhonkapi chief said, "Well, then, I choose fire." They agreed on that, and the two-heart told him, "Tell your people you are going to have a big dance in four days."

The kikmongwi did that. The crier chief went around the

---

[1]Note here the same motivation for destruction that appears in the Palatkwapi story. And as in the Awatovi story, as well, the chief arranges for the destruction of his own village.

[2]A version of this story given in Voth, *Traditions of Hopi*, pp. 241–44 calls the sorcerers Yayaponchatu.

village announcing there would be a dance. And when that day came the people started dancing, not dances praying for rain and good crops, but men and women dancing together. While this was going on, someone was sitting on one of the roofs and he called out, "There are some people coming. They are coming from the direction of the peach trees." Well, it was those powakas, those witch people, and they were all dressed in kachina kilts and masks, with eagle feathers in their hair. They were dressed something like the Somaikoli Kachinas, the Blind Ones.[3] They went all round the village four times, chanting,

Ha - ha - ah,   ee - hee - hee.

Something like that. Then they came into the plaza and danced there. I can't tell you [the meaning of] what they were chanting. Probably powaka language. One of those powaka men, I guess he was a priest or medicine man, carried around a bowl of sacred meal stuck with four prayer feathers, and when the dancing was over he started off south toward those [San Francisco] Peaks carrying the cornmeal and feathers with him. Well, after that, the dancers went home, and the Pivanhonkapi people went back down in the kiva and started gambling and carrying on again, the way they were before.

Well, four nights later there was a man sitting on top of the kiva and he saw a kind of spark, a fire, on the top of the peaks. He called down to the people [in the kiva], "Say, there's a kind of fire burning on the peaks. It looks funny to me." Some of the people came up and looked. They said, "Yes, it's there, all right, but I guess it doesn't mean anything." The next night the man was again sitting on the top of the kiva, and he saw the fire again, much larger. He told them [the people in the kiva], "Say, that fire is getting to look pretty big to me." So they came up and looked. They said, "Yes, it looks funny. But it's a long distance from here. Nothing to worry about." And they went down again.

[3]As noted elsewhere, there was a link between Somaikoli and the Yayas. See texts 45 and 46.

Then on the third night they saw the fire burning again, and it had sure spread. It was coming north. It seemed to be coming toward Oraibi Mesa. So they started to worry about that. Well, on the fourth night that prairie fire reached almost to the bottom of the mesa, and they could hear the sound of it. It didn't look very good for them.

Of course Oraibi was south of Pivanhonkapi, and the fire came to them first. When the kikmongwi of Oraibi saw that the fire was coming on them, he called for all the people to come to the kiva to decide what to do. And while they were all down there talking, the grandedame, Gogyeng Sowuhti, came to the top and stamped on the kiva roof.[4] They told her to come down and they welcomed her. She told them, "That fire isn't meant for us, it is meant for Pivanhonkapi because they are evil people over there. So I have come to let you know what to do to save this village. Here are two arrows. Take them down to the foot of the mesa and stick one of them in the ground on the east side, and the other one stick in the ground on the west side." They did that, and then Gogyeng Sowuhti went down below and spun a spiderweb from one arrow to another. She said, "Now, moisten that spiderweb with water." The people did that, and the part of the fire that reached that place stopped and died out. And so Oraibi was saved with the help of Spider Old Woman.

The fire went right around Oraibi on two sides. And it kept right on going until it reached Pivanhonkapi. When the people there saw what was happening, they grabbed whatever they could to save, and then they fled out of there. The flames burnt everything up. The roofs fell in and the walls turned black. So Pivanhonkapi came to its end. I can't tell you where those people went. They were scattered. Maybe some of them went back to Kawestima, north of Kayenta, or maybe some went back to Navajo Mountain, that's where the Snake and Horn clans came from. But we Sun Clan people don't know the details. You have to go to the Horn and Snake clan people to get their story about that. I don't even know what clans were living up there at Pivahonkapi. But I do know that the old ruins of Pivanhonkapi are

---

[4]The customary way of announcing one's presence.

there. I think you can still see some of the walls standing. I've been over there and seen them, but maybe they are all down by now, nothing left but broken pottery.

Chuka (Don C. Talayesva)
Oraibi, July 1970

————20————

The Races at Tsikuvi

Why the Payupki People Departed

Long ago there were people living in a village called Tsikuvi.[1] The men from that village were supposed to be fast runners, the men and the boys. There was also another village north of Tsikuvi called Payupki.[2] There weren't so many people living in Payupki. The people in Tsikuvi did strenuous dances during the winter months, and the people from Payupki would come and watch. Payupki had only one good runner. He noticed one day that the people of Tsikuvi were having races at their racing grounds. He told the chief what he had seen. The chief went to the edge of the mesa to observe. The races were over by that time, but he saw the chakmongwi [crier chief] of Tsikuvi going around from kiva to kiva announcing races to come the next day.

So he told his runner to go over there the next morning to race with the Tsikuvi young men and find out how good they

[1]The ruins of Tsikuvi are on a lower shelf of Second Mesa a short distance north of Shipaulovi and Mishongnovi.

[2]The site of Payupki is on a point of Second Mesa a little north of Tsikuvi. Most of this village has been obliterated, but at the time of writing, a few walls were still standing. The Payupkis were an Eastern Pueblo group who settled for a short time in Hopi country, then returned to the Rio Grande. From the edge of the mesa, Tsikuvi, on the lower ledge, was clearly visible.

were. When the boy saw the young men going to their racing grounds, he went down from Payupki. When he got to the racing grounds, all the runners were getting ready. The people were glad to see him. He said he would like to race with them. They said, "Fine, come on." So they formed a line, and when the signal was given they started running. Soon some of the runners fell behind, and the Payupki boy found himself in third place. Then pretty soon he found himself up in the second place, right behind the first runner. When the first runner saw him, he began to run a little faster. The Payupki boy didn't try to catch him, just ran behind. After the race, he came back home, and he told the chief what he had learned, that if he had wanted to he could have caught up with the first runner [and won].

The chief told him to practice running every day. He said they might have a race with Tsikuvi some time, and that the boy should be prepared. So the boy went out to practice every day at the Payupki racing ground. One day the people saw the chief of Tsikuvi coming up the trail to Payupki. They went to the kiva to wait and find out why he was coming. Soon they heard the Tsikuvi chief say "hai"[3] at the entrance. They all answered, "Hai." He started making his way down the ladder. He came down and sat beside the chief of Payupki. The Payupki chief picked up his pipe and filled it with tobacco. He lighted it. He took a few puffs and handed it to the chief of Tsikuvi. The Tsikuvi chief smoked until he finished the tobacco, and handed the pipe back. Then the Payupki chief asked the purpose of the other man's visit. The chief of Tsikuvi said, "I came to tell you that four days from tomorrow we will hold a race. I want your people to come and race with us. Bring anything that you have for prizes, anything that you want to bet against anyone. This race is just for pleasure." After that he went out.

The days went by, and the night before the races were to take place, the men were in the kiva making plans. Over in Tsikuvi also, they were in the kiva discussing these things, and while they were talking they heard somebody coming down the ladder. They saw that it was an old lady, Spider Old Lady, who lived in their village. She came down with her bag of herbs and

[3]Or "ha'i."

things and stopped at the first floor. The Tsikuvi men were not very glad to see her. They said, "What does she want down here? We don't want her." They told her to go back home and go to bed. Somebody gave her a push, and so she went up the ladder again. She was very angry. She decided to go to the other village.

So she went to her house and picked up all her things, and then she went to Payupki. When she got there she went to the kiva and started going down. When they heard her, someone called, "Come in." She went down the ladder real slow. Everybody was glad to see her. She came down to the first floor, and the chief stood up and said, "Come down and sit with me." So she went down and sat by the chief. He put some tobacco in his pipe. He lighted it, took a few puffs, and handed it to the Old Spider Lady. He said, "My daughter." She answered, saying, "My father."[4] She started smoking. She smoked with a flourish. She puffed out great big [clouds]. Everyone was smiling at her because they were thinking that she was an old lady and would soon become dizzy and fall over. But she smoked very well, all the tobacco that was in the pipe. Then the chief asked her the reason for her visit.

She said, "Yes, I have come here to try to help you. I was at my own kiva in my own village, but they did not treat me well. They chased me out. That is why I've come here to try to help you win the race. They are planning bad things for your runner. So I have brought all my medicines with me." The chief said, "It is fine that you are here to help us." The Spider Lady said, "Bring me your best runner, the one that will race tomorrow." She took something out of her bag, a little bowl. She put the bowl down and took out a bundle of something, then she took out another bundle. She took a pinch of something out of each of the bundles and put it into the bowl. She asked for water, so the chief sent a boy out with a water jug to get some water. He came back, put the jug of water down by the Spider Lady. She

[4]Though the chief is much younger than Spider Old Woman, he calls her "daughter" because he is regarded as the father of the village, and all the inhabitants of the village are his "children." The expression of relationship terms always accompanies smoking in the kiva.

poured some water into her bowl. She stirred it with her fingers, around and around. Then she asked the boy [runner] to step forward so she could rub his legs with this medicine. The chief said to the boy, "It is all right for you to come down so that the Spider Lady can put some of this medicine on your legs."

So the boy came down and the Spider Lady put the medicine on him, first one leg, then the other. Finally she said, "That will do. This will help you tomorrow." She said, "The men over in the other village are planning to stay up all night, doing whatever they are going to do to make sure the race will be won by them. But it is best for us to go to sleep and rest." That was what the chief wanted also. The old lady cleaned her bowl out and put it into her bag and tied it with a string. She asked if anyone had a room in his house for a visitor. One man answered, "We have a spare room in our house where you can sleep." He went to his house and told his wife, and the two of them went into the spare room and started a fire and brought food for her to eat. They fixed up bedding for Spider Lady. Everybody slept.

The next day they saw the men of Tsikuvi going down the trail to their racing grounds. So the Payupki people picked up their things [prizes] and went down also. The chief of Tsikuvi was glad to see them. "Are your people all here?" "Yes, we are all here." And so the races started right away. First was the short distance run. Each side offered its best runner, the boy from Payupki and Tsikuvi's fastest runner. From a certain point each of them went out in a circle, and when they met they started to race. They both ran well, but the Payupki boy won, and so the Payupki people took prizes from the Tsikuvi people. The runners rested a little bit, then they raced again, a little farther this time. The boy from Payupki won again. He won all the races. The people of Tsikuvi were not very happy about it and about losing all the things they'd brought for betting. The Payupki people started putting their things [winnings] in bundles to carry them home. The Tsikuvi chief told them that next year there would be another meet, and he would let them know. He told them to go home with this thought in mind.

The Payupki people returned to their village and went straight to their kiva with their bundles. They showed one another the things they had won—woven belts and moccasins and things like that. Old Lady Spider was very happy. One of the men gave her a dress that he'd won, and somebody gave her a woven belt. She received many things. After that, Old Lady Spider continued living in Payupki. The boy runner decided that he was going to practice running every day to become even better than he already was.

The boy had a sister, and she was always grinding corn. One day she saw him practicing, and when he came home she said she'd seen him running and she didn't believe he could run very well. She said she would race him the next day. The next day she went down to the racing grounds with her brother. He said, "You go on down the dip and up the rise, and wait for my signal. I'll give you this head start. When you hear the signal, start running." So she went down the dip and up the hill. And while she was waiting, she put her skirt up and tucked it under her belt. He gave the signal and they started running. He chased her. He came down the dip and up the hill. And when he came up the hill he saw that his sister was way off, ahead of him. He ran very hard. She reached the turning point. She passed her brother still going. She said, "You are not running." Soon she came to the finish line. She stopped there and put her skirt down, then she went home up the trail.

Her brother finally came to the finish line. He was very surprised. He rested a while, then he went back up to the village. He found his sister grinding corn. He said, "My sister, aren't you tired from running?" She said, "I don't call that running." She went on grinding. She said, "I will race you again tomorrow." Her brother said, "All right."

The next day they went down to the racing grounds again. This time she said she would start out with him. So they stood at their mark. She fixed her skirt up under her belt real tight. Her brother gave the signal and they started running. They went down the dip and up the hill and straight on. Her brother was behind her again. She came to the turn, made the turn, and started back. She met her brother still going. She said, "Run, my brother, you are not running. Try harder." She went on and reached the starting point. There she put her skirt down and went home. When her brother got home, his sister was grinding again. He said, "My sister, aren't you tired from running?"

She said, "No, I'm not tired. I could run much faster. The way you are running, you will not win any races."

The next day they went down again [to the racing grounds]. This time she told her brother to start from the hilltop. He went down the dip and up the hill and waited. The girl fixed her skirt and tightened her belt. Then she said, "Run, my brother." They started running. Before he was halfway she was even with him. She passed him. She made the turn, came back [to where her brother was going the other way] and said, "Run, my brother, you are not running. Try harder." She reached the finish line way ahead of him. The boy saw that his sister could run like he hadn't ever seen anyone run. It seemed that her feet hardly touched the ground. When he came home, she was grinding again. It was then that he decided he would tell the chief about his sister.

So he went to the chief's house. He told the chief about his sister. He said he thought his sister should be the runner for the next meet. The days went by. Soon it was time again for the races. And one day they saw the chief of Tsikuvi making his way up to their village. So the people gathered down at the kiva. The chief arrived and said, "Hai." They answered, "Hai." He came down the ladder into the kiva, and the Payupki chief invited him to sit with him. He fixed the tobacco again in the pipe and took a few puffs and gave it to the chief of Tsikuvi. He smoked. He smoked it all and handed it back to the chief of Payupki. Then he asked the reason for his visit. He said, "Yes, I have come to tell you that is about time that we held a meet. Four days from tomorrow we will hold a race at our racing grounds again. I would be happy if you would all come down. So this is what I have come to tell you." He came out of the kiva and went back to his village.

Then the days went by real fast. The night before the racing was to take place, the men of Tsikuvi missed their Old Spider Lady. They hadn't seen her for a long time. They asked each other if anyone had seen her recently, and they were sort of waiting for her to help them. The chief asked one of the men to go to her house to bring her down. But they remembered that they had not treated her well and [thought] that she might not be interested. So one of the men went out to her house, and then he came back and said that Old Spider Lady wasn't home. Her place had not been lived in for quite a while. The men said that maybe she had become angry and moved out of the village to some other village. So they said, "Oh, well, we'll get along without her."

And at the other kiva at Payupki, she was there with the men. When they were through smoking, the Old Spider Lady said, "Now I will fix my medicine and rub it on the runner's legs." They told her that it was the girl [who would run]. I forgot to say that when the Tsikuvi chief came to Payupki they told him that a girl would race for them this time. He said, "Is she the only one that you have?" They said, "Yes, she seems to be the best one we have now." The chief of Tsikuvi said, "All right. If she is the only one you have, then I guess it is all right."

So the Spider Lady asked the girl to step down. Her brother said she wasn't down there [in the kiva]. He went to his house to get her, and he brought her in. The Old Spider Lady mixed her medicine in the bowl and stirred it around with her fingers. And she rubbed this [medicine] on the girl's legs and feet, first one side and then the other side. When she was through she said that the men at Tsikuvi were planning bad things for the Payupki runner. This medicine should ward off the bad [medicine] and help her, so she won't be hurt. Then everybody came out of the kiva and went to their homes to bed.

The next day, when they saw the men of Tsikuvi going down the trail, the Payupki people gathered their things [i.e., prizes] to take along. This time the women were going with them, and they took their grinding stones, anything that women used in the home that could be carried. They would bet these things against the other village [runner]. They carried all these things on their backs. When they reached the racing grounds, the people of the other village were already there.

The chief of Tsikuvi said, "Are your people all here?" And the chief of Payupki said, "Yes, I think we are all here, so the racing will start right away. Bring out your runner." So they brought out their girl, and she had this ateu'eu about her shoulders. The chief of Tsikuvi said, "Does she want to take off that ateu'eu?" They asked her, and she said no, she would keep it on. But she put up her skirt in front and tightened her belt so that it wouldn't come loose.

And they took the two runners down to the starting place. They made a circle, came together, and started off. The people saw that she could run. She really could run, she flew along. She finished ahead of the other runner. They had another race, then another, then another until the last one. They were to start from this end and run to a certain place and then come back. The Old Spider Lady was there with the Payupki people. She made herself small and climbed onto the girl's ear, so that she could tell her what to do. So the runners made a circle, came together, and started off.

The girl could really run. By the time they reached the turning point, the girl had left the boy a few feet behind. The Old Lady said, "Run, my daughter, run!" Then suddenly something made a swishing sound right past them. They saw that it was a white dove. The Old Lady said, "You see what is happening. The boy has turned into a dove." The dove is supposed to be very swift. The white dove was flying way ahead of them. [So] the Old Lady gave a signal to the one sitting on top of the mesa, a hawk. It was her bird. She gave the signal and the hawk came swooping down and hit the dove [from above]. The dove went rolling [on the ground]. That gave the girl a chance to catch up. She passed the dove. But before she had gone very far, the dove caught up and passed her again. Spider Old Lady told the hawk to strike again. So the hawk came down again and sent the dove rolling. He did that four times, and after that Old Spider Lady said, "Now they will try something different. When I tell you to jump sideways to your right, you must jump quickly."

Pretty soon the Old Woman gave the signal to jump. "Jump, my daughter." The girl jumped to the right. Just then something landed where she had been [a moment before]. The girl went on running. Spider Lady said, "Next time when I say jump, jump to your left." Pretty soon she said, "Now!" The girl jumped to her left, and the thing, whatever it was, missed her. It went on like that till the fourth time. [Spider Lady] said, "One more time, and then you must jump straight up." The next time she gave the signal the girl jumped straight up, and something landed right [where the girl had been]. It missed her, and that was the last time.

The girl went on. Spider Old Lady said, "Now there isn't anything more [to worry about]." The girl kept running as fast as she could. Pretty soon the people at the racing grounds where the race had started saw her coming. They said, "Someone is coming." But they could see only one runner. The next one was not yet in sight. Then, pretty soon, they saw the second runner coming [in the distance]. And they saw that the girl was ahead and the boy was lagging far behind. Finally she came to the finish line. The Spider Lady told her, "Run past the finish line, up to that pile of rocks, and then come back, the way the Tsikuvi runners do." So the girl came on, and the people saw that her feet were hardly touching the ground. She was not even tired. She ran to the pile of rocks and came back.

The people of Tsikuvi were wondering how come their runner was so far behind. So the [Tsikuvi] chief sent men to get him. When they reached him, he was tired out. They scolded him. "Hurry up, the girl is up to the finish line already. You are beaten." He said he was too tired to run any more. The men brought him back walking. When he reached the finish line the Tsikuvi people were not very glad to see him. They were sort of scolding him.

Before this last race, the women of Tsikuvi said that their men had bet so heavily that they had lost everything. They didn't have any prizes left to bet on the final race. The Tsikuvi women said that if their runner lost, the people of Payupki could take them [the Tsikuvi women] as prizes. The Tsikuvi men said, "That's all right if you go with the Payupki people. We can get along without you." So when the girl runner came in first, the Tsikuvi women stepped over to join the Payupkis, the women and the young girls. The Payupki people picked up all their things, what they had brought and all their winnings. The Tsikuvi men went back to their village. They weren't very happy.

When the Payupkis got to their village on the mesa they went to the plaza and put everything down and looked at the things they had won. They gave some things to the Spider Woman, a string of turquoise beads and two strands of turquoise earrings. She was very happy about that. The women of Tsikuvi were all bunched together. They were all noticing that the men and boys were very handsome, and they were commenting that this one or that one was very good-looking, saying, "I'd like to get to know him." Another one would choose someone else. They were talking like that, choosing the men and the boys. They were in-

terrupted by the Spider Woman, who said the women of Tsikuvi
were to be taken down into the kiva. So they all went down into
the kiva, and the Spider Woman said that the men and the boys
were to leave the Tsikuvi women and girls alone, because, she
said, "We don't know what is going to happen in the future.
The Tsikuvi men may be planning to come and take their women
back. So you men and boys, leave the women alone." And the
chief said, "It shall be so." Then he said, "Anyone who has room
in his[5] home, if he is willing, should take one of these women
in until we build homes for them."

So the men went out of the kiva to their houses and told
their wives about it, and so they got busy and made room for
the Tsikuvi women. Most of them had rooms where they kept
corn, roomy places where one or two persons could live for the
time being. The men returned to the kiva and told the chief that
there was room for all of the Tsikuvi women and girls. Two or
three of them could share a room. So they took the women home
to their places. The men chopped wood for them [for their fires].
They said they would provide corn for them and other things to
eat. The village lived on that way.

At first the men of Tsikuvi did not feel very bad about losing their wives. They said they could work just as well as the
women. They had seen their wives grind corn, and it looked easy.
The men could do that, and they could shell corn, and they could
make piki. The women had left a supply of piki in their homes,
so the men had this to eat. Some of them who didn't want to
cook anything went to another man's house, and they would fix
some food together. But as time went on, they used up all the
piki [that the women had left behind], and soon they used up
all the corn flour. They said they would grind corn and make
piki. So they got busy shelling corn. Some of them who weren't
very good at this scattered the corn all over the floor. They had
to pick up corn from all over the place. When they got through
with that they would start grinding. They had these matas that
the women grind on. They'd sit down behind this grinding stone,
and they'd take a mataki, a long piece of rock just wide enough

[5]Strictly speaking, the homes belonged to the women, though in an in-
formal way the men would speak of the homes as their own.

to hold. They'd put the corn between the mata and the mataki
and start grinding. The men had a time doing that, because the
corn was slippery and would slide right under the mataki and
whole kernels would come out underneath, instead of being
cracked. They tried and tried and soon they managed to grind
some. They didn't know it was so hard, that it was so much work.
It took a lot of time to grind corn, enough to last them for a while.

Some of them decided to make piki, the way their wives
did. And so they went to the piki house and made a fire under
the big black flat stone that they use [for baking piki]. When it
was good and hot—of course, they had mixed the batter already,
the flour and water and the juice from a certain kind of bush
ashes—with their hands they would spread this batter across
the hot stone. They discovered that it was not so easy. They
would burn their hands and shake their hands around to cool
them. Before they were through covering the stone with batter,
the front part was already curling up, and they made the piki so
heavy that when they were through they had to put it out to
dry. The piki dried in hard sheets so that it had to be soaked in
water before they could eat it.

This went on for a long while, till they decided they could
not go on living this way. They wanted their wives back. So they
got together in the kiva and talked about it and decided that the
next day they would go to look for material to make bows and
arrows. The next day they went looking for materials, and they
came back with a whole lot [of these things]. They made arrows
first. They peeled off the bark, and they warmed [the arrow
shafts] near the fire so they could be straightened out. When
they were all nice and straight, they put them on the floor. They
worked this way for several days, until they were through with
straightening the sticks. Then they went after material to make
bows. They brought these [sticks] back and started peeling them
and whittling them. This went on for several days, and then they
wanted feathers for the arrows, so they went after them. Finally
they had enough bows and arrows to take along with them [on
an expedition against Payupki].[6]

By now in Payupki the [Tsikuvi] women were living in new

[6]The narrator made no mention of arrow points.

houses in groups of three, and they were well taken care of. The men chopped wood and brought it in for them. They killed some of their cattle that they had a whole herd of, enough so that everyone was supplied with meat. They dried some of the meat for future use. The Tsikuvi women were very happy here.

Then one day the Old Spider Lady called the men together again, and she told them that she had been over to the other village and found the men in the kiva making bows and arrows and talking about when they would come to Payupki. They were planning to take back their wives and also [the other] women of Payupki. She told the men to look for their horses early in the morning and round up the cattle and put them in the corral.[7] She said that the next morning they would start out early and that they should have their wives fix them lunches to take along. They would drive the cattle east until they came to the end of the south wall and then turn right, make a crossing there, turn right till they came to a high hill. They would climb this and turn to the east again. This wasn't just a hill, it was a plateau. Then they would travel east till they came to a canyon. They would find a place to drive their cattle down and follow the canyon until they came to the end, and there they would find water for their horses and their cattle.[8] They must not waste time anywhere.

So early the next morning they started rounding up their cattle. They put them in the corral. The women gave the men their lunches, cornmeal and piki, and the following day they started driving their cattle east. They drove along the south wall until they came to a place where the Spider Woman had told them to cross south. They traveled south until they came to the hill. They climbed up and traveled east, coming to a place the Spider Lady called Awatovi. They passed this and came to a canyon, and they looked for a place to drive their cattle down. They went down into the canyon and followed all the way to the end,

[7]There were no horses or cattle among the Hopis until after the arrival of the Spanish. This tale takes place during the Spanish period. The Payupkis came to Hopi country to get away from the Spaniards along the Rio Grande.

[8]The narrator is describing actual terrain between Payupki, on Second Mesa, and Jeddito Wash, though the precise canyon is not indicated. There are numerous canyons in this area.

and there they found water. When their animals had gotten enough water, they started east again.

Back at Payupki, the Old Lady Spider had called the women together and said that they would follow the men. The next morning early, they picked up their things and got started down the hill. The Old Lady came down last, and she was carrying a big jug. She set it down. She said, "We cannot take along some of these things you have in your bundles, like beads and things that you won from the Tsikuvi people. They are heavy, and they will interfere with our traveling. When you are tired, they will become heavy." The women put all their treasures into the jug. They sealed it up with a rock and dug a hole in the ground deep enough to bury it. They put the jug in and covered it up with dirt. Then they started east, following the tracks of the men. They traveled until they came to the crossing, went south, climbed the hill and turned east, and finally went down into the canyon. The poor women were tired, some of them, but they rested only a little while and started out again. They were afraid that the men of Tsikuvi would follow them and catch up with them. So they traveled like that, day and night, until they caught up with the men and the cattle.

After that they all traveled together for days, until they came to a [certain] place. There they saw a man coming toward them, driving a good-sized herd of cattle. They stopped and waited for him. When he came up to them, he spoke to them in a strange tongue and nobody understood.[9] But Old Lady Spider understood and she spoke to him. She turned around to the chief and said, "The man wants to gamble with us for our cattle." The chief said that they had traveled so far that they shouldn't take a chance on losing their cattle. But the man said that that was the only way that he would let them go, so they decided to try.

Spider Lady said, "You all know each other well, and you know which one can shoot the straightest and the hardest." And so they picked out a man who could shoot straight and hard.[10] Old Lady Spider said, "I want to speak to one of your

[9]After the story was finished, the narrator added, "The man with the strange language was a Castilla, a Spaniard."

[10]The narrator indicates, without spelling it out, that the contest will be in shooting, as becomes clear a few lines further on.

kaletakas."[11] And so a man came up and stood before her, and she was giving him instructions what to say when she gave the signal. The stranger said he would try first. He had a strange looking stick in his hand. He raised that to his shoulder. He pressed something and there was a big bang. He had hit the stump, but it didn't crack right in half the way he said [it would]. He had said that they should crack that stump in half, and the one who could do it would be the winner.

So it was their turn. The man [who would shoot] stepped up, and the Old Lady gave the signal, and the kaletaka said, "Place your arrow on your bow." The next signal was, "Take aim." And the next signal, "Let your arrow fly." When the kaletaka said, "Place your arrow," a cloud formed right over them, and it turned dark. And at the last, when the man let his arrow go, there was a big clap of thunder and lightning [came down] at the same time, and they saw that the stump had fallen apart. The [strange] man was surprised. They walked up to the stump, and an arrow was imbedded in it. The stranger was very astonished that the Payupki man could shoot this way. And so the people increased their herd right there and traveled on east, until days later they came to a nice, wide stream of water, either it was a stream or a river. The Old Lady said, "Here is the place I chose for us to live." And so they settled right there, and the next day they started gathering material to build their new homes. This is where they stayed. There is supposed to be a village there [now] called Payupki, right below Sioki, in New Mexico. Maybe it's still there, we don't know.[12]

The men that were left behind in Tsikuvi tried to follow them, but they could not catch them so they gave up and went back home and continued living the way they were after they lost their women.

Tsakaptamana
Moencopi, March 1969

[11]A warrior.
[12]The narrator's tradition was that Payupki, like Tsikuvi, was a Hopi village, and that it was Hopis who migrated to the Rio Grande and settled there. See footnote 2.

————21————

The Village
at Queungofovi

Yes! This story is about the beginning of Mishongnovi and Shipaulovi.

Many years ago, according to my grandma, my grandpa, my own father, and especially my uncle—the old people told me a story about Queungofovi, meaning round rock up on top—round stones on top of the little mesa. That mesa belonged to the Nuvangnyam, the Snow Clan. Snow Clan people. They owned that mesa. Now, there were no buildings up on top except one house. That was before the Mishongnovi people lived down below over on the west side of the [Second] Mesa. The people were there [at Queungofovi] for years and years.

And there was some kind of a bird called teukchi, a mean bird. The people said he would come out only at noontime, about one o'clock in Hopi time. He would come out and fly [around]. He was bigger than an eagle. His wings would [stretch] out, as if they were made of plastic. He would go [flying] all day, about two or three hours, then he would return. But somehow he must not have been getting anything [to take] home, so he picked on the people living on the west side of Queungofovi. If the children were out playing, he would come and grab one of them and carry him away with his [claws], and his wings carried him over [the village] and took him home. That went on quite some time, so the head people there at Queungofovi all got together to figure out what they were going to do. They wanted to kill the bird, but there was no way of killing him. He'd never come out. His home was over by Corn Rock, but not as high as that one.[1] Down below was a big cave, like, way down underneath. There was a spring there, all [muddy] in the hole.

[1]This mythological predator operating in the vicinity of Corn Rock is very reminiscent of a story about a predatory hawk at virtually the same site. See text 71, "Grey Hawk and the Field Mouse."

That was his home. And they would go in there with spears and bows and arrows and never come out. He knew what he was doing. He didn't want to get killed.

So they decided to move away from that place. They came over here to Old Shongopovi, not the present village. It's down below [the mesatop] on that little hill. Their higher-ups asked the head man at Shongopovi if they could move there, asked him to take one, two, three, four days to think over whether he would accept them or not. So they came [on the fourth day] and the head man at Shongopovi said, "No, you can't come over here unless you have some kind of a possession [i.e., talent or magic] that will be helpful to us."

They said they didn't have anything. "All right. I and my four higher up men have been talking about this thing. Our enemies have been coming [frequently], stealing our crops from the fields when the corn is mature. At harvest time the Apaches have been coming in on horseback with sacks and watching and waiting till evening when the owners of the fields go home. Then they come in and harvest the corn, fill up their sacks and go home. They never raise anything themselves, just raid on other people. At first they just took corn, but later on they began taking girls and women, kidnaped them. This happened four different times. Our important men have agreed to accept you if you will be our protectors. They say you can make your home right over there near Corn Rock [below present day Mishongnovi] and watch for any enemies that are coming. If the enemies should come, you are the ones who will fight for us. This is going to be your job.[2] You can settle over there. That land is all Shongopovi land."

The people were happy and started moving over. But they did not all go over there. Some of them stopped at this little butte called Changaieuteika. We call that place Changaieuteika, Seven Houses Point, because there were only seven houses there. Some

---

[2]We encounter here a theme central to the story of the Tewas' establishment on First Mesa. Tewas from the Rio Grande village of Tsewageh, tradition says, came to Hopi country to be protectors of the village of Walpi. See Courlander, *The Fourth World of the Hopis*, pp. 164–174, and Yava, *Big Falling Snow*, pp. 26–34.

of the ones who stayed were related to Shongopovi people, and so they let them stay there. They didn't come down into Shongopovi, but later they moved over to Shipaulovi, next to Mishongnovi. So the Shipaulovis are part Shongopovis, and all through the years they held their initiations down below at Old Shongopovi.

When the Spanish came, the Hopis [of Old Shongopovi] came up here to the top of the mesa, and Old Shongopovi became ruins. The people came up here so they could see the enemy coming.

Lomaheungva (Porter Timeche)
Shongopovi, June 1981

2
RECOLLECTIONS
AND
EXPLANATIONS

———22———

The Emergence
as a Children's Story

I'm familiar with that children's story. They want to block the real story [of origins] until the children are initiated into the [kiva] societies, that's why they tell this story [in the meantime]. They tell the story of how the people were in the [under]world, and when they came up they found out that Masauwu was over here. They say that there was a young girl [who came up with them]. They thought that she was a good girl, but afterward they found out that she was a witch, a witch woman. The reason that they'd come up was that they'd wanted to avoid that bad stuff down there. That was the reason they'd moved out. But that's a children's story.

[They tell] the other stories after you've been initiated, after you've become new-born again. They baptize you[1] and give you "the mother," a perfect corn [ear], perfect stock, good kernels. That's our principal food, that's the reason they use it as their "mother." And then when you become educated,[2] that's when you're born again, you get your new name.[3] Then you are warned not to tell the children about the secret things. This is like some

[1]The traditional Hopi washing of the head with yucca suds, not Christian baptism.
[2]That is, when a person has learned the rituals and beliefs of the kiva society.
[3]Persons are given new names after initiation and at the time of burial. See text 26.

[white] lodges, they don't tell you anything [about what they've learned]. So we have two kinds of stories [about origins], the children's story and the men's story. Most of those stories they told Voth[4] were not the true, secret stories of the religion. I read some of the Voth stories the Smithsonian Institution had from the Hopis. Some places he was altogether wrong.

In the old days when someone wanted to make [up] a story for children to work in between the serious parts of a ritual or ceremony, he went to the kikmongwi to ask permission. They'd smoke, and afterward the chief would ask him, "Now, what is it you want?" "Well, I'm making a story. If it's permissible I'll go and tell the story." "What character do you put in the story?" He would tell him. Then the kikmongwi would ask the chakmongwi, the town crier. He would ask if it would be all right for this man to tell this story. The chakmongwi would say, "Well, that's all right. Go ahead." The reason for this was so as to not distort the stories belonging to any clan.[5]

Homer Cooyama
Kikeuchmovi, July 1970

————23————

The Deity Masauwu

Masauwu is very supreme in the universe, but he's an evil[1] supreme. He's in the atmosphere. He's in the spirit. But he's not

---

[4]A Mennonite missionary. See text 39.

[5]This narrator's opinion that the story of the emergence was a stopgap for the young is unusual. The story is generally accepted as part of adult tradition, and it is alluded to or dramatized in various rituals.

[1]Hopis frequently use the word *evil* to characterize Masauwu, probably in the sense of "malevolent." Albert Yava, who provided many of the texts in this volume, said of Masauwu: "People claim that he is either evil or good. It's according to the way you conduct yourself. If you are good, he'll bless you with good spirits. If you're bad, he'll destroy you."

good. There are people who belong to the Masauwu Clan, or the Ghost Clan. They say he lives right with us here, unseen. But he can appear to you as a person, and he disappears. He can show [himself] by his burning fire or he can show himself in different forms. The Hopis know that. When I got this double pneumonia, before I caught it, my wife saw the fire up there way at midnight, it went up three times. She prayed hard that nothing would happen. And after about four days I got it. I was ready to go off from this world. But she prayed hard, and that saved me.

And then myself, when I was at the Riverside [California] School in 1914, there too I saw a fire three times. First it was there, then it went down, then it went up. Big fire, up this high. You could see it clear, but I was the only one that saw it. I was the captain of Company E, and I was watching as we were bringing down the flag. It was during the winter, and I saw that fire. That same night I got a letter that my first cousin's mother had died. This fellow [left the school and] went home.

Another time, back here [New Oraibi], there was going to be a butterfly dance up in Old Oraibi. And we young men were going up there for a rehearsal for the butterfly dance, during the night. And we young men had a little [lantern] device we'd made, a can with a little wire [handle] on it and pitch inside. We took that little can along. Before we got halfway to Oraibi, we saw a fire coming, moving. And we knew that it was Masauwu. He moved. Before we got to the top of the cliff, we beat it back, threw everything away. So we know that this evil spirit is around.

One time there was going to be a basket dance, and two of us were sitting out in the evening, myself and the man who was sponsoring the basket dance. We saw a fire coming down from a certain place, and it went down into the kiva. As soon as it went down, this man who was sponsoring the dance went down with a lantern. In a little while the fire came up again and went up the hill. And that was bad news too.

[Things like this] make the Hopis believe Masauwu is always evil. They have to worship that Masauwu. They make a prayer for him and everything.

According to the [creation or emergence] story, Masauwu was already up here when the people came. But they know that

Masauwu had been already thrown out by some spirit, like Satan
in the Bible, thrown out and burned up. But he had a strong
spirit or power. He was thrown into a place where stuff was
burned, but he survived. That's why this figure has no hair, that's
the way they represent him in costume. No hair, and blood all
over, just eyes and nose, he looks terrible. Real neglected, never
took a bath. That's the way he looks when they present him. I
saw that the last time the Ghost Clan portrayed him. They go
out and hunt rabbits and collect the blood, and they put that all
over him. He wears a rabbit skin cape, the fur inside and the
skin outside. He looks fierce. These things, what they do to him,
people don't know [generally], but I know because I'm Coyote
Clan and we're related to the Ghost Clan, the Fire Clan. That's
how they picture him. He has a mask, too, that makes him look
like a warrior.

Now, they have a pumpkin filled with ashes in the Masauwu
ceremony. That is a prophecy. It is Masauwu's pumpkin. Today
I figure that this represents the atomic bomb, because ashes
represent "burned up." I'll give you an illustration. One time I
had a pumpkin in the stove. I didn't put a hole in it [for the steam
to escape]. I just left it there. And all at once the thing exploded
and knocked everything around. See how powerful it is? This is
a prophecy of the atomic bomb.

Homer Cooyama
Kikeuchmovi, July 1970

———24———

The Land of the Dead[1]

About that place where the dead live, we don't hear so much
about it over here in Walpi. The Oraibis claim that it is their story.

---

[1]Compare with versions in Voth, *Tradition of the Hopi*, pp. 114–19, and
Yava, *Big Falling Snow*, pp. 98 ff.

The spirits of the dead are supposed to go down there. They have their own village, just like up here in Hopiland, but it isn't made of hard substance, like rocks, but, you might say, [of] fog, something like that. From what I heard, everything is the other way around, just the opposite. Those people—not really people, but the breath of people—don't eat solid food, only the part you can smell. They cook the meat and eat the smell of it, then they throw the meat away. That's what I heard. The young folks have rabbit hunts, just like here, but they don't hunt rabbits, only grasshoppers and crickets. They say down there that the dead spirits are alive and that us live people up here are dead. That's what I heard from my uncle, but he told me it is an Oraibi story.

That place where the dead ones are is called Maski. That word *mas* means dead. It's the town of the dead. Masauwu, that's the name of the dead spirit who owned all this land around here. Before we Hopis arrived, he lived up there where the Snake Rock is, right at the edge of the plaza in Walpi. That's where he slept. They say he was thrown into the fire down there in Maski, but he didn't die. He crawled out of the fire. He was burnt pretty bad, all over his skin, and his hair was all burned off. He was pretty terrible looking, with a red head and blood all over him. The Oraibis tell you that the big fire is still burning down in Maski, waiting for bad people to be thrown into it. When a person dies his spirit or his soul goes down—it looks just like the person when he was alive—and there are two people waiting for him at a fork [of the trail], a One Horn priest and a Two Horn Priest. They argue over him, whether he was a good man or a bad man when he was alive, and if he was bad they throw him in the pit [of fire].

According to those Oraibis, you go west when you die to Grand Canyon, over where the Oraibis go for their salt. Somewhere around there. They claim that the sipapuni is there too, the place where we Hopis all came out of the underworld. Around there somewhere is the road to Maski. That's where the dead spirits go. And they have all kinds of punishments for the bad ones.

They [the Oraibis] have that story about a young man who went to Maski and got a look at it and then came back. They tell it when somebody wants to know what it's like. Well, this young

man is supposed to have told his father that he wanted to go
down there and see for himself. His father said, "My son, no
one can go down to Maski except a dead spirit or soul." But the
boy said, "Well, just the same I want to go down and see it. Then
when I come back I can tell you what it's like."

It made the boy's father pretty sad to hear that. But he sent
for a medicine man to come and help his boy go. The medicine
man told the boy, "You don't have to go. It's not your time yet.
When you die, then it will be time [enough]." But the young
man said, "No, I want to go now." So the medicine man told
him to lie down on his blanket, and he covered him with an ova[2]
and rubbed some kind of medicine on him. After a while that
boy stopped breathing, just like he was dead. But his spirit, we
call it breath, got up and went out of the house and started walking west on a trail. He went through some cactus fields, four of
them, and after some time he came to the edge of Grand Canyon. But he didn't know how to go down, or where to go from
there. While he was standing there a kaletaka (warrior), an old
man, a priest, came up and told him to take off his kilt and
put it on the ground. He did that. Then the Kaletaka told
him to stand on it, and he did that. Then the kilt just lifted
up and floated over the canyon a ways and set him down at
the bottom.

There was a trail, still going west, and he went along that
way. He began to see a lot of dead spirits walking along real slow.
They were trying to climb sand hills, but they kept slipping back.
Couldn't get anywhere. Then further along he saw some more
dead spirits, masauwus, carrying heavy loads. He saw women
all bent over, with loads of matas and matakis on their backs.
They had real narrow forehead straps on their foreheads, and
it cut into their skin and pained them. All these people were
masauwus who were being punished for things they had done
[when alive]. They walked a little way, then rested, then walked,
then rested. The way they were going would take them maybe
four years to reach Maski.

Then the boy came to the fork, and there was a One Horn
and a Two Horn priest there. They saw he wasn't really dead

[2]A so-called bridal robe.

and asked him what he wanted. He said he just wanted to see what it was like down there, to see if it was true. They said, "No, you can't come here till you die." And the boy said, "Well, as you can see, this isn't my real body, just the spirit. My real body is up at Oraibi." They said, "Well, we can see what has happened. Some medicine man has separated your iksi [breath] from your living body. But still you aren't really dead yet." The boy told them, "I have come all this way to see what it is like. I'd like to look around and then I'll go back." Finally they said, "Okay, if you are really going back. Come over here and we'll show you something." They took him a little ways down the right-hand trail and showed him a big roaring fire in a deep pit. That fire was something. It was like a volcano, giving out sparks and ashes. Had a kind of blue flame. Well, they said to the boy, "Take a look at that. That's where all the evil ones go. When you were coming here on the trail you saw some of them. Those people were trying to go fast, but they weren't getting anywhere. They've been on the way four years.[3] They did pretty bad things when they were alive, and now they're getting punished. Some of those men you saw, when other men were in their fields working hard, the way Hopis are supposed to do, those fellows seduced their wives, maybe raped them. Or they didn't respect the chief, who is supposed to be the father of the village, or didn't take care of the old people. And those women, they played around a lot with men, or they didn't take care of their children. When they get here we'll decide if they can be forgiven. But if they've been too evil, they can't be excused, and we'll toss them into the pit." Just then a man came along and they grabbed him. They said, "This one was too bad, we can't excuse him." They took him by his hands and feet and tossed him down into the fire.

After that, they took the boy back to the fork and let him go on the other trail to the village where the dead spirits were living. He saw a bunch of kids on a rabbit hunt, but they were hunting grasshoppers and crickets and things like that. They saw him coming and began to yell, "Look out, here comes a masauwu!" You see, they called him a dead spirit. They acted like they were

[3]The narrator meant to convey that they would be on the trail four years before arriving at the fork.

alive and he was dead.[4] They ran like anything. Well, he got to
the village where the people were living. That village looked just
like his own village, Oraibi. He even saw some old people he
knew when they were alive. There were women and kids as well
as men, but nobody paid any attention to him. He thought he
would go on top of a roof and started to climb a ladder, but the
steps, the rungs, just broke under him and he couldn't go up.
Those steps were made out of cornstalks or sunflower stalks, and

[4]In his "Archeological Expedition to Arizona in 1895," p. 647, Jesse Walter
Fewkes describes the experiences of dead spirits ("breath-bodies," as he for-
tuitously translates the term) in more detail, stressing the purification aspects
of the fiery ordeal:

> There are two roads from the grave to the Below. One of these is a
> straight way connected with the path of the sun into the Underworld.
> There is a branch trail which divides from this straight way, passing from
> fires to a lake or ocean. At the fork of the road sits Tokonaka, and when
> the breath-body comes to this place this chief looks it over and, if satis-
> fied, he says, "You are very good; go on." Then the breath-body passes
> along the straight way to the far west, to the early *Sipapû*, the Underworld
> from which it came, the home of Müiyinwû. Another breath-body comes
> to the fork in the road, and the chief says, "You are bad," and he con-
> ducts it along the crooked path to the place of the first fire pit, where sits
> a second chief, Tokonaka, who throws the bad breath-body into the fire,
> and after a time it emerges purified, for it was not wholly bad. The chief
> says, "You are good now," and carries it back to the first chief, who ac-
> cepts the breath-body and sends it along the straight road to the west.
>   If, on emerging from the first fire, the soul is still unpurified, or not
> sufficiently so to be accepted, it is taken to the second fire pit and cast
> into it. If it emerges from this thoroughly purified, in the opinion of the
> judge, it is immediately transformed into a prayer-beetle. All the beetles
> we now see in the valleys or among the mesas were once evil Hopi. If, on
> coming out of the second fire pit, the breath-body is still considered bad
> by the chief, he takes it to the third fire, and, if there be no evil in it when
> it emerges from this pit, it is metamorphosed into an ant, but if unpurified
> by these three fires—that is, if the chief still finds evil left in the breath-
> body—he takes it to a fourth fire and again casts it into the flames, where
> it is utterly consumed, the only residue being soot on the side of the pit.

The explanation that the "breath-spirits" climb out of the fire relates to the
fragmentary tradition that Masauwu, the deity of death, crawled out of a fiery
pit where he was badly burned and disfigured.

they wouldn't hold a live person. Only dead spirits could climb them. So after a while he went back to where the One Horn and Two Horn [priests] were, and he told them he was going home. They said, "Well, you can tell the people what it's like down here, but after this no one who's alive should ever try to get in. Only when your time comes. Then you'll get tested and we'll see which way [trail] you have to take."

So the boy went on, went back the same way [he'd come]. His kilt took him back to the top of the cliff. And he went through the four cactus fields, got his clothes pretty torn up and ragged. He got to his house and went in and laid down on his blanket. The medicine man worked on him and pretty soon he came to life again, you might say. He told his father everything he'd seen, and that no one was ever supposed to try to go there [to Maski] while he was still living. That place was only for the dead spirits.

That's an Oraibi story about Maski, the way I heard it. Here on First Mesa we don't know too much about it. Maybe someone over there can give you the whole thing. It doesn't have anything to do with Walpi or my [Tobacco] clan.

Pautiwa (Ned Zeena)
Walpi, August 1969

————25————

Burial in Oraibi

The one thing that [all] Hopis stick by is their religion, these genuine ceremonials that they practice down in the kiva, New Birth Again. That is something that really means something, how people are going to turn out at this end. And it's true, the way they practice down in the kiva. They have seven numbers, and four, and on the death of a person they have three numbers. When a person dies, the day of his death is one, then two, three. And on the fourth day they are making preparations for the grave. Then another day they call a New Day, on which they make a mush without salt of any kind, and they place that at the grave. And from there they call it Third Day. The first three days they have fasted. On the Third Day they have offered some food to that grave, and that's when he came out. . . . [several words unintelligible].

The body is always facing west. In case the dead individual is a very religious person, a priest maybe, or some other very outstanding person, they sit him up just like this. They make a little bench, like, in the grave. They say that when they are alive they are always worshiping the horizon when the sun comes up. They don't really worship the sun, but every morning when they get up they know that day is coming. If you happen to live on that kind of day, you know your heart is growing. But when they are dead they can't worship any more. They are buried facing west because that is where the sun is going.

Homer Cooyama,
Kikeuchmovi, July 1970

————26————

Burial on First Mesa

When the people came out of the underworld there was a prophecy that a good bahana, or white man, would some day come to the Hopis from the east to guide them and bring harmony and a good life. That special bahana never arrived. He's still expected, though, especially among old, tradition-minded people. For this reason, important personages—village officials, clan chiefs, and leaders in the kiva societies—usually are buried facing the east so that they can recognize and welcome the good bahana when he makes his appearance. Their bodies are dressed in the proper ceremonial costumes to explain who they were when they were living. Sometimes they are buried sitting up. Or they can be buried with their feet toward the east, so that if they were to sit up they would be looking eastward. Even people who aren't important personages can be buried this way if it is known that they wanted it, or if their families want it. Hopis and Tewas alike on First Mesa follow this tradition.

I remember that when my stepfather Peki died, I came home from Keam's Canyon to bury him. We placed him in his grave sitting up, facing toward the east. We didn't have any caskets in those days. He only had a blanket around him. The same way with Peki's sister. When she died, I carried her down to the burial place from the mesatop on my back. We buried her right next to Peki, facing in the same direction. Of course there was always a ritual in the house before the body was taken to the graveyard. The main part of it was the headwashing of the corpse with yucca suds. People used to undergo headwashing at all critical points in their lives—when they were given their first names, when they were married, when they were initiated into fraternities, and so on. This was the last headwashing. It was done by the grandmother, you might say, the oldest woman in the [father's] clan, and after she was finished she whispered a secret name into the dead person's ear. That was the name he or she would take into the next world, wherever that is. They placed cotton over the dead person's face—not cloth, but raw unspun cotton—with two holes for the eyes and one for the mouth. It was a cotton mask, you might say, tied with a cord around the forehead. The cord also held four turkey feathers pointing downward over the masked face. The reason for the white cotton was to make the person appear as white and unblemished as possible before the Great Spirit.

After the burial there was a feast, and the choicest part of the food, usually the heart, was put in a bowl and taken down to the grave and placed on top. Another bowl with yucca roots, which had been used in the headwashing, was also placed on the grave.

Nuvayoiyava (Albert Yava)
Tewa Village, June 1977

———27———

Harvesting Eagles, I

The people used to keep eagles on top of their houses. They still do that some places over there [in the other villages]. Well, it's a story that the white men don't believe. When we [our ancestors] went through here, well, they left some children behind. Those children became eagles. That's why all the clans through here, maybe certain clans, can pick [take] the eagles. Maybe in this direction there's another clan can [take] those eagles. Each clan has its own [eagles]. That's why they treat them just like babies. They make cradles [cradleboards] when they're going after eagles. When they catch them the eagles are small and they put them in the [cradleboards]. They bring them home like that. And then they wash the eagles' heads, just like humans, and they name their eagles, just the way Hopis do [with their own children]. They give them names and then they put them up on top of their houses. Then they feed them. You're not supposed to feed them just anything, you're supposed to feed them rabbit meat.

And then when they grow up, about that time they have a Home [Niman] Dance. Then the kachinas bring the children dolls or maybe bows and arrows. And they give that flat doll to the eagle. When the dance is over, the next day, they kill the eagle. They don't shoot the eagle, they put their thumb down here [in the eagle's throat] and close their windpipe and kill them that way. They don't shoot them or anything like that. Before they kill the eagle, though, they wash its hair again. They remove all the feathers. Then they bury them just like humans. Like the white man does, they put flowers on certain graves. They put the eagle's doll there. Eagles are buried just like humans. The feathers are kept for ceremonial use, for making prayer feathers and things like that.

We don't just go out and get [any] eagles. We've got to go

where the eagles belong to my clan. They're golden eagles, just one kind. You can only go where it's yours. All this way clear up to Lee's Ferry,[1] that belongs to the Bear Clan. If there are any eagles there, they're Bear Clan eagles. And then over this [other] way it belongs to the Kachina Clan. Like my father, they have a place over there where they get their eagles north of Red Lake. There's a Red Lake Trading Post up just about twenty-five miles. There's ruins over there too. Over this way, it's ours [Reed Clan], down this ridge clear back, about fifteen miles. This is where we get our eagles. We used to have an eagle on top of our house, down below [in Lower Moencopi]. Sometimes its hard to get the eagles. They have to tie somebody with a rope and lower him to the eagle's nest from above. It's about May when they go out for them. Then the Home Dances are in August.

Uwaikwiota
Moencopi, August 1968

———28———

Harvesting Eagles, II

We need eagle feathers for our ceremonies. Feathers of the whole eagle, except the head and feet. It's all useful. Our members of the Bear Clan, we had two this year. Our properties for eagles run from Grand Falls, below Leupp—that little part of the canyon—start from there all the way down to just about two miles above Cameron. All that little canyon, that's our property. The nests are here, maybe here, here, and there, and [also] way down below. We go on set dates for our eagle hunt. That's when they

[1] About fifty-five miles north of Moencopi and Tuba City.

[the young eagles] are ready to jump, before they jump. After they jump you can't catch them. May 18, before they jump, that's when we go. Sometimes they've already jumped. Other times they [haven't yet] jumped, shows they're a little too young, and we have a hard time getting them down.

One time they had to hang me down from the top—way down—and I kept circling around [on the end of the rope trying to get to] the nest. The eagles were a little young yet, they still had the little white feathers on their heads and weren't able to fly down. So I finally got hold of the rock, and they threw me another rope and I tied the eagles and they pulled them up. I had a hard time getting up. My uncle hadn't told me what to do. Going down is easier. There was a big bulge in the rock and the [eagles'] cave was underneath. And every time they pulled me up and I came to the bulge, my hands got all scraped up. And my uncle had never told me [what to do about] that. I yelled, and they were way up on top. And down below me, there was water there and big black stones. If I fell there'd be a dead Hopi down there. I kept looking at that and trying to forget it.

They threw down another rope and I put it around me. Then finally my uncle yelled, I could hardly hear him. He said to have the rope tied here [under my armpits], here [around my waist], and down here [under my crotch], and then I wouldn't have to hold the rope with my hands. "Put your hands on the wall," he told me. He knew all about it, our big uncle. Amos was his name. He was a much older man. I finally did that, put my hands against the wall, and went walking up just like that with my hands and bare feet.

We went below [in the canyon] looking for eagle droppings. Whenever we saw that white stuff [on the cliff walls] we knew that there were nests up above. We went under the white marks and if we found rabbit bones or pieces of snakes or prairie dogs we knew the eagle was there. We'd take three cans and tie them to the end of a rope and shake them. The young eagles who were big enough to jump would fly out, but once they hit the ground down in the canyon they couldn't fly because they didn't know how yet. They always landed alive, but they could only run around, and we'd pick them up. They'd fight and try to get away, and grab you with their claws. The more they fought you, the more their claws would go in. My grandpa and dad told me that whenever they do that you should get hold of their arm and press it real tight, and after a while their nails would get numb and their claws would open up.

Lomaheungva (Porter Timeche)
Shongopovi, June 1981

————29————

Harvesting Eagles, III[1]

Eagles are killed by some Hopis just after the Niman ceremonies are over. Men go out and capture fledgling eagles by climbing down from the cliffs. They take them home, sometimes carrying them in cradleboards as if they were babies. The eagles are kept tied by the feet on roofs. The people who catch them take good care of them, hunt rabbits for them to eat. After the Niman Dance they kill the eagles by putting a finger in their throats and pressing on their windpipes. Then they remove the feathers and down, which are used for sacred rituals. That down, called breath feathers, is considered specially important. When the feathers have been removed, the eagle has a ceremonial burial. They give it a carved doll as a present to take up to the eagle afterworld. Tradition says that there is another land up there in the sky, with tall mountains. Eagles are supposed to go there, breed to replenish their numbers, and after that return to the earth. Behind all this is the belief that human children were once transformed into eagles and cared for by eagle mothers and fathers. This explains why young eagles are carried in cradleboards when they are captured, and given dolls as presents. According to

[1]Transcription edited by narrator.

this belief it's the human children in the form of eagles who provide the Hopis with feathers for their rituals. Over in Shongopovi and some of the other villages they still go out to capture young eagles for this purpose, but it's not done on First Mesa.

I never liked this mistreatment of eagles. It is cruel. Somebody ought to put a stop to it. Our eagles are vanishing. It won't be long before they're gone. We [Hopi-]Tewas never catch eagles. The Zunis and Lagunas capture them, but they don't kill them, just keep them tied by one foot until they die of old age. That's pretty cruel too. But I think this capturing of eagles is dying out. The question is whether the eagle rituals or the eagles will die out first. I suppose that tradition came in here with one of those clan migrations and belongs only to certain groups, because it wasn't followed by a good many people.

Nuvayoiyava (Albert Yava)
Tewa Village, July 1970

————30————

Kachina Fraternity Whippings

The Kachina Clan people came [to Walpi] from Burnt Corn ruins, over near Piñon. I've never seen that ruins, but some people have and they say that the village must have been burnt to the ground. You can see the foundations and some of the rooms. Rooms where they used to store their corn still have corn in them, and the corn is burnt as if the houses had been destroyed by fire. I don't know where the Kachina Clan came from before they got to this village, but according to what I hear they came from there to First Mesa, to Walpi. Whenever you hear a story about a clan coming into Hopi country, there are always a number of stops it makes on the way, usually four in all, or Walpi or Oraibi may be the fourth stop. That's the way the Kachina Clan came, making stops at different places, staying there for a while, then coming on. And whenever they have some particular sacred ceremony they sing about the journey and how they finally arrived here. They have to tell it exactly as it happened, that's the way they remember their history. I can't say if it is true, but some of those old time Kachina Clan people say they were actually kachinas who came.

The Kachina Clan has a big part to play in the Bean Planting Ceremony, we call it Powamu, which comes in February. That's supposed to be when the kachinas return to the village from where they've been living. People say the kachinas have been staying at San Francisco Peak, but I've also heard that they live in other places too. When the Kachina Society initiation is held, down in the kiva they tell the clan story. That's when the initiates get whipped. Down in the kiva is a person telling the story, sort of singing it, and the initiates are sitting there pretty scared. The story tells about how the clan was coming. He names all the places and the person who was leading. They did this and that, lived at one place until a certain thing happened, then they moved again. They moved on and came to a certain spring and settled again. They came to Wepo, but they didn't stay there long because they were invited to come up to Walpi and initiate all the young men. They kept coming. They came to the Gap. They came up those steep stairs where Hano is now. Then they came to that shrine where Sichomovi is, but there wasn't any village there then. Then they came to the gate, that narrow place in the mesa. The chanting tells all these details.

The chanter says, "Yes, they're coming, they're getting closer." The initiates are getting pretty scared; they know something is about to happen. "I believe they're here now!" Then the Whipper Kachinas come down the ladder into the kiva. The first one down is Teumas, the mother. She's the one with crow feathers at the sides of her mask. She's carrying a plaque with cornmeal in it, and she's going, "Hoo hoo-oo!" After her come the Tunwups, they're the Whippers. They have pretty fierce masks, a horn on each side and a great wide mouth with zigzag teeth, and they're carrying a bundle of sticks in each hand, willow sticks usually, sometimes yucca sticks. They whip the initiates. They don't tickle

them, they really lay it on. A boy's sponsor can take some of
that whipping on himself. He goes forward and the Tunwups
beat him. Sometimes those fierce Tunwups get out of hand and
whip anybody else who happens to be standing around.

What I've said is about how it happens in Walpi. Over in
Hano, after each whipping the Tunwups wave their sticks in the
air to purify everybody.

Anonymous
Walpi, August 1970

————31————

Hopi Slaves
in Santa Fe

My grandmother used to tell us about when the first Spaniards came over to Old Oraibi. They captured some of the Hopis
and used them as slaves. My grandmother was one of them.
They took them clear back to Santa Fe someplace. At that time
the Hopis didn't know how to speak Spanish. But they used
prayersticks [to communicate]. I think the prayersticks had a
meaning to them, they were like a message or a letter. Well the
head men of the village wanted to get their people back from
Santa Fe, so they made those things, I don't know how many.
It's not really a stick, it has a string attached. You twist the string
so that the strands open up and you put a feather in there, then
you let go of the string and it twists back, then you tie it. The
head men of the village made those and gave them to a man
who carried them to Santa Fe, where the Spaniards had their
headquarters. He gave them to whoever was in charge there, and
when the person looked at the prayer things he knew what they
meant.

He went around and gathered all the Hopis who'd been captured [and sent them home]. And he punished all the Spaniards
who had done that. The man who was in charge, it hadn't been

his order to capture slaves. They say that they tied those Spaniards who'd taken the slaves and tied them to logs and whipped them to make them pay. The Hopi slaves were all brought back to Old Oraibi. That's what my grandmother used to tell me.

Uwaikwiota
Moencopi, August 1968

————32————

Homecoming of a Hopi Slave

The Spanish gave us hard times. They captured Hopi women and children and made slaves out of them. You can see that documented in books. When the Spanish were operating around here and in New Mexico, even after the revolt of 1680, sometimes they carried off some children and young women and took them to Santa Fe or Mexico and forced them to work, that is, made slaves out of them. This isn't a make-believe story, it is true. I believe the Spanish used to do that right down to the time of the Treaty of Guadalupe Hidalgo in 1848, maybe even later. Of course the white man still had his own slaves and he didn't worry too much about Indians being carried off by Spaniards or Mexicans. (We call them both, Spaniards and white Mexicans, Castillas. We call Mexican Indians Siu Castillas, meaning Onion Castillas, because they eat so much chili and onions.)

One of my cousins who died not long ago had an uncle—his father's brother—who was sold to the Castillas by Hopis when he was quite young. His name was Weupa, meaning Tall or Long. He was taken down into Mexico and nobody around here expected to ever hear from him again. But one day he reappeared. I was herding sheep out there in the valley, and out of nowhere Weupa showed up. He told me who he was, that he was my cousin's uncle, and I invited him to stay with me at the sheep camp for a while.

After we ate our dinner that night I asked him, "Now, where have you been all this time?"

He said, "Way down in Chihuahua, also in Sonora. I've been in many parts of Mexico."

I asked him what he was doing down there.

He said, "I herded sheep for my Papá. The man I worked for, I called him that. He took good care of me. He didn't treat me like a slave but like one of the family. When I worked for him I wasn't a slave any more."

I asked him how he got captured by the Castillas.

He said, "They didn't capture me. I was sold by my own people when I was still small. The village was having a famine at the time, and I guess it was hard to get enough to eat. So my family sold me to the Castillas. That's how it was. I was taken by a rich man down there who had lots of sheep in different parts of the country. When I was grown and in my prime he asked me if I wanted to go back to my people. So eventually I left him, moved around a lot, herded sheep here and there, and drifted north till I got home."

He told me about his experiences in Mexico, said he had met other Indians who had been sold to the Castillas. He said he knew some Hopi women in Sonora who had been captured, but they didn't want to come back. They had lived there so long they felt they were Mexicans.

Nuvayoiyava (Albert Yava)
Tewa Village, July 1970

———33———

The Pueblo Revolt
Against the Spanish

A First Mesa Account

The village leaders and the people were always thinking about how they might get rid of the Castillas—that's what they called the Spanish. Then one time they got word from the Eastern Pueblos that some kind of uprising was being planned. They sent a delegation over there, representing the main Hopi villages, and found out that the Eastern Pueblos had gotten together and were preparing a revolt under the leadership of a Tewa named Popay, who came from San Juan or Santa Clara, which had been called Kapo until the Spanish renamed it. In Tewa, Popay means water-bug—mosquito larva—and they say he was called that because he was always in motion. In Hopi they call him Pa'ateu. He was probably a Water Clan man. He was the driving force of the revolt. After he got the Tewas to back him up, he went to the other pueblos organizing and getting support.

Well, the Hopis joined forces with the Eastern Pueblos. A particular day had been set for the beginning of the attack against the Castillas. The Hopi delegation brought back a buckskin thong with a number of knots in it, indicating the days to go before the uprising. The last knot on the thong represented the day when all the villages on the Rio Grande side and the Hopi side were supposed to go into action. But after the Hopi delegation returned home, Popay learned that someone had revealed plans for the uprising to the Spanish, and so he moved the date of the attack ahead. As a result, the uprising along the Rio Grande began before the Hopis came to that last knot in the thong. The date was August 10, 1680. The Eastern Pueblos struck hard, killed a lot of Spaniards, and drove the rest of them south into Mexico. Of course, all that didn't happen on the first day. After the first attack, the Indians just kept pressing the Castillas until they were gone from Pueblo country.

Back here in the Hopi villages, the revolt started a couple of days later. In Oraibi, a war party attacked the church and the outbuildings. It seems that some of the padres and their assistants were away at the time, having gone somewhere for supplies. They say over there that the Badger Clan warriors took the lead. They killed two padres, their Indian assistants, and a few Spanish soldiers who were stationed in the village. They dragged the bodies away and threw them in deep washes. After that they looted the church, stripping out all the paraphernalia. The church livestock was divided among the clans. The One Horn Society took the steel lances of the Castilla soldiers and put them in the kiva as a record of the event. After that, the people razed the church to the ground, stone by stone and beam by beam. They scattered the stones in all directions, and stacked up the beams for future use. The large church bells were hauled away and sealed up in a secret crypt.

At Keuchaptevela, over here on First Mesa, the church was torn down the same way, and the big bells were taken out in the valley and buried at a place of drifting sand. On top of the mesa they laid out a line of stones pointing to where the bells were buried. In later years, people sometimes went to the line of stones and sighted along it to see whether the sand might have drifted away and uncovered the bells. Our One Horn Society on First Mesa has some souvenirs of the church, some small bells that look like sleigh bells. We ring those bells sometimes when we are chanting in a ceremony. All the villages tore down their churches. In Awatovi everything was torn down except some of the outbuildings, which were later converted into living quarters by some of the families. Of course, the Hopis didn't have to confront Spanish military forces, but what they did took some courage because it invited reprisals by the Spaniards. After that they waited, expecting that one day or another the Castillas would arrive to punish them. The Keuchaptevela people moved their village to the top of the mesa, where Walpi is today, for more security. Other villages also moved to higher ground. Awatovi already was on top of Antelope Mesa. In time it began to look as if the Castillas weren't coming back. They were gradually resuming their control over the Eastern Pueblos, and I guess they were too preoccupied with that to think much about the Hopi villages.

Nuvayoiyava (Albert Yava)
Tewa Village, July 1970

———34———

Oraibi and the Pueblo Revolt

When the Catholics had their church at Old Oraibi, things were like they are around here now, everybody was starting to get kind of wild. And pretty soon the chief's wife started going to the parties. The chief didn't like it.[1] So the chief went to Zuni, west of Gallup. All the chiefs from all the villages toward Santa Fe were there. I guess they'd sent out a message for the chiefs to come. The Catholics were scattered all through those villages, and the people were doing the same thing as at Oraibi, growing wild. The chief from Old Oraibi wanted all the Catholics to be killed because they were making the people go crazy.[2]

So this chief from Old Oraibi gave them strings with knots, and every string had the same number of knots. Every chief took a knotted string home with him. The next day they untied one knot. The next day another. When they untied the last knot, that was the day they were supposed to kill the Catholics. When the time came in Old Oraibi, one of the kachinas killed the priest over there. This is not a story; this is what really happened. Over in New Mexico the Pueblos killed their priests. But some say that there were people who hid the priests, because there were a lot of Catholic converts who wanted to save them. They didn't want to kill them. Just lately over in Old Oraibi they found some cement blocks where the church used to be. The blocks had holes in them. I guess they were used to set posts in.

Uwaikwiota
Moencopi, August 1968

———35———

An Oraibi Raid Against Walpi

There was a young married couple who were tending to their field in the valley. They were newlyweds, and they were sort of playing around, doing silly things. The woman was fixing the man's hair to look like a girl's. And she put some of her

---

[1]This Moencopi-Oraibi version of events employs the "last straw" motivation found in the Palatkwa and Awatovi stories and is clearly an interpolation of a free-floating motif.

[2]Most Hopi accounts agree with those heard in the Rio Grande villages, that the revolt originated among the Pueblos under the leadership of a Tewa named Popay. This version casts the Oraibi chief in the leadership role.

clothes on him. Then she fixed her hair to look like a man's, and
I guess she made her clothing look like a man's too. That was
when a party of Oraibis came on a raid. It was a small party.
Instead of running, the Walpi man started to fight, and the
woman stood aside. It looked to the Oraibis as if the woman was
fighting back, because the man had his hair in the woman's style,
heh'eh they call it. And it looked as if the man was standing
back and letting the woman do the fighting. It seemed as if the
woman was shooting arrows and the man was doing nothing,
and it puzzled them.

But of course the Walpi man was outnumbered and things
were looking bad for him. He had a dog up in the village. The
dog was up on top of the houses when he heard the man call. He
jumped down and ran out to the field and attacked the Oraibis.
He was pretty fierce, and the Oraibis backed off and went away.
To commemorate that event, someone drew a dog on the rocks
right where it happened. They call that place Puweuvetaka, The
Dog Chased Them Away. The Oraibis don't like to hear that story,
or the name of that place. The rock is down there near the ruins
of Koechaptevela. It was only a small raid, of course, but the
Oraibis did make some serious raids against Keuchaptevela. In
those days the Hopi villages didn't consider themselves the same
people. Every village was a people unto itself, and sometimes
the villages were hostile toward one another.

Nuvayoiyava (Albert Yava)
Tewa Village, June 1976

————36————

The "Hanos"[1]

The Hopis here in Walpi were having trouble with the
Paiutes, Navajos, I don't know which tribes they were. But there

---

[1]Hano is the name by which many Hopis refer to Tewa Village, based on
their belief that the people who came to First Mesa in response to the Hopi

was a lot of killing and the Hopis wanted help. They sent some people over near Taos somewhere, that's where Hano was. They sent for the Hanos to come and help them. They made some prayer feathers and two men carried them to the Hanos. But they didn't want to come and help us. I don't know exactly which village it was, but it was somewhere around Taos.[2] The Hopis went there four times. The fourth time was the last time, then the Hanos wanted to come. The Hopis were going to give them a place to stay here, and the Hanos could become Hopis. This was what the Hopis promised. These Tewas [sic] wanted to become Hopis. The Hopis gave them land here to raise their food. This is how it happened that we have these people here on First Mesa.

Pautiwa (Ned Zeena)
Walpi, August 1969

———37———

First Mesa Pottery

Some Hopis say they taught us Tewas in Tewa Village how to make pottery. That's all wrong, of course. Tewas were making pottery back in Tsewageh before they came here. At one time the people on First Mesa had just about stopped making pottery altogether. One of the few people still making pottery then was my great-grandmother, White Corn. She was making pots when most of the Walpis weren't doing it anymore. Her daughter —that's my grandmother on my mother's side—was Nampeyo.

petition were "Hanos" or T'anos. The people of Tewa Village consider themselves to be Tewas, an assertion supported by their continued use of the Tewa language. The Rio Grande Tewa villages also regard the people of Hano or Tewa Village as Tewas. An extended, detailed account of the coming of the Tewas to First Mesa is to be found in Yava, *Big Falling Snow*, pp. 26 ff.

[2]The village from which these eastern people came to Hopi country was Tsewageh, near Santa Cruz Creek, east of Española, New Mexico.

She and her husband—my grandfather—went to Sikyatki and found some old pottery there. She got the designs of the old pottery and began to make pots in that style. She also went to other ruins. There's a ruins coming out of Keam's Canyon, up on that big point to the right. Down below there's a kind of ridge, and from there you can look down and see other ruins. That's where some of Nampeyo's pottery designs came from. All those old designs Nampeyo was using were different from what the First Mesa people had been putting on their pots. Some of Nampeyo's designs also came from Awatovi. Then other First Mesa women began doing the same thing, and pottery revived. Nampeyo improved on her mother's work, and she became very well known.

> Dewey Healing
> Tewa Village, June 1976

————38————

Moencopi and Tuba City

I was born over in Old Oraibi. My mother told me that I was born in 1885, one year after they established Keam's Canyon [school?]. That's the way she remembered, it was a year after that. But when I started to go to school, the government just guessed at it and gave me 1895 instead. My people came over here to Moencopi to live. Of course, the Hopis lived here long before, a long time ago. But they moved to Oraibi, Old Oraibi. They lived there a long time, but they found that there was a lot of water here, and at Oraibi they didn't have much water. So some of those Hopis came back to the old village down there [lower Moencopi] and planted some vegetables, irrigated the fields, just small pieces [of land].

Of course at that time there were no Navajos, no white men, just the Hopis, by themselves. The farmers [from Oraibi] came out here, starting at daylight. Started running down here and when they got here they worked their farms. Towards sundown they started running home. Of course at that time they were good runners, they'd been practicing since they were kids. That's the way they trained us old-timers. Between Oraibi and here it's forty-some miles, and you have to run home again toward sundown. And next morning, come back again. That's the way they'd been doing. But after harvest time they'd just leave the place and stay home in Oraibi, doing ceremonials in winter time. Only one fellow named Tubi stayed here in the winter, he and his wife. Did that for some years, while the rest of them stayed home. By that time a few Paiutes were around. They were enemies of the Hopis, from Utah.

This man Tubi wanted somebody to protect him [from the Paiutes]. Before that Mormons came around, those missionaries, in Oraibi. They made friends with the Hopis. I don't know how long afterwards, Tubi wanted to go to Utah with them. He went with them to Salt Lake City. Jacob Henlein was the head man. Tubi and his wife went. They stayed there one year, then they came home again. He asked the Mormons to come over there where he was, so he'd be safe. Some years afterwards the Mormons came, fifteen families. And they stayed up there on top, where we live now [upper Moencopi] and the old man stayed below.

At that time the only school was at Keam's Canyon. The Hopis used to send their children to Keam's Canyon from here. It was a long way. In those days they didn't have anything to ride but burros. The Hopis down here wanted the government to build a school close to the village so they wouldn't have to send their kids clear to Keam's Canyon. So the government picked out a place up here at Blue Canyon, about ten miles from Moencopi, maybe twelve, in this wash. Used to be a trading post there. The man left the building and the government built it up again for a school for the Hopis. That was in 1900, I was here then, so I saw it myself. After two or three years, it was still too far. The Hopis wanted a school over here. So the government bought this place from the Mormons. I think they paid just $450[1]

[1]A misrecollection. The amount was considerably higher.

for the property, the houses, orchards. They had a lot of orchards. I used to work picking apples and peaches and apricots. I was a kid then. In 1904 they started to build the school over here. The Mormons had to leave. They said the money wasn't enough. But the government told them that if they didn't want it, they could go away empty. They had to go, in 1904, in July. They went in all directions. Some went to Salt Lake, and some went east and other places. Not many Hopis became Mormons, maybe a lot of the kids. But because the old man Tubi was here, they called this Tuba City.

I don't see how the Navajos could claim this place. They came in late. They used to come over to Oraibi and fight with the Hopis for the food. They'd take the stock. Sometimes they'd kill the Hopis, fight with them with arrows. Wherever they saw a sheepherder they'd kill him and take the sheep and horses. Hopis used to have a lot of sheep and cattle. You could see the footprints of the cattle up in this canyon, and in Coal Canyon they made a real trail in the sandstone where they went down to the water. There's water down there in Coal Canyon, it comes into Moencopi Wash. The Navajos are still like that. They'll take anything they can.

Louis Numkena, Sr.
Moencopi, August 1968

———39———

Comments on Voth[1]

Voth was a German. He first established his mission across the river [i.e., the wash] there, and my father was the first one to be acquainted with him. He was a Mennonite man. He was

[1]H.R. Voth, author of numerous studies of Hopi life. See Introduction, pp. xviii–xix.

also sent out by the Smithsonian Institution.[2] Most people who came out here [in those days] were Germans, teachers who could handle the situation. They're not soft people, they're pretty rough people. And it happened that we moved over there and I lived there during that time. It was September 1906 when the Oraibi Split happened. Before that I lived up in Old Oraibi, where I was born in 1894. There weren't any white people around in those days. Everything I learned was authentic. There wasn't any white man's interference yet.

I knew Voth pretty well. He used to force his way into the kiva. My father happened to be his right-hand man, and later when he went back to Kansas City he took my father along. That is, after he left here, in about two years he came and got my father to go back with him. There Voth made repairs on a lot of ritual paraphernalia that the Hopis had sold him. Some of those things were duplicates [reproductions], some were the originals, altars and things like that. My father did that work for him. Voth even had a collection of skulls. Later we found out that he was working with the Smithsonian Institution.[3]

Oraibi was the main place where he took down information and recorded Hopi traditions. I think now that there weren't many people who could speak English, and Mr. Voth didn't have a very big Hopi vocabulary. He depended a lot on guesswork. Mr. Coin[4] was the only one around here who could speak English, but he couldn't interpret things in the right positions [i.e., way]. Voth spoke Hopi a little bit. Hopis speak two ways, the higher and the lower language. He picked up some of the language, but he didn't know it too well. He took his information and stories down by hand, and he didn't know enough Hopi to do it well.[5] Used a lot of guesswork. But I suppose he had a lot of associates back east to help him.

There were two main things the Hopis were looking for in

[2]A misrecollection. Actually, the Field Columbian Museum.
[3]See footnote 2.
[4]As heard.
[5]An introductory note, by George A. Dorsey, in Voth's *Traditions of the Hopi* says that the stories in that collection "were collected in the vernacular and without an interpretor."

the old days, a promised land and a promised person. These
things were prophesied. Religious Hopis are still looking for the
promised place where they are supposed to settle. We've discussed these things many times in the kiva. The person they are
expecting is said to be a bahana, a white man, who will arrive in
great glory. Everybody knows this belief. And so when the first
white man came to stay in Oraibi, they were looking for someone who could speak Hopi and all kinds of languages. Well, Voth
spoke a little Hopi. And when he came they thought he was a
god. He'd studied the Hopi language before he came, but he
spoke brokenly. But we thought that was marvelous. That's the
man, we thought, that we'd been expecting. But after while we
found out that he wasn't the man.

Homer Cooyama
Kikeuchmovi, July 1970

————40————

The Split at Oraibi

An Oraibi Account

I can tell you exactly how it happened because I was involved
in that business. I was about sixteen years old then. There was
this group in Oraibi that was hostile to the whites. That was the
problem. We all used to live peaceably together when I was a
young boy, but about the time I was old enough to be in school
we began to separate from our old way of life. And this group
that was hostile to the government refused to send their children
to school. They didn't want to get help from the government.
They wanted to be left alone to go their own way.
    It got to be pretty bad in the village. Things got turned up-
side down. When we friendly people had our ceremonies they
[the Hostiles] had theirs by themselves. We were not living peace-

ably for quite a while, till 1906. That was when we decided to do something. It was on September the 8th, 1906, that it happened. We drove those hostile people from the village, out that way, and kept them gathered there. During the afternoon it was getting pretty bad. Yukioma, who was head of the Hostiles, wanted his people to stay in Oraibi. He wanted us [the Friendlies] to leave the village. So about three o'clock he made four lines on the ground and then he said, "Well, it has to be done this way now, that when you pass me over these lines it will be done. We're going to have a [push]-of-war. If you push us over [the lines] we are the ones to leave."

So our chief called a lot of those strong men to do the work. Said, "Well, we'll get together and push each other. We'll push them back that way. If we pass them over the four lines it will be done." We had a hard struggle. Both of our chiefs were in the center, and they had a hard time to get their breath. And then we drove them over the four lines. Then it was done; that's what Yukioma said. Before the setting of the sun, he [and his group] departed. Our chief said to them, "You people are supposed to go out where you came from, Kawestima, to live." That's out toward [Kayenta].[1]

After the Hostiles left, someone carved three or four footprints in the rock showing where they went out toward the west. [Two fellows] named Robert Silena and Charles Addington carved the words that Yukioma had said. When the Hostiles got to the place where they were going to stay, Hotevilla, they cut down some trees and made temporary hogans at first, then afterwards they made their stone houses.

Our chief at that time was Tawakwaptewa, and his second lieutenant from Moencopi was Frank Shiamptiwa.[2]

Chuka (Don C. Talayesva)
Oraibi, July 1970

---

[1]The narrator said Canada, which the editor has changed to Kayenta.

[2]Another account of the push-of-war by Don Talayesva, the same narrator, appears in his book *Sun Chief*, pp. 109–10. Compare also with the account given by Tuwahoyiwma, pp. 302–4 of *Book of the Hopi*, by Frank Waters and White Bear Fredericks.

————*41*————

The Burning of the Altars[1]

The breakup of Oraibi brought an end to all the important rituals and kiva organizations there. The Hotevillas claim that they took the rituals with them, but they left all the ritual paraphernalia behind in Oraibi when they went away.

Eventually all the paraphernalia [left in Oraibi] was destroyed by a Bow Clan man named Johnson, a convert to the Mennonite Church. His Indian name was Tawaletstiwa. He was in charge of those objects, and when he became a Christian he took the Wuwuchim and Two Horn altars and all the other ritual objects of those two kiva societies and burned them. He made a big public display of it, announcing in advance what he was going to do. Quite a few people assembled and watched the bonfire. I was in Oraibi the day it happened. I had to take a wagonload of supplies to New Oraibi from Keam's [Canyon], and when I arrived I saw the crowd over on the north side watching Johnson destroy the altars and other paraphernalia. He took the responsibility on himself because it was his people, the Bow Clan, who had brought those traditions from Awatovi. The paraphernalia that he burned must have been copies of the originals—that is what First Mesa people believe, because First Mesa traditions say that the altars and other sacred things were brought from Awatovi to Walpi by a Tobacco Clan man. But whether the sacred objects were originals or copies, they were accepted in Oraibi as the real thing and they were essential to the proper carrying out of rituals.

So neither the Oraibis nor the Hotevillas had the sacred objects any more. But it was not just the burning of the altars that doomed the rituals in Oraibi. Some of the people who had gone to Hotevilla were leaders in the kiva societies. They had a lot of the knowledge and the secrets in their heads. The continuity was broken.

[1]This text also appears in Albert Yava, *Big Falling Snow*. It was read in transcript and edited by Mr. Yava.

After the Hostiles departed, the Oraibi chief, Tawaquaptewa, understood that the old life was gone for good. He said, "We can't live in those old ways any more. Now we have to look to the white man's ways. Our rituals are gone, our clan system is gone. The clan landholdings are finished. If people need land for their gardens, let them take fields that aren't being used by somebody else." Tawaquaptewa was the last real chief of Oraibi. He was buried in his Eototo Kachina costume. Eototo is supposed to represent the Fire, or Masauwu, Clan. Burying the chief in that costume meant the end of Oraibi's history and rituals, and an end of the clans' control over the fields and lands around Oraibi. Masauwu had given out those lands, and the chief being buried that way signified that the gift was revoked, that henceforth the Oraibis were on their own without any ceremonial connections to the past.[2]

Nuvayoiyava (Albert Yava)
Tewa Village, June 1977

———42———

Oraibi Before the Split

Before the split, Old Oraibi was a very complicated society. We were involved with different organizations, with fraternities, with groups [comparable to] the Masons, many things we don't know too much about today. There were fourteen kivas in Old Oraibi before the breakup. Each organization had its high priests. The kivas were located in three different areas. One was for the common people. The kivas in the middle area were for the high priests, officials in the big, important societies. And in the back area was where they had special shrines where they kept all

[2]Tradition says that Tawaquaptewa designated Myron Poliquaptewa of the Parrot Clan to perform chiefly duties for four years, after which the village was not supposed to have a kikmongwi. However, Myron's sister, Mina Lansa, took over the chieftainship and acted as Oraibi's kikmongwi until her death in 1979.

kinds of sacred objects—things that had to do with kachinas, ancient pottery pieces connected with some important ritual or commemorating some significant mystery in our religious beliefs. All those things were placed in appropriate shrines. Only the high priestly officials could go there.

We who had never been initiated above a certain level had to stay away from the pahoki [shrine] area and the most sacred kivas unless we were invited to come. It was a very elaborate religious system. An outsider could never completely understand it. That is why it was important to have initiations into the societies every year, so that new members could be brought in to learn the traditions and keep them going properly. In 1906, when we had the split and drove out the Hostiles, we blew up the whole thing.

I told white men sometimes, "You are the ones who spoiled everything, the way you brought education in here and insisted everything had to go the white man's way. You are the ones who destroyed our religion." Of course, that may sound too hard. But before the white man moved in on us and sent missionaries in the Hopis had been practicing their old religion according to their prophecies and the supervision of the high priests who had inherited the knowledge, and according to the ritual calendar of the clans and the kiva societies. We also had a sun watcher, an astronomer you might say, who kept track of where the sun came up every day and told the people when it rose at a certain particular point, meaning that a certain ceremony should take place. Every clan had a particular responsibility, it had to do special things for the village. My own clan, the Coyote, had the responsibility of taking the lead to protect the village in time of danger. When the Catholic priests were thrown out back in the 1600s some time, we took the responsibility in that and in tearing down the Catholic mission. Every clan had something particular to do for the village. It was very complicated. We had a village chief, a war chief, a crier chief, and many other officials who carried out their tasks. If there were difficulties between kiva societies or clans, they were discussed and thrashed out in council in the kivas, and whatever was decided down there was carried out. You could say that we had a wonderful social organization that really worked.

Then the government came in and forced us to do things, threatening us, shooting guns over our heads, chasing us all around Oraibi. I was one of those who were chased around, when I was a little kid. They sent a lot of Hopi and Navaho police from Keam's Canyon to force the people to send their kids to the government school. We felt very much under threat. For that reason, Oraibi people felt very hostile against the government and what it was doing. That whole affair of the Oraibi split was stirred up by the government, which forced the people to take sides. I'm sure the village had had troubles before, but they were all settled in council in the kivas. This time Oraibi broke wide open and there was no way you could put it back the way it was. Of course, now we are kind of reconciled to the white man's way. But having grown up and lived here so many years I will never forget those things.

No outsider can ever hear everything that really happened, because most of the people who were involved have died away; they're gone forever. But I participated in the kachina ceremonials for a long time. I take part nearly every time there is a ceremony. I know all the processes, how they're performed and what they're for. My parents had very high positions in the ceremonial life, and they told me many things. That's how I have some ideas about what it was all like before the white man and the missionaries intruded on us.

I think you can read something about the destruction of our altars when the village split up. There are some books and articles on it. All the sacred altars and paraphernalia of the main kivas were brought here originally by the Bow Clan when Awatovi was destroyed. So you could say that the Bow Clan in Oraibi was responsible for them in a particular way. After the split, a high official in that clan named Johnson—his Indian name was Tawaletstiwa—burned everything. He's an old man now. He was a converted Christian, and after the split he took all the stuff out of the kivas and burned it. A lot of people were pretty shocked by what he did. It's a peculiar thing, what I'm going to tell about what happened after that. Johnson is the only one of those Bow Clan people who is left. After the altars were burned, the Bow Clan had a whole series of misfortunes. Their people died off one after another, or went insane, or developed some kind of condition where they had fits. Johnson is the only one that's still here.[1]

Oraibi used to have a very high standard of moral living before things broke up. We had a great deal of knowledge about the traditions that other villages didn't have. Compared to what we had, some of the other villages were, you might say, backward. They looked to us for religious leadership.[2]

Homer Cooyama
Kikeuchmovi, July 1970

————43————

Government Water in Moencopi

That water tank on the other side of the road hasn't been there too long. We [traditionalists] didn't have anything to say about it. The government and the Friendlies worked it out between them. Nobody asked us. Those houses in the upper village have water piped in, they belong to the Friendlies. My house is on the edge of the upper village, but our people are mostly down on Old Moencopi, down below. Because the Friendlies cooperate, they are getting the water. One of them came to me and said, "If you dig a ditch for pipes, we can put water in your house." I asked him, "Who is making the rules about these things? I never heard it discussed in the kiva [in the lower village]. You come to me and tell me to do this and do that, but I never heard it discussed in the council. That is the way you people work. You have your own meetings and then you tell us what we can do and what we can't do." He said, "Well, that is the

---

[1]Now deceased.

[2]The original taped material given by Cooyama has been enlarged somewhat in this text by the addition of explanations given by the narrator at a later date.

way it works under the new constitution. The government has to deal with somebody, and you don't want to deal with them. You voted against the constitution." I told him, "Yes, we already had a traditional government going in Moencopi. You people set up a new government. You turned your back on our traditions, and now you seem to be the ones who can tell us to do this or do that. We don't want your water. We'll get our water the old way."

We still carry our water from the old spring down below. It's quite a distance from here. When we lived in Old Moencopi it wasn't so far. But from here it's a long distance. Once in a while we can bring up some water in the pickup, but a lot of the time the women have to carry the water in pails. So getting our water is even harder than it used to be. And somehow we need even more water now than then. It takes an awful lot of water to fill a washing machine.

Even though we don't go along with the Friendlies taking over decisions the way they are doing, we are hospitable to government people if they come to talk to us. We try to tell them what's wrong with the setup. We tell them most of the people in Moencopi never voted for the constitution under the Reorganization Act, and the way things have been reorganized doesn't conform to our system. We tell them we had our own chief and our own way of doing things all along, and it worked fine for us. They tell us, "Well, maybe you didn't vote *for* the reorganization, but you didn't vote *against* it, either." We tell them, "Why should we vote? We had our own government here, then someone comes in and tells us we have to vote on a different system. Outsiders were telling us to vote on something we didn't ask for. It had nothing to do with us. That's why we didn't vote. And a few people voted yes, so they have power over government funds and projects and the majority of us don't have anything to say about anything. So we'll go our way and they can go theirs if they want to abandon the old ways." I can tell you, we don't feel very good toward those Friendlies. (They call themselves Progressives.)

Some of the government people make a point of coming to talk to us traditionalists, even though they are supposed to deal with the elected group. Agriculture agents go around looking at our fields and making suggestions. I remember when I was working one of our fields over in Pasture Canyon an Agriculture agent came down and looked at the sand dunes drifting over the fields. Every so many years the sand drifts in that way and covers everything. You can't plant, and that field is lost until maybe a few years later the sand blows away, goes somewhere else. This agent suggested that we put up snow fences at certain places to stop the drifting. But nobody did anything about that. They thought that the white man was trying to sell us snow fences. People have fields at different places, and when the sand moves in on one field they let it be and do their farming in the other fields.

Most people listen to the Agriculture agents, but when the agents try to tell us how to grow corn, that's something else again. One agent tried to convince me to grow those great big ears of hybrid corn. He took out a hybrid ear and showed me it had about six times as many kernels as a Hopi ear. I told him we'd been experimenting with corn from the beginning of our history and knew which varieties would grow and which wouldn't. He kept saying, "Try it. What do you have to lose?" Finally I agreed to putting some hybrid corn in one part of the field. Well, the Hopi corn grew just as it usually did. It has deep roots. The hybrid corn grew up about a foot or two, set there a while and then died. When the agent came out again to see how his corn was doing, he just stood there and shook his head. There wasn't an ear large enough to feed a half-starved crow.

Uwaikwiota
Moencopi, August 1968

————44————

Women as Chiefs

The first chief of Moencopi was a woman, "Queen" Nash-ilehwi. I've known her. She was Corn Clan. I don't know how it happened that they had a woman chief there. She had brothers there during that time, but they were not [made chief]. They were the helpers of that woman. That's how they worked, all togeth-er. There weren't any other [legitimate] women chiefs. Mina [Lansa] at Oraibi supposedly made herself chief, but she is not. She was not anointed. This fellow named Myron [Poliquaptewa] was supposed to be the one to lead the people, and he was anointed [appointed]. But she was allowed to take that kingdom away from him.[1] And we have not been living so peaceably.

Chuka (Don C. Talayesva)
Oraibi, July 1970

———45———

The Yaya Fraternity, I

The Yayas [on First Mesa] used to use the Aal or Horn Kiva, that one right on the edge of the cliff in Walpi. Of course we still use that kiva, but not the Yayas any more, they are gone. The Yayas were pretty good, they were witches. One time up there in Walpi village they did something. Down below Walpi where Huckovi used to be, there was a man built a house there and made a garden. He had a scarecrow in his field, made out of straw to scare the crows away. That scarecrow came right up to the plaza. The Yayas were calling him to come up, and I heard he did, clear up to the mesa.

Those guys were witches. They liked to show what they could do. But I guess they got into trouble with the village one time. They were wild. They gave whisky and beer to the girls and got them drunk and started raping them. The village stopped the Yaya business, took all their things [paraphernalia] away. North of the gap on top of the mesa there's a big cave there. All

[1]See footnote 2 under "The Burning of the Altars," text 41.

the Yaya stuff is in that cave now, it's walled up. Inside are the old pahos, baskets, plaques, and other things that the Yayas used. That cave is about two miles from the gap. Those Yayas said they could do anything. They even showed the people that they could fly [from the top of the cliff] to the bottom, and nobody was hurt. They weren't separate people, they were Hopis. One thing they had was the Blind Kachinas, the Somaikoli. We still have them sometimes.[1]

Pautiwa (Ned Zeena)
Walpi, August 1969

———46———

The Yaya Fraternity, II

Each Hopi village has different information about the Yayas. Up in Walpi it was the Reed Clan that practiced the Yaya ceremonies. They kept their paraphernalia way down in a back room, in a cellar. They had some extraordinary performances for people to see. They had stick swallowers who would put long sticks into their mouths and down their throats. They had a skull that they would call, and it would come rolling to them through the plaza. That was the Yaya fraternity on First Mesa. They were affiliated with the Blind Kachina group, the Somaikoli. That's under the Reed Clan. They wore eagle feathers or cornhusks in their hair. They acted kind of rough, broke things up. Wanted people to know how wild they were. If you had a smokepot on your roof, they might go up there and throw it down. They gave the people a lot of trouble. But they're gone now.

Nuvayoiyava (Albert Yava)
Tewa Village, June 1976

[1]Somaikoli is a Reed Clan ceremony today.

————47————

The Yaponcha People

I have heard of the Yaponcha people but can't say much about them.[1] It could be that they were not really Hopi, because our hair is naturally straight and smooth. Yaponcha means that one's hair is unruly and mussed, "big-headed." Yayaponcha means a large group of Yaponchas. When we were kids and didn't comb our hair, my uncle and mother would say I was Yaponcha.

Tsakaptamana
Moencopi, May 1969

————48————

Hippies in Shongopovi

I'm not against everything new. If there's something new that is good for us without destroying our traditions, I have no objection to it. I certainly don't like the way those missionaries

[1]Some Hopis in the Second and Third Mesa villages understood Yaponcha (or Yayaponcha) to be the same as the Yayas of First Mesa, apparently in error. While Oraibis recognized the Yaya group as a secret society, there was also a tradition that the Yayaponcha were a separate group with a language and village of their own. In Voth, *The Traditions of the Hopi*, p. 123, an informant says: "North of the present peach orchards . . . lived the Yayaponchatu. These are not Hopi, but they are beings something like the skeletons. They have white faces and white bodies, disheveled hair, and wear kilts of black and white striped cloth. They understand the fire and more than once caused the villages to be destroyed by fire." It is possible that the Yaya Society on First Mesa was built on this tradition.

According to Bert Puhueyestewa, one of my Mishongnovi informants, Yaponcha is the name of a wind spirit or deity, also identified with fire. The "disheveled hair" cited by Voth and the "mussed" hair described in this text appear to be the wind spirit's trademark.

have been coming up here and knocking on doors. That's harmful to our traditional ways. They ought to stay out of the village. They want us to drop our own Hopi religion and take on theirs, become Mormons or Mennonites or Seventh Day Adventists. They aren't shy about telling us how backward we are and how we will go to hell if we don't give up the Hopi religion. What they are telling us is to stop being Hopis and be something else. I would like it if they could stop the missionaries from coming into the village. But we are told, "No, you can't stop them from coming, because it's freedom of speech. Under the American Constitution you can't stop people from talking." So they come and come, one after the other. You can stop people from bringing cameras into the village to take pictures of the ceremonies, but you can't stop the missionaries. So when they come to me I am hospitable, the way Hopis are supposed to be. I listen, but I don't say anything. One time, though, I gave a long talk to one of those missionaries and told him why I thought he ought to give up being a Mormon and become a Hopi. I never saw him again after that.

There was that time when the hippies came over here and sort of took over the village, as if they owned it. They just camped in the plaza and went around, going into people's houses and things like that. We didn't want them but they refused to go. Shongopovi people had to avoid them by going inside and closing their doors. Those hippies offended our way of life. They hugged each other and kissed in public as if they didn't have anything else to do and nowhere else to go. I went out there and spoke to some of them. I said, "Why are you here? Why do you behave this way, doing anything that comes into your head? We do not like the way you are behaving. It's not our way. It's improper."

They said, "What's wrong with what we are doing? We are here because we're on your side. You have been put down by the establishment, and we are against the establishment." I told them, "No, you are not on our side. You don't behave well. Whatever you want, you take it. Whatever you want to do, you do it. There are rules in the world. You can't be just anything you want." They said, "The rules are wrong." I said, "Don't you believe there is a Great Spirit somewhere that created us and is watching us?" They said, "No, we don't believe it." I said, "Well, then, who created you? Do you think you created yourself?" They didn't say anything. Finally the Hopi police came and made them get out.[1]

Those hippies set a pretty bad example for our own young people. We don't seem to be able to guide the young people the way we used to. We try, but they say, "You are going by the old ways; it isn't that way anymore." It's pretty hard for us because the young people are being sent away to schools, and you can't guide them when they aren't in the village. Quite a number of young girls come home pregnant. I don't say that sort of thing didn't happen in the old days. But when we had our children growing up in the village and being initiated into the kiva fraternities we had a better chance to teach them the right way of living. The women could teach the girls and show by their own behavior what was right. Boys would get teaching from their fathers and their [ritual and clan] uncles who sponsored them and guided them. Of course, the ones who go away to school are getting an education they can't get here. Maybe that will help them in days to come. I hope so, because there's no doubt the world is changing. But I hate to see them lose the old life.

Some of the young people believe I am too strict about everything. They call me the old guard, though not to my face. When I kill an eagle and take out the downy feathers—breath feathers, we call them—some people think I'm old-fashioned.

---

[1]The "Hippie Invasion," as many Hopis call it, occurred in 1967. According to various informants, the hippies came to the villages in response to an invitation from an ultratraditionalist group centered in Hotevilla which called itself the "Hopi Independent Nation." This Hopi group, hostile to any form of cooperation with the U.S. government or the Hopi Tribal Council, seemingly sought ties with a variety of protest movements outside the reservation. The Hopi newspaper *Qua′töqti* observed in its issue of September 12, 1974 that "one of the early black activist groups, Congress of Racial Equality, came on the reservation" and allegedly used the Hotevilla traditionalists to further their own cause. Referring to the "Hippie Invasion," *Qua′töqti* says that "the 'Flower Children' arrived in large numbers and camped around Hotevilla. Village women reportedly complained bitterly about the sex habits of the 'invaders' and their less-than-tidy looks."

It's right after the Niman [Home-Going] ceremony that we do this. The downy feathers are sacred to us. We use them for prayers and rituals in the kiva. Perhaps it is old-fashioned. Many families don't do it any more. But to me it is part of the old way that saw us through many difficulties.

I'm not against "progress," but I have to know what it means. I don't accept everything the white man offers us. I look at things and ask myself, "Is it good for us or bad for us?" Some things, many things, that are good, I say to myself, "This can't hurt us. It can help us." I accept it, and try to use it in a good way. I am building a new house for myself over on the other side of the village. I work on it almost every day. I build it the old way, with stone slabs. You lay the slabs one on the other and shim them up so they are firm. I enjoy building the old way. It's as if I am preserving something that many people are forgetting. But inside the new house I have another man building me a wall to separate the rooms. He's building the wall of cement blocks. That's something I've accepted that's good. One thing he did that's not the old way or the new way is that he forgot to put a doorway in the wall to get from one room to another. So he'll have to fix that.

One thing we Hopis have always needed is water. We used to have to bring water from the springs down below. It was hard for the women, because they used to carry it in jars, and there was only so much they could carry. Now the government has put water tanks on most of the mesas for us. That's something good, but I often wish the young people understood how we had to get our water before. It troubles me that they take it for granted that the tanks are there. Here and there on the mesas you sometimes see windmills that bring water up from the ground. I'd have to say that is something good. In my new house I'll have glass in the windows, and I'd have to say that is good too. Anything that will help our children and grandchildren have a better life will be good. I don't mean an easy life. It is our tradition that people should work for everything they get. But our tradition doesn't say that our life should be harsh. I don't want our children facing harsh things when they grow up. I want to see them prepared for what is ahead. I can't see into the future or know what they'll have to meet. But we can help them now to be prepared. That's why I am working with the Save the Children group, which is helping many of our kids get an education. I also work when I can with the Tribal Government to help improve things on the Reservation. You might say, though, that I still have one foot firmly planted in the past. I am Bear Clan and I belong to the Wuwuchim Society, and these things tell me who I am.

Peter Nuvamsa, Sr.
Shongopovi, August 1969

———49———

Hopi Religion and the Missionaries[1]

We old-timers can see that there has been a steady drift away from our traditional attitude toward nature and the universe. What I'm talking about is not the dancing and the kiva paraphernalia, all those visible things. They are only a means of expressing what we feel about the world. I am talking about the feelings and attitudes behind the kiva rituals. We feel that the world is good. We are grateful to be alive. We are conscious that all men are brothers. We sense that we are related to other living creatures. Life is to be valued and preserved. If you see a grain of corn on the ground, pick it up and take care of it, because it has life inside. When you go out of your house in the morning and see the sun rising, pause a moment to think about it. That sun brings warmth to the things that grow in the fields. If there's a cloud in the sky, look at it and remember that it brings rain to a dry land. When you take water from a spring, be aware that it is a gift of nature.

[1]This segment is extracted from Yava, *Big Falling Snow*, 1978.

All those stories we tell about men changing into bears or deer, and then changing back, you can look at them as primitive ideas if you want to, but they really express our certainty that the dividing line between humans and animals is very slim, and that we are here to share what is given to us. We seek a way of communicating with the source of life, so we have prayers and kachinas. I think we are probably as successful at this effort to communicate as Christians are. You don't hear as much about the Great Spirit in our traditions as you do about those lesser spirits that are sacred to particular clans and kiva societies, but I believe we are constantly aware that it exists, and that without it we would not be here. You can say that we have not lost our sense of wonder about the universe and existence.

This knowledge is supposed to be translated into personal good behavior, into the way we act toward other individuals, our clan and our village. If you meet a person, you greet him. If he is a stranger or someone you know, it is all the same. If someone comes to the village from another place, even if he belongs to a different tribe, feed him. Keep your mind cleansed of evil. We have purification rituals to accomplish this. Be generous with whatever you have. Avoid injuring others. Respect older people. No matter how they appear to you, they have had hard experiences and have acquired knowledge from living. Do not injure others by violence or gossip. Now, if all these ideas don't meet the highest standards of the different Christian churches that have been busy trying to convert us, I'd like to know why.

Still, we have had a long line of missionaries parading through the villages. First were the Catholics, but they were thrown out—unfortunately not without some sad events, such as the massacre and destruction at Awatovi. Then there were Mennonites, Mormons, Jehovah's Witnesses, Seventh Day Adventists, and Baptists. You will find churches in or close to all the villages now. The missionaries came telling the Hopis and Tewas that the old traditional ways were barbaric, and each one claimed to have the true faith, the only one that paid respect to the Great Spirit. Because of that old tradition that a good bahana [white man] would come some day, the Hopis and Tewas listened, some of them wondering if this missionary or that missionary was the right one.

I remember a man who was in charge of the Sunlight Mission back around 1912. He approached me and said, "Say, Yava, what do you think about all those things that are going on in the villages?"

I said, "What kind of things do you mean?"

He said, "Well, all those things that are going on in the kivas. Don't you think they are pretty bad?"

I said, "I know that you are trying to convert me to your church. Maybe that would be all right, I can't say. Maybe you have a good church. But I have been doing a lot of thinking about what you missionaries are doing and the way you are doing it. The first thing you do is to say that the Hopi and Tewa religious practices are barbaric, and after that you convince a few people here and there that they have to become Christians so as not to go to hell. But I don't think you are doing very well. You don't catch more than a few stragglers. One reason for that is that you don't really know anything about what Hopis and Tewas believe in. You just assume that they don't know the difference between right and wrong. I thought that Christians were supposed to have humility, but I don't see any humility in that. How can you just assume that we're barbaric? Have you ever taken the trouble to study our ways and find out what our religious beliefs are? If you are ever going to be successful with your converting of Hopis and Tewas, you are going to have to know a lot more about us."

He said, "Yava, I believe you're right about that."

I suppose he and some other missionaries made an effort to know more about us, but they all came with that fixed idea that the poor barbaric Indians had to be saved, so they only learned what they wanted to.

I myself have listened to these missionaries. They come to my house sometimes, and I invite them in and hear everything they have to say. Sometimes I have gone to one church or another on Sunday. Of course, a great deal of what they say is interesting. But I have not heard anything yet to persuade me that what they have is superior to what we Tewas and Hopis have. All I can tell those missionaries is that it is a matter of conscience. I tell them that if a person believes in the Indian way and lives according to what Indians believe is a good way of life, that is okay. And if a person is a Baptist or a Mormon and lives according to what Baptists and Mormons believe is a good way of life, that is okay too. That is a choice everybody should have, and the missionaries should stop putting themselves forward as the only ones who know the difference between good and evil.

I don't believe any of the Christian denominations has something valuable that we don't already have. "If a man falls down, help him to get up." That is our belief. Do the Christian churches have anything better than that? I don't think so. In fact, you have to judge those churches by the way Christians act in their everyday lives. And too often we have seen a man fall down and a Christian walk right by, in a way of speaking. "Share what you have." We believe in that, but we have had long experience with the white man. Sometimes he has shared what he has, other times he has taken away what we have. "If you see something edible, take a part of it, only what you need." Too often the white man has eaten everything up.

One thing is clear. The Hopis and Tewas who convert from our traditional religion have taken themselves out of our traditional ways. The missionaries have had a great deal to do with the destruction of Hopi-Tewa religion. In a way, they are competing with each other to see who can do the most destruction. I guess you can't blame the missionaries too much. They are doing what they believe they are supposed to do. If our traditional religion is passing, you have to blame the Hopis and Tewas themselves. There is one fellow over in Oraibi who was lamenting that the Hopi religious beliefs were disappearing. I said to him. "Why are you crying? You yourself joined the Mennonites a long time ago. You talk about the Hopi way, but you deserted it. So who are the people who should be blamed? The ones who stayed or the ones who left?"

> Nuvayoiyava (Albert Yava)
> Tewa Village, date unrecorded

————50————

Ancestral Boundaries, I

When it came time for the migrating clans to become the Hopi people, there were certain staging areas from which they came to the three mesas. They were the last staging points of a long series of migrations. Some of these places are identified by their Hopi names, like Kawestima, those ruins over by Betatakin north of Kayenta. And Tokonave, Navajo Mountain. And Wupatki, near Flagstaff, is another one. And Chevelon Cliffs, south of Winslow. Another one is at Lupton Point. It's primarily a shrine with a lot of petroglyphs. And north from there it goes to White House [ruins] at Canyon de Chelly, then back to Loloma Point and over to Navajo Mountain. These points mark the boundaries of what the Hopis consider to be their ancestral lands.

Eugene Sekaquaptewa
Kikeuchmovi, June 1981

―――51―――

Ancestral Boundaries, II

There are eight major Hopi shrines that mark the extent of our traditional Hopi country. One is at Tokonave, Black Mountain (the whites call it Navajo Mountain) in the north. Another is on the Supai Trail west of Grand Canyon Village. One is at Kawestima, those ruins north of Kayenta. Another one is near Williams [Arizona]. It is called Tesaktumo, meaning Grass Hill. Another is on the San Francisco Peaks. Another shrine is on Woodruff Mountain south of Holbrook. Another is at a place called Namiteika, near Lupton. Another is on the Apache Trail on the Mongollon Rim. I have been to all of these shrines except one. They mark the lands we Hopis have always claimed as ours. All the land between the shrines belonged to us.

Bert Puhueyestewa
Mishongnovi, June 1981

———52———

Visit to Washington[1]

You get the feeling sometimes that white men believe anything you tell them, especially if you tell them what they want
to hear. From us Indians they want to hear talk that makes us
sound like we're pretty uncivilized. There was one time when
the Department of the Interior invited some of us Hopis and
Tewas to Washington for a conference on Indian affairs. They
didn't particularly want to hear from us, but they wanted a bunch
of us circulating around in Indian clothes. They had a big dinner in some hotel, and we Indians were mixed at the tables with
the white guests so that everyone could have an Indian close by
them to talk to and ask questions like, "How do you like our
country, anyway?" They served a lot of champagne, and some
of us never had champagne before and thought it was something
like Seven-Up, so before the dinner was over we had a few dancing Indians in the dining room.

After dinner someone came to me and said there was a radio
station set up in one of the hotel rooms, asked me if I'd go up
there and be interviewed. So I did go up like they asked. There
was a man sitting at a table, and he asked me to sit down. Then
he started to ask me a lot of questions about our Hopi and Tewa
customs.

He said, "Well, I guess you people are having a lot of dances
out there in Arizona now."

I said, "Maybe you're right. They do a lot of dancing out
there."

He said, "I suppose your people are dancing to make it
rain."

I said, "They are? I haven't heard about that."

He said, "What I mean is, whenever they do a kachina dance
they are praying for rain. Isn't that so?"

I said, "Well, I have been to a lot of kachina dances, but half
the time I don't know what they are singing."

[1]From notes taken by hand.

He said, "You're putting me on, aren't you?"

I said, "No, I didn't know it if they were praying for rain. But you can never tell about Indians."

He said, "Well, I have been doing a lot of reading about the Bean Dance and the Snake Dance, and according to everything I've read on the subject, whenever they do those dances they are trying to make it rain."

I said as far as I was concerned they were just doing a lot of funny things with beans and snakes, and I couldn't say for sure about the rain part.

He said, "Well, now, you're a real Hopi, aren't you?"

I said, "No, I'm a Tewa, but if you want to you can call me a Tewa-Hopi."

He said, "Well, even if you're a Tewa-Hopi instead of just a Hopi, you've got to know something about the rain dances. Some of our people have been out on your mesas and seen those dances, and they said that because the Hopis were praying for rain, sooner or later the rain came, sometimes the next night or maybe even while the dancing was going on."

I said, "I sure am surprised to hear that. You mean they danced for rain and then the rain came? Maybe it would have rained anyway."

This fellow was getting pretty put out with me. He said, "Look, you are an Indian, and I'm sure you know that they have rain dances."

I said, "Yes, we Indians are always having dances of one kind or another. We sure like to dance."

He said, "You mean that they don't believe all that, about dancing to make it rain, and then the rain comes?"

I said, "I can't tell you if I believe it or not, because I haven't read all those articles you are talking about. But I'll sure think about it. It's pretty interesting."

He said, "Mr. Healing, I can tell you one thing. You are the first Hopi I ever talked to who didn't tell me positively that they have the rain dance to make the rain come down and then it rains."

I said, "Well, I am glad to have the information, and when I get back home I'm going to look into it."

Dewey Healing
Tewa Village, July 1977

3
ADVENTURES
AND
EXPLOITS

The Boy and the Eagle[1]

Aliksai!

Ho!

In the village, the people were living there. Living in one house was a boy who owned two eagles. He had a sister, mother, and father. The boy kept his eagles tied [by one leg] on top of the house. One day he went out to hunt rabbits for them to eat. His sister was making piki. The eagles got hungry and started getting into her piki dough. She got angry and picked up a stick and hit one of them over the head and killed him. She buried the dead eagle in the ashes. So there was just one eagle left. When the boy returned he brought a rabbit that he'd killed. He went up on top of the house and saw only one eagle there. He asked the eagle [that was still there] where the other one was. The eagle told him that that the girl had killed the other one for getting in the piki dough.

Usually they pound the rabbit meat up and feed it to the eagles, and the eagle told the boy to do that. The eagle ate the rabbit meat, and when he was finished he told the boy to go down and get his ceremonial clothes because he was going to take him up to his [the eagle's] home. The boy went down and

[1]Compare with "Chórzhvūkíqölö and the Eagles," in Voth, *The Traditions of the Hopi*, pp. 159 ff.; "Tsorwukiqlö and His Eagles," in Malotki, *Hopitutuwutsi*, pp. 151 ff.; and "Joshokiklay and the Eagle," in Courlander, *People of the Short Blue Corn*, pp. 50 ff.

got his ceremonial clothes, his kilt, the bells that go around the legs, everything he'd wear at a dance. He put all these things on, just as if there was going to be a ceremony.

The boy's father, mother, and sister had gone out to the father's field to hoe weeds. The eagle told the boy to take off the rope he was tied with. He spread out his wings, like this, and told the boy to lie on top of him. He said they were going down to their father's field, and that when they were over the field he [the boy] would start singing. He told this to the boy, and the boy laid down on top of the eagle. The eagle took off and started flying, and pretty soon he came to the father's field. He started circling the place where the father had his cornfield. Pretty soon his sister noticed that there was something flying overhead, so she looked up there and saw her brother on top of the eagle. The eagle told the boy to start singing, so he started singing and his sister recognized her brother's voice and told her mother that he was up there riding the eagle. The eagle circled the field for a while, then went up higher, higher. Then the sister, mother, and father laid down [on their backs] to watch where the eagle was taking the boy. Finally they couldn't see them any more.

The eagle went up through the sky [into what they call] Tokpela, another world up there. He took the boy to a ledge, a high cliff where there was no way of getting down. The eagle put the boy there. "This is where you stay." The eagle left him. The boy laid there all day. There was just enough space for him to lie down. He got tired of lying there. He got thirsty. He didn't know how to get down. The cliff was just straight down. So he just laid there and laid there. About towards afternoon he heard somebody. So he looked around. There was a little bird. Came up to him and started talking with him. Said he felt sorry for him that the eagle had left him up there. He said he'd brought the boy a little food and a little water, in his mouth I guess. The boy ate that and felt a little better. The little bird told him, "Well, I'm going to get you down from here." He went down again, this little bird. The boy waited and waited, and pretty soon the bird came back up again. He had no feathers on. He had stuck his feathers in the little cracks in the rock clear up to where the boy was. That little bird just had no clothes on. The boy was thinking, "How is this bird going to get me down? He just a little one. How is he going to get me down?" The little bird told the boy he was going to carry him down on his back. Told the boy to close his eyes and not to open them. If once he opened his eyes they were going to fall from that cliff.

The boy got on the little bird's back, and the bird started [climbing down] on the feathers. Those feathers were steps. Finally they reached the ground. Then the little bird started going up [again], pulling out the feathers and sticking them back [in his skin]. When he came down he was all dressed up again. The little bird left the boy, but [before going] he told him that there was somebody living not very far from there. "You'll find him," he said.

So he started going where the little bird had told him. Pretty soon he got tired, and he started to sit down, but he heard someone, "Don't sit on me." He heard somebody say that, and he looked around. He didn't know who it was. He tried to sit down again, and [a voice] said, "Don't sit on me." Then he looked down, and there was that little spider. It was [Spider] Grandmother, Gogyeng Sowuhti, Spider Old Lady. "When you're rested up," she said, "you can come into the house." "How am I going to get in there?" he said. "Well, just sit down and go like this [narrator indicated a wriggling motion] and you'll have a hole there," she said. So he did that, and sure enough there was a kiva underneath. He got in there and this old lady fed him. He stayed there with Grandmother for a while. He went around hunting deer and antelope, and they had a lot of meat to eat.

One time Grandmother told him not to go in this [particular] direction. There was a wicked man living over there. "If he catches you he's going to gamble with you for your life." That's how wicked this old man was. "He is Hasokata, who commands the north wind to blow. He has long white hair and long eyebrows and eyelashes."[2] But you know how young boys are. He wanted to find out for himself. He started wandering over there.

[2]The narrator inserted this identification later, after he had finished the original narration.

Pretty soon he came to a sort of kiva. He looked inside. The old man had seen him coming, and told the boy to enter. They started playing [gambling]. The game was totolos [totolospi]. You play it by throwing bamboo sticks split in half. That was the game they played, and the boy lost. This old man, North Wind, put him up on the ledge of the kiva. Then he went to a door and opened it, and the north wind came out. He took all the boy's clothes off. The boy started freezing up there on the ledge. He just laid there freezing.

Pretty soon his Grandmother worried about him. She started looking for him and found him over there. The old lady couldn't do anything [much], but she stuck a turkey feather on the boy's back to keep him warm, that soft feather. The old lady went back to her house. She went up on top like a village crier and made an announcement for all her relatives, all her clan people, to come to her house. Soon they came, kachinas of different kinds. They grouped up and then they went to Hasokata's place. When they got there the boy was about to freeze. They started going down in the kiva. They were going to gamble with the wicked old man for the boy's life. The kachinas went down. They put sand on the floor. They planted corn, melon, squash, and everything. This is the way they were going to gamble. They were going to try to raise the plants up, make them grow. Hasokata was going to use his cold [wind]. If the plants would come up and mature and have corn or melons, the kachinas would win. That was the contest. The North Wind opened the door and the cold air started coming. The kachinas started dancing, all different kinds [of dances].[3] Pretty soon the corn was coming up, growing. The kachinas were winning, getting the best of North Wind Old Man. They were singing all kinds of songs. The corn had corn ears. The kachinas won that contest. They beat this old man. So they went up and untied this little boy. And they tied up the old man.

It started to rain.[4] The water started going down in the kiva, so the kachinas began to go out. The kiva was getting full of water. They left the old man there because he lost the contest.

[3]The group was Mixed or Soyohim Kachinas.
[4]It is implied that the kachinas caused the rain to fall.

Pretty soon the water was up to his neck. So he started crying. He was singing:

"Vainamokay kwing eu . . . huh huh huh!"

That "huh huh huh" was water going down into his mouth; he was swallowing it. He was about ready to drown.

"Vainamokay kwing eu . . . huh huh huh!"

The old man just drowned in there pretty soon. So they all went home then. The kachinas were everything, all kinds. I guess Spider Old Lady was Kachina Clan; she was everything.[5] So those kachinas went back where they came from. Grandmother told the boy to go out hunting deer. He'd go out hunting and bring one in, and they'd skin it up and then have the meat dried up. They'd stack it up, and pretty soon they had a whole stack of dried meat. The Grandmother told the boy he was going back home, and that's why he was killing the deer, so he could take the meat home when the time came. The way they stack that meat up and tie it in a way that you can't lose any of it, they just use one rope. That's the way his grandmother fixed it for him.

So the boy started going home from there. Pretty soon he got close to the village. (See, that's the way the story is. He's way up there and now he's down here.)[6] When he was getting close to the village, somebody saw him coming and recognized him, so they went back running to his house to tell his folks that his boy was coming home. But his folks didn't believe it because he'd been gone a long time, and maybe it was somebody else. [People] kept going to his house, telling his folks that he was coming home. They couldn't believe it because they'd been worrying about him and where he'd gone, and they'd got sick with it, and they'd just been laying down. Finally he got home, and sure enough it was their boy.

[5]Meaning that Spider Grandmother is related to all kachinas.

[6]A version of this story in Voth, *Traditions of the Hopi*, pp. 159 ff., explains that Spider Grandmother carries him down on a strand of spiderweb.

And after that whenever he had an eagle, his sister never killed it any more, because it's a cruelty to animals, and that's what the moral is.

The boy's name was Joshokiklay.

The songs that the kachinas sang in North Wind's kiva are long ones. They are talking about rain, talking about talavai, morning. Talking about the rain and lightening. Talks about yoiseumala, little stone things [shaped like] tires. They race with them. Have stone races. They're having stone races up there. That's the way the clouds throw their rain and lightning.

Uwaikwiota
Moencopi, August 1968

———54———

The Boy Who Crossed the Great Water

Aliksai!

East of Nuvatikyaovi, or Flagstaff, and west of Oraibi there was a place called Sowiteuyeuka. In this place there was once a village where many people lived. There were many children in that village, except that there were more boys than girls. The chief had one son, and this was a source of worry [that the boy would not find a wife]. And one evening after they had had their meal, the chief asked his son to stay and talk with him. So they sat down, and the chief said, "My son, I have something that I want you to do for me." And the boy—his name was Deveh—said, "Yes, my father, what do you wish to ask of me?" And his father said, "Yes, I have been thinking that I would want you to start racing tomorrow [i.e., practicing], and from then on you will race every day. You will start from here to the south, from the village [towards] the south, and then to the east towards the rising sun, and you will run till you are very tired. Then you can turn around and come back home again."

The boy said, "Is that what you wanted to tell me?" and the father said, "Yes, that is what I want you to do." And the boy said, "All right, I will start tomorrow." So they went to bed. And the next morning early, the boy started out towards the south of the village. [At a certain place] he started running towards the east, and he ran and he ran until he was tired. He had gone quite a way. When he became tired he turned around and started back. When he was halfway back he could hardly run any more. Then he would walk a while and run again. Finally he came back to his starting place, and he came on home from there. He went to his house, and his mother and father were glad to see him. So then they had their breakfast. After breakfast the father said that the boy would race every other day, instead of every day. He would race one day and rest one day.

So the next day the boy didn't run. The following day, early again, he went out toward the south and then started running. His father had told him to try to not let anybody see him, so they would not know what he was doing. The boy went running toward the sun. He ran and ran till he reached the place where he had turned around the time before, and he ran past it quite a ways. He finally became tired and turned back. Then he would run and walk, run and walk until he came home to the village. Several days after that his father asked him, after they had had their evening meal, how he was progressing. The boy said he was doing fine. He had passed three marks already. His father said, "That is fine. I am very glad. Now you have reached the place where, next time, you will climb the rise, and when you look towards the east you will see the flat lands, and way in the distance you will see a high rise, a lone rock formation. That is what you will try to reach. When you are finally strong enough you will reach that, circle it, and come home running, the way you started out."

The boy thought that was quite a ways, and he wondered if he could do it. He told his father, "Is that what you expect of me, my father?" And his father said, "Yes, that is what I want you to do." And so the boy said, "I will try. I will try not to disappoint you." His father said, "When you have finally come home without tiring, I will give you something else to do." And so after that the boy started running again. A few days later, he finally did reach the rock formation and circled it, but that was about all he could do. He was very tired, and so he started walking home, walking and then running again. He told his father he had reached the place but that he was too tired to run home. His father said that the next time the boy went out, his mother would fix lunch for him, and when he got tired he could sit down and eat. His father knew that it was a long way to run without eating anything. So the next time, his mother gave him a lunch to take. He went out, ran to the rock, circled it, and started back. Then he became very tired and sat down and had his lunch and came on home. After a while he was able to reach the rock and come home running.

And [that time] he told his father [what he had accomplished]. "Father, I have something to tell you." "Yes, my son, how are you coming along in your running? Have you reached the rock?" And his son said, "I have reached the rock; I have circled it, and I have finally come home running without tiring too much." His father was very happy. He said, "Thank you, my son, I am very glad that you are now strong enough. Now you will rest for two days, and on the third day I will tell you what I want you to do next." And so he rested, didn't do any running at all. The third day came, and after the evening meal his father said, "Now, my son, I have something else for you to do."

The father got up and went into the next room. He came back out carrying something in his hand. It was wrapped up, and he put it down before him and unwrapped it. He told his son, "Now I have this all ready for you." It was a ball and a stick, a playing stick [for the game nahoydadatsia]. The ball was covered with buckskin, it was real tough and was a good running ball. When hit, it would travel far. The father explained to the boy that he would hit this ball while running. He would hit it as hard as he could, and then he would run after it and as soon as it landed he would hit it again with all his might. That was what the father wanted him to do. His son said, "I will try to do as you want." His father said, "When you are strong enough you will reach the rock and you will circle it and you will come back running, the way you did before. [Then] I will have something else for you to do."

And so the boy went the next day with his ball and his playing stick. He went down the south side of the village and then toward the east. He put his ball down and hit it as hard as he could. Then he ran after it. He went along that way. And soon he became tired and turned around and started back home again. [He did this for a number of days.] His father asked him, "My son, how are you doing?" And Deveh said, "I am doing fine. Tomorrow maybe I will reach the rock and circle it." His father was glad. The boy went on practicing. Soon he found that he could almost catch up with the ball as it flew in the air. He would hit the ball and run and arrive almost at the same time that the ball landed. When at last he was able to arrive back at the village running, he reported to his father. He said, "My father, I have come home running, the way I started out." His father was very glad that he had done this. He said, "Now you will rest for two more days. And on the third day I will tell you what I want you to do next. I have something else for you to do."

The second day passed, and after their evening meal when the mother finished clearing everything away, the father said, "Now, my son, I have something else for you to do." He got up and went into the next room and brought out something, a bow with four arrows. He said, "Now, my son, I made this for you to practice with." He put the things down in front of him. He said, "Tomorrow morning I want you to go to the west side of the village and hide these things somewhere and come on back home.[1] You will watch the sun today [tomorrow] and when it goes to the west, when it is sliding down, then you will be down at the place where you hid your arrows, and you will shoot them toward the setting sun. You will mark a place for yourself on the ground and you will shoot straight towards the sun. Watch it as it flies along. And then when you think it has landed, you will shoot the next arrow, and watch again. Maybe you will see it. Maybe it will disappear, and you will see the sun as it shines on the feather. But you will have to use your imagination in looking for your arrow. You will think that this is about the place where

[1]The reason for hiding the bows and arrows is so that other villagers will not suspect what is going on.

they landed. You will shoot all of your arrows that way. Then you will go and look for them, and you will find them all and you will hide them again, and then come on back home."

So with this the boy left his parents and went to bed. The next morning early he picked up his arrows and his bow and started towards the west side of the village. He went out among the rocks and the bushes and he hid his bow and arrows there. Then he came on back home. That afternoon he waited around until the time came for him to go. He went down toward the west side of the village, went out to find his bow and arrows. By the time he found them, the sun was sliding down toward the west, toward the horizon, and he made a mark for himself on the ground. He shot his first arrow. He pulled as hard as he could on the bow and watched his arrow fly toward the sun. Then finally it disappeared. Then he started his next arrow. The he waited a while and started his third arrow. When he had shot all of them, he started out to find them. He walked along toward the sun, and thought, "Maybe it landed about here." So he went back and forth toward the north and south until he found one arrow, his first. Then he looked for his second arrow and found it a little further west. The third arrow he found a little way from there. Then he found his last arrow, [still] further away.

After that he came back to the starting point. He hid his bow and arrows somewhere and went home. He did that for several days, and each time he went to look for his arrows he found them further west. A couple of days later he reported to his father. "Father, I have found my arrows today at the point where the trail turns around a hill." His father was glad and said, "I am very happy, my son, that your arms are now strong enough. Wait three days and I will tell you what I want you to do next. So the third day came, and that evening after their supper he sat down with his father. And his father brought out his pipe and tobacco and he smoked. He smoked until he was finished. Then the son knew that his father was going to tell him. His father cleaned his pipe and put it away. He said, "Now, my son, I am going to tell you why you have been making yourself ready. You are going on a journey tomorrow morning, a long journey. That is what I have been preparing you for." His son said, "All right, my father, I did not know that I was going on a journey. I did not know what I was preparing myself for."

His father said, "Yes, you are going on a journey tomorrow morning early. You will start out before it is daylight. You will go out of the village by a roundabout way and then go towards the west, and you will finally reach the place where you last found your arrows, quite a ways away from here. You will reach the place, go around the bend, follow the faint trail that you see. This trail leads straight west. It will soon disappear. You will keep going straight west, not turning left or right at any time. And you are to hurry. Run as fast as you have been practicing. Do not save [spare] yourself. You will become hungry. When you feel that you are hungry, you will open up your sack—your mother will prepare your lunch for you—you will open up your sack and you will eat as you go, and drink some of your water, but do not eat too much, just enough to get your strength back, and then start running again. And then you will finally reach a high mound. It will look blue in the distance, but when you reach it, it will be green. It will be full of grass. That [place] will be the very edge. You will climb to the top, and you will stop and look out over the water."

"You will not be there very long. You will watch and then you will imagine a place that you think will be narrow [enough] to go across. When you have made up your mind on this, go down to the edge of the water and watch as the water comes in. It is never still, it is always moving. And when the water comes in toward the shore and then goes back, that is the place where you will dig holes for both of your heels, and you will stand in the holes.[2] And from there you will shoot your arrow."

The father got up and went into the next room and came back with a bow and two arrows. He said, "This is the arrow that you will shoot.[3] Look at it well so that you will not forget. You will place it on your bow and shoot as hard as you can, and watch. Watch your arrow, it will soon disappear, but do not take your eyes off of where it went. Then, if you do it right, you will see something white coming towards you. Make yourself ready as it comes. When it comes closer you will see that there will be

[2]That is, he will stand on that part of the beach from which the wave has receded.

[3]Designating one of the two arrows.

a path for you, a clear path for you to run on.[4] As soon as this white thing reaches you, you will run as fast as you can. Do not save [spare] yourself; run as you have never run before, because if you don't, the water will swallow you up. And as soon as you reach land you will hear a slam right behind you and the water will come back together again. You will look for your arrow, and when you find it, leave it as it is[5] and mark the spot so you will know it when you come back again. And from there you will have to be on your own. I cannot tell you which way to go from there. You will have to decide that for yourself. That is where I will leave it up to you. I will wait for you for four days. If on the fourth day, when the sun is setting, [you have not returned] I will know that you are not coming back."

This made the boy sad, and he said, "I am sad, my father, I did not know it would be this way. I will try to come back for you and do as you want me to."

His father said, "You will go to bed here in our house to-night, so that you will start out early tomorrow morning." He put the bow and the arrows away, and the boy went to bed, but he didn't sleep well because he was worried. He didn't know if he was going to return from this journey. He thought for a long time, and finally went to sleep. His mother and father stayed up all night. His father smoked and prayed, then he smoked again. His mother was getting his meal ready. She had made the piki and she had made the ground cornmeal made out of baked sweet corn. They had made a bag for him to carry his lunch in, it had a strap on it. They had fixed a jug for him to carry his water in, and it also had a strap. The father had made a bag for his arrows. It had a strap also.

The first thing the boy knew, he was being awakened by his mother. "Wake up, my son, it is time for you to get ready to go." So he got up and got dressed. He went into the [other] room, and there he found his father. Then they had their breakfast. After breakfast his father said, "My son, come here and I will

---

[4]As is made clear a few lines further on, the water parts, and he will run between two walls of water.

[5]The narrator explained later: "A Hopi will never use the same arrow twice."

dress you.[6] First your mother will comb your hair." She got out her brush *[sic]* and combed his hair. His father went into the other room and brought out a bundle. He unwrapped it and took out a pair of [leggings] and put them on the boy. He put on a new pair of moccasins. Then, next, a white kachina skirt with designs on it. Next he put on the boy a turquoise-blue shirt, which was worn in those days with some kind of ribbon on the shoulder. Then he put around the boy's neck a string of turquoise beads. He put on a belt around the white [kachina] skirt. He tied small belts around the leggings at his knees. Last of all he put a white fluffy feather on top of the boy's head. And he said, "Now it is time for you to leave." He put the strap of the lunch bag on the boy's shoulder, and the bag of arrows too.

So the boy left the house, going out of the village by a round-about way, and he went on. He came to the bend of the road and followed a faint trail. Then he started running as fast as he could because his father had told him he should hurry. Finally the faint trail disappeared, and he kept going straight toward the west. About noontime he began to get tired. So he took out some of his piki and his dosi, and he put it in his mouth and drank some water. He didn't stop, but kept walking while he was eating. Then he started running as fast as he could.

In the late afternoon he came to the mound that his father had spoken of. It was green when he reached it, with a lot of grass on it. He climbed up to the top. He saw the water. There was water as far as he could see. Like his father said, it was never still. He wondered how far this water [extended]. He couldn't tell how far the water went, where it ended and where the sky started. He went down the slope to the edge of the water. He saw the water stirring around with foam on it, with waves coming to the shore. At the very edge of the water he stood and made a place for his heels. He had to try with all his strength to shoot his arrow as far as he could. The he took out his arrow, and he said to his arrow, "Fly straight, and may you see us both safely across." Then he put it to his bow and he stretched it as far as it would go, and then he shot. He watched it fly across the

[6]That is, with ceremonial clothes.

water, then finally it disappeared, but he kept his eye right on
the place where it disappeared.

Soon after that he saw something coming. It came nearer,
and when it came right up to him he saw that there was a path
to follow, on the ground.[7] He started running as fast as he could.
With all his might he ran. He ran like he never did before. He
felt he was getting tired, but then he thought, "Oh, no, I must
not give up now." So he went on, trying harder all the time.
Then he saw land. He was encouraged and tried harder. As soon
as he got to the edge of the [land] he gave a big leap, and right
after that there was a big slam right behind him. And when he
turned around he saw that all the water had come together again.
There was no more path. He stood there looking at the water,
and after [a few moments] he looked around for his arrow. He
looked and there it was in the sand, almost hidden, only the
feather part sticking out. He didn't take the arrow out. He left it
there so he wouldn't forget the place when he came back this
way again.

There was a mound there by the shore, and he climbed up.
He looked around and saw strange country, a strange place he
had never been. He didn't know which to go. He saw a hill a
little way from there. He decided to go to the hill. Maybe there
was a cave there in the hill, where he could spend the night.
The next morning maybe he would climb the rest of the hill and
look around to decide which way he would travel. So he started
for the hill. When he got there he started climbing, and halfway
up he saw that there was a cave. He saw bones lying around as
if some animal had been in there. He cleaned the cave out for
himself and by then it was dark. He sat down and ate some more
of his piki and dosi and drank some of his water. He put his
lunch [bag] and water [jug] away in a corner. Then he took off
his kachina skirt and belt. He thought, "I will go to sleep now
so I will be rested for tomorrow." He lay down in a corner and
put the kachina skirt over him. It almost covered him from head
to toe. Then he went to sleep.

When he woke up it was morning, almost light, and he

[7]That is to say, the water parted, forming a wall on each side.

could see a little bit. He ate a little more of his dosi and piki and drank some water and started climbing to the top [of the hill]. When he reached the top he stood looking around. He could see way off in the distance. To the south he could see some mountains, and he decided that that would be the place he would head for. To the east and the west there was not anything, and he thought that [toward the south] there might be some water and grass. Perhaps some people would be living in that direction.

So he came down the hill and started running toward the south. He ran, he ran as fast as he could. Finally he stopped. He looked at the ground and thought he saw a footprint. He was glad. He thought, "Maybe there are some people around here." [The footprints] were heading toward the south. He was encouraged by this and started running again. When he became tired he would walk, and then he would run again. The mountains were coming closer to him. They were blue [before], and now they weren't blue anymore. He came to a sandy place and stopped again, and this time he saw some more footprints. There were two [persons]. They headed south where he was going. He was glad and hurried on, running. As he came closer to this high mesa he thought he saw somebody coming toward him, a little figure [in the distance]. He couldn't tell if it was an animal or a man. Pretty soon he saw that it was a person.

He kept running, and the man came up to him. He said, "You are a stranger." And Deveh said, "Yes, I am a stranger to this land." The man said, "You are a stranger from some other place, for you are dressed differently. I will go back and tell my chief. Take care as you come along." With this he turned around and started running back.

The boy looked at the mesa, and right next to the mesa there was a lone butte, a rock formation standing straight up. At first he had thought it was connected to the mesa, but as he came up he saw that it was separate. On this rock formation at the very top there was an eagle that was kept there for the purpose of looking out for strangers. The eagle had a sharp eye, could look far off. It was the chief's eagle. When the eagle saw Deveh coming he flew to the village, to the chief's house. He went to the [entrance] and the chief said, "Come in." The eagle said, "I have seen a stranger coming this way. He is a real stranger, for he is dressed in a strange costume." The chief said, "Thank you. I will send a man out to meet him." And so the eagle went back out to his post. (That was why this man had come [running] out to meet him.)

The man climbed the mesa and disappeared. Soon another man came running out. He did the same thing. He stopped the boy and said, "You are a stranger." And Deveh said, "Yes, I am a stranger." And the man said, "I will go back and tell my chief. You take care in coming." He turned around and started running back to the village again. Then a third one came just as the boy was at the foot of the mesa, and they said the same thing again. A fourth man came when the boy was ready to climb the mesa. He said, "You are the stranger I have been sent out to meet. Come up and I will show you where the chief lives. He may or he may not want to see you." Deveh said, "Oh, is that so?" "Yes, follow me up." The man turned around and started going up the trail, and Deveh followed him. When they got to the top there was still another place to climb.

The man turned around and said, "You wait here. I will go up and tell my chief that you are here." Then he went up the ladder to the next [level] and disappeared. Soon the boy saw a man standing up above. The man said, "You are the stranger they told me about, and you are indeed a stranger." Deveh said, "Yes, I am a stranger." The chief told him, "Come on up. I will take you to my house." So he climbed the ladder and [followed] the chief to his house. When they got there, the chief said, "Come on in and sit down. You are welcome here." And he told his wife, "Prepare some food for this man, because he must be hungry, he must have traveled far." His wife got busy and prepared something and put it in front of Deveh. He was surprised at the language of these people, because it was the same as his. He started eating. He had piki and dosi in a bowl.

He thought that when he was eating, these people would talk with him, but they did not. [After a while] the chief said, "You may be interested in watching the people here entertain themselves. You can go out of this house, turn east, then turn right, and there you will see the plaza. You will see lots of men and women on top of the houses watching them play ball." So the boy came out of the house and then he went east and to the right. Then he was on top of a house, and he looked down into the plaza. There were a lot of men and women on top of the houses, cheering and laughing, because there was a game going on between the boys and the girls. They were having a good time.

Deveh thought, "I'll just sit here and watch them play." So he sat down and watched. He thought that the girls could really play well. What they were playing was what he had been practicing.[8] They buried the ball in the middle of the plaza. Then a girl and a boy stood on opposite sides with their sticks, and one would hit first and the other one would hit next, and pretty soon they had hit away all the sand and could see the ball. As soon as the ball appeared the next one would hit it with all his might and the ball would come flying out, and everyone started hitting it back and forth. And at the end of the plaza on each side there was a place where they drove this ball to determine the winner. The boys seemed to be losing. The girls were better players. After a while they noticed Deveh up there. They sent a little girl up to tell him to come down and play with them.

Deveh decided, "Oh, well, I will play." He went down to the plaza and they already had brought out a stick for him. He saw that the girls had all put up their skirts under their belts in front, so that their legs [in front] were all bare. That was the way that they played, and that was the reason that the boys were losing, because they were watching the girls' legs. Deveh saw what was happening, but he was doing the same thing as the other boys, watching the girls' legs. Pretty soon the boys lost their game.

Then a girl came up to him, and she said, "Thank you, I have won this away from you because you lost the game." She took away his moccasins. They played another game and Deveh played with them again and he kept losing his clothing. Next he lost his belt, and the next time he lost his skirt, then his socks [i.e., leggings], then his shirt, all his clothes, then his beads. The only thing he had left was the feather on the top of his head. Then he lost the feather too. It was the last thing he had. When

[8]Nahoydadatsia, or shinny.

he had lost everything, he quit. He went back to the house where the chief was, and when he came into the house the chief laughed at him. He really laughed, didn't seem sorry for him at all. Of course he had known all along what would happen to the boy. Evidently it had happened before.

So they had their supper and went to bed. In the morning at breakfast time someone came in and said, "We will be holding a contest with your guest. We will all go down below and have a contest with him. He will run a race with our runners." The chief said, "I am sure our guest will be willing to take on this contest with our runner." After they ate, he went into another room and brought out something wrapped up, something longish, and he put a strap on it and put it over his shoulder. He said, "Let us go. The people are going down already." So the woman hurriedly cleaned off the place where they ate [and they went out]. The boy had to go with them. They made their way to the [lower] ground.

When they got down there, the chief said to Deveh, "Take a few paces over to the east side, and I will stay here." And as the people came down he said, "Anyone who would like to take [the side of] my guest here, step over to his side. And whoever wants to be on my side will stay here by me." The boy said, "Well, I don't think anyone will come on my side, because nobody knows me." Nobody stepped on his side until later, when more people came down [from the village heights]. Then a thin, smallish, not very good-looking young girl said, "I will be on his side." She came over to where Deveh was standing. She said, "I will be on your side." And finally, when some more people came down, a bigger girl came to his side.

The chief said, "All right, we will go on with the contest. Bring out our runner." They went into the crowd and came out with a boy, a tall boy who looked like a good runner. They stood him beside Deveh, who thought, "Well, he looks like a good runner. I don't think I have a chance against him." But the little girl told him that when they started out Deveh should not [press] too close to the other runner because something might happen on the way. She warned him about that. She said, "We will both hope that you come home first."

The chief said [to the runners], "You both come up to this

line and stand here, and I will give you a push at the same time and you will start out." He took down the thing he had hanging from his shoulder [which he had brought from his house] and unwrapped it. It was a large knife. Then the boy [understood] that this had all been planned. The chief said, "If we lose this race, if our runner loses, then you will take this knife and kill us all. And if you lose, then we will kill you with it." He stuck this sword into the ground.[9]

So [the two runners] stood on the line and the chief put his hands on their shoulders and gave them a push and said, "Run!" And so they started running, and the runner [from the village] shot right out and was ahead, right from the beginning. Deveh wasn't very happy about what the chief had said, that they would be running for so many lives. He thought for sure that he would be the loser. The other boy was an expert runner and went way ahead. But then Deveh said, "Well, maybe I will have a chance. I will try hard." He kept the other runner in sight. They ran towards the north. The chief had said they would run to the north till they came to the edge of the water. Then one of them would go to the left and the other would go to the right and they would circle the water.[10] When they had circled it they would come back to the place where they started, and then return [to the village].

Soon they went down a dip, then up again, then down some more dips and up again. Pretty soon they came to another dip and when the first runner went down and came up it was [i.e., he had become] a deer. The deer looked back at the boy, sort of went around in a circle, and started out again. The boy Deveh thought, "Well, so this is what I am running against. I will have no chance against him because he is a swift runner." However, he tried. He was quite a distance behind now, because a deer runs real fast. Deveh came up to the edge of the water and saw the hoofprints of the deer turning to the left, and when he saw that he turned to the right, and ran along the edge of the water,

[9]The knife in the ground, indicating that death will come to the loser (or the losing side, collectively), is a free-floating motif appearing in numerous stories.

[10]Obviously this cannot be the same body of water that Deveh had to cross earlier, but the narrator did not explain.

wondering when he would meet up with the other runner. Finally they did somewhere [on the other side] and passed each other and came on, and pretty soon they came back to the place [where they had turned in different directions]. The deer was still ahead, running back toward the mesa. The boy kept running and finally caught sight of the other runner. He saw that [at a certain spot] the deer made a kind of circle. He could tell from the footprints on the ground [that the deer had run in a circle]. The boy avoided running or stepping into the circle.[11] He would sort of go around it. The deer wasn't doing so well [now] and the boy was catching up to him.

Finally Deveh did catch up with him. He said, "I will go first for a while," and the deer didn't say anything to him. He passed the deer and then slowed down and the deer ran in front again. Then the boy passed the deer again, and as he passed him he gave the deer a slap on the rump and said, "Run, you are not running." The deer gave a little jump but he could not run any more; he was walking. So the boy was encouraged by this and ran harder, and soon he caught sight of the people standing there waiting for them. The little girl had already seen Deveh coming, and she said, "Our runner is coming first, but do not say anything, we will make believe we don't see him yet." She was the one with the good eyesight. After a while people began to see someone coming. "Oh, there is someone coming. It must be our runner." But when he came closer, they discovered that it was Deveh, their guest, who was coming first. They couldn't see the other one. When Deveh crossed the finish line the girls were there to catch his arms and lead him over to one side and make him sit down. The little girl had brought a bowl, and she brought a jug of water and she put some dosi in the water, and after he had rested a while she had him drink this. She said, "It will bring your strength back." He drank it and was refreshed.

Finally the other runner came in, turned into a man again. He was barely walking and when he crossed the line he fell over. The men from his side came and picked him up. Then the chief

---

[11]The making of the circle is obviously witchcraft or sorcery.

said to Deveh, "Now that we have lost this race you have a right to kill us with this knife, with this sword." He took the knife and handed it to Deveh. Deveh accepted it. Then a girl stepped up and handed him the belt [she had taken from him during the stick ball game]. She said, "Here is your belt. Since you have beaten us in this race, I will give it back to you." She handed it to him. Then another girl came up with his moccasins. She said, "Here are your moccasins." And another one came up with his skirt, and so on, until he had gotten all of his things back, including the feather. He started dressing himself with the things they had given back to him.

When he was through, he stood there thinking what he should do. He called the chief over to him. He said, "Come over here." The chief came to him. "Turn around." He turned around, and as soon as he did, Deveh struck with the knife at the chief's neck, and the chief's head [fell and] went rolling away from the body. The chief's body moved around and jerked until it finally lay still. Then Deveh called the runner to come up. He came out of the crowd and came up to him. "Turn around." He turned around and Deveh struck with the knife again and the head came off and the body jerked around and pretty soon lay still. There were two of them [killed].

Deveh put the knife down. "There is one more thing that I want to do. This will be all the killing I am going to do now, but there is something else that I want from you. I am going to pick out all the girls I want and I am going to take them home to where I came from." And do he went over to the crowd and went among them, picking out the girls he wanted to take home. He said, "I will take you," and he went up to another girl and said, "I will take you." And he picked out I don't know how many, but quite a few. And he selected some young women who had small children. He left only the older people there.

He put them all in a bunch and told them that they must go up to the village and prepare lunch [to carry on the trip]. He told them to hurry, and he told the rest of the people to go on back home. So the girls and young women went up to the village and made hurry-up lunch [for the trip]. Deveh was thinking that some of them would not want to come, but he waited and they all showed up, even those with small children. Then he said, "Let us go, because we have to hurry." So they started out. It was late afternoon, and he wanted them to go as far as they could before dark. So they started out hurrying, running and then walking, and running again. He was surprised at the girls and the young women with children, how strong they were, how far they had gone without any sign of being tired. He thought about the games they played in their village, and he [supposed] that this must be the reason for their strength. Soon they were almost at the place where Deveh had crossed the water. Finally they reached the place. Deveh said, "Here is where we will cross. Come over here and I will tell you."

So they all gathered, and he said, "I'm going to shoot my arrow. Watch and you will see something coming where I've shot my arrow, something that will come traveling towards us. As soon as it reaches us, you'll all start running as fast as you can. I'm going to be right behind you." He got his arrow out. He shot his arrow as hard as he could, and then he watched. Soon he could see it [coming], and he said, "There it is, watch it closely." So it came traveling to them, this white thing, and they all saw it. Soon it was close to them, and he said, "Get ready to run." Soon as it [reached] them there was a clear path in front of them and he told them, "Run!" They started running. "Run as fast as you can!"

The little thin girl, his friend, was the best runner of them all; she was way ahead of everybody and nobody could catch up with her. Pretty soon the ones with babies looked like they were slowing down, so Deveh would take a baby from one of them and run with it, and he would grab a woman by the hand and pull her along. Somehow they all got across, and as soon as they did there was a big slam right behind them. They turned around and [saw that] the water had come together again. There was no more path. They were all happy. They said, "Thank you [that] we all came across safely." And they thanked the arrow.

Deveh told them, "Now that we are across we will go up to the mound, on top here, and we're going to sit down and eat. Eat well, because we are going to travel all night; we're not going to sleep anywhere." They went up to the top, and there they opened up their lunches and brought out their water and started eating. When they were satisfied they put their things away. It was then about time for the sun to set. Deveh told them, "We must hurry and be on our way." So they started out.

In the village that they had left, the menfolks there were all very angry that Deveh had taken all the young girls and women. The boys had had their sweethearts taken away and the men had had their wives taken away. These were the ones that wanted to go after them. So they decided to go before the sun was up. They fixed their lunches and before daylight they started out. They started out running and followed the footprints of the women. Soon they came to the edge of the ocean, and that's where the footprints disappeared. They went up and down along the shore looking.

One of them remembered that there was a place for crossing [the ocean] under water, a tunnel. He told the men to look for a huge shell that covered [the entrance]. They went back and forth and found the huge shell close to where Deveh's arrow [had landed]. The great big shell was turned down over the opening. They dug away the sand that was on top of it, got hold of the edge and lifted it up. There was a great big hole there. So he told them, "Go on in, you young ones first. Run as fast as you can, and when you reach the other side do not wait for us. Lift up the lid [on the other side] and go after them." So the young boys went in first and the men followed, closing the lid after them. Then they ran and ran until they got to the other end. They got together and pushed the lid away.

Then they started running again. They found the footprints of the boy and the women who were with him. They followed as fast as they could. They were strong, much stronger than the women, and they were gaining on them.

The chief of Deveh's village, his father, was worried. The sun was going down and soon it would be dark. He thought, "He must be on his way home." But he didn't know and he was worried. He got on top of his house and said, "My strong messenger in the east, will you come to my house right away." He went back into his house and sat down. Pretty soon somebody came in. "Come in, I want to speak with you." He came in, and it was a dove [who entered]. The chief told him, "Four days ago my son went on a journey. He's due back today at sundown, but he has not yet arrived. Will you go and see if he is coming or if he is having trouble. You know which way to go, so go without wasting any time. When you see them do not stop, but go further and see if there is anybody following them."

So the dove went out of the house and flew toward the west. [After a while] he saw them. They all looked pitiful. The girls and especially the women were tired and looked hungry and thirsty. The boy was having trouble. He would carry one [woman or girl] for a little way, then put her down and go back and get another one. The dove felt sorry. He did what the chief asked and went farther. Before he had gone very far he saw that there were men and boys following them. They were coming fast and gaining on them. The dove turned back and flew to the chief's house. He said, "Your son is coming but he is having trouble with the girls and the women. They seem to be tired, and he is tiring himself out, too, carrying one for a ways and then going back for another one. I am afraid that the men will catch up with them soon. They are right behind them." The chief said, "Thank you, that is what I want to know. I will ask my other messenger to come. You may go home." The dove went out.

The chief came out of the house again and went to the top. He said, "My strong messenger in the north, will you come? I would like to talk with you. And hurry." He went back into the house. He sat down. He filled his pipe and started smoking. Somebody came [to the entrance] and said, "Are you here?" He said, "Yes, I am here." The person entered. It was an owl. He said, "You have something that you want me to do for you." The chief said, "Yes, I have something that I want you to do for me. Four days ago my son went on a journey toward the setting sun. In four days he was to return. I sent my other messenger to see if he is coming. He has come back and told me that my son is on the way home, except that he is having trouble. He is bringing some girls and women. They are tired. He is having trouble, he is tired himself. So there is something I want you to do. When I have this tobacco in my pipe going good and hot, you will take [the pipe] and go to the west and you will see my son coming with the girls. You will pass them and farther west you will see some men coming. They are strong, and my other messenger said they are catching up. When you come up to them you will [puff on the pipe and] blow smoke down onto them. In that way I hope they will be slowed down."

And so the owl picked up the pipe and went out. He started to fly west, and soon he saw the chief's son and the women coming. He saw that they were having trouble, like the chief said. He passed them and went farther west and saw the men who were coming. He perched himself upon a rock, high up, and started puffing on the pipe. He would get a mouthful of smoke, and it would all come out [of his mouth] in a lump and go down towards the ground, and when it hit the ground it would explode and the air would be filled with smoke. Pretty soon the smoke was getting so thick that by the time the men reached that place they couldn't find the footprints. They looked around and they said, "What is happening? It is getting dark and we cannot see the footprints." They bent their heads real low to look for the footprints. They couldn't see. The owl was busy putting smoke down to them. They huddled together and stopped for a while. They were standing around, [waiting] for whatever it was to clear so that they could go on. When the owl used up all of the tobacco, he picked up the pipe and came on back to the chief's house and told him he had done what the chief wanted him to do. He thought that [what he had done] would slow them up, because he had seen them milling around when he left them, but they were right behind the women, and he was afraid they would catch up anyway.

So the chief thanked him and said for him to go on back to his home. The he waited a while. And he got the fire going good and hot in the fireplace, put a lot of wood in it and it started burning real fast. Then he waited for it to die down so he could do what he was thinking [of doing]. When the fire died down a little he got his brush and started brushing down the walls. There was a lot of hot soot on the walls and he swept it down in a pile. He was so busy that he didn't hear anybody come in until someone spoke to him. "Did you want to see me? I am here." He turned around, and there was a crow. He was sitting there waiting for him.

He said, "Yes, I sent for you. I wanted you in a hurry. Wait until I am through and I will tell you what I want." So he hurried brushing down the walls, and he had a whole pile of soot there. When he was through he said, "This is all that I can gather of the soot. It is still hot. I want you to take this and slow the men down. Four days ago my son went toward the setting sun, and today he is supposed to be back and I am waiting for him. He has trouble with the people he is bringing here, and I have sent my other messengers and they came back telling me these men that are following them have almost caught up with them. So I want you to see if you can slow them down. I want you to put all of this [soot] in between your feathers and take it to the men who are following them. When you are right on top of them you will shake yourself and put this hot soot on them, and this will slow them down, I am hoping. You know how to do this and so I will leave it up to you."

So he came away as the crow hopped to the fireplace. The crow stood right there by the pile of soot and put soot right in between his feathers on the left side. And when it was full, he started on the right side, in between the feathers. When it was full he started on his tail. When that was full, he started filling his fine feathers. He did something so that these fine feathers puffed up and there was a lot of room in there. Soon he had all of this soot taken up and he came jumping out. He said, "What should I do now? I have picked up all the soot and there isn't any more, although there is still room in my feathers." But the chief said, "That is all that I can get, and so it will have to do. Be on your way now. Hurry as fast as you can."

The crow got out of the house and he started flying, but he could not flap his wings so well, fearing that the soot would start dropping out. He went as easy as he could. He reached the women and Deveh, and like his father had said, Deveh was having a hard time with the girls. The crow felt sorry for him. He went past them and soon, not far behind, he met the men who were after them. As soon as he got [above] them he started shaking himself, and pretty soon the air was filled with soot, it got dark all of a sudden. And the men felt the warmth of it. Soon [the air] got hot, and they felt it stinging on their skin, the hotness of the soot. And they started rubbing their arms, their bodies, trying to get the heat off. The crow was busy shaking himself right on top of them, and the men were rubbing themselves.

They found that their skin was getting blistered and their hair was getting thin. Their hair was not long anymore, it was short and shriveled up and tangled. They were milling around and wondering what had happened to them. Then one of them said, "Somebody has put something on us, and I'm afraid we can't fight this off." So they stood around, and pretty soon the stinging was not so bad and the air was clearing.

They could see that something had happened to them. They looked at each other, and one of them said [to another], "Something happened to you. You look different. Your long hair is gone, and it is all curled up tight into frazzles, and your lips are thick and your skin has turned black. You are all scorched." They were talking among themselves like this. They were surprised. And while they were talking they began talking differently, and it wasn't the Hopi language any more. They were talking a different language. They could not understand what had happened. Finally they became very angry and said they would catch the boy and kill him. They started traveling again, all black men, their hair singed.

They found the footprints and started following them. Soon they saw the boy and the women. Deveh looked around and saw the men coming. He said, "Well, I am sure they will be upon us soon and there is nothing I can do. I cannot get you all home to my place. There is no help coming my way, so I will just take these two [girls] who have befriended me." He chose the skinny little girl and the other girl who had been on his side when he raced with the deer. He chose those two to take home with him. So when the men came up close he said [to the other girls and women], "I will leave you now, because if I don't, they will kill me." So he got the two girls by the arm and started running towards home again.

Then the men caught up with the women, and the women were afraid of them, these men with the shiny bodies and singed hair and the thick lips. They didn't want to be caught by them, and they were all crying and screaming. [The men] were not talking Hopi at all. The women didn't want to go with them. But they were caught, and soon they were turned around. The men just picked them up and carried them back. They carried them on their backs. The women were their wives and sweethearts,

and each one took a girl or woman. They went back to where
they had come out of the tunnel, which they hadn't bothered to
close when they came out, so it was open already when they
got there. They entered the tunnel and went across. When they
reached the other end they opened it and came out. The last
few men who had entered the tunnel closed it behind them and
then went on, and when they came out at the other side they
closed the tunnel up with the huge shell and went on their way.
They carried the women until they were tired. By this time the
women were rested and could walk along by themselves for a
while. Finally they got home. The people there were surprised
that these black men had brought the women back. Since the
women were their wives, the men lived with them. And soon
they started having babies that looked like their fathers. Several
years after that, there were no more people [there] who spoke
the Hopi language, they were all black, with kinky hair and shiny
bodies.[12]

Deveh, when he got home, brought the two girls to his father, and his father was very happy that the boy came home with

[12]Although some revisionist versions of the emergence myth now say that
all races emerged at the same time from the Third World, it is generally believed
that the people of the Southwest saw their first black person at the time of
Spanish intrusion early in the sixteenth century. Estevan, a Negro (described
as "Moorish") who had travelled with Cabeza de Vaca in the latter's explora-
tion of Texas, headed a scouting party for Fray Marcos de Niza into Zuni
country in 1539. At first accepted by the Zunis, he aroused their hostility by his
manners and arrogance, and he was killed before the arrival of Fray Marcos at
the Zuni village of Hawikuh.

According to tradition, Estevan also appeared in Hopiland. Albert Yava
stated: "The Zunis killed him. He came to Hopiland with a bunch of Spaniards.
They brought him out here. He claimed to be a kind of guide, claimed to be a
Mexican Indian. But he was a Negro. That's why they called him Black Mexican. That is what they called Negroes. He was out here, according to old-
timers. Then he went back to Zuni and began to monopolize the womenfolks.
Where he got his turquoise nobody knew, but he brought a lot of turquoise
and gave it to his lady friends. The Zunis didn't like it, so they killed him."

Hopis first saw blacks in numbers when some of the villages resisted send-
ing their children to government schools early in this century. Black troops
entered Third Mesa villages to round up the school-age children and take them
to Keam's Canyon.

at least these two [girls]. Deveh decided he would have the little skinny girl for a sister, and he would have the older girl for his wife. His father was very sorry that the other women were taken back, because there would have been enough women to go around, and many children.

Tsakaptamana
Moencopi, April 1969

————55————

A Wife Who Joined
a Secret Society

Aliksai!

In Oraibi there was a man and his wife and only one girl-child. As always, the man wanted a son, but there was only this girl-child. She was a pretty little girl. As time went on, she grew, and finally she was a teenager. One day she and her chums decided that they would have a grinding—what would you call it?—a grinding marathon or a grinding spree. Girls would get together sometimes and grind corn for four days straight. They wouldn't do anything else but grind corn. They'd finish one batch and start another. So one day she and her friends decided they would do this. This was only for unmarried girls. She had four friends she wanted to do this with at her house. Her mother had four [five?] grinding stones, four fine ones and one coarse one to grind corn into coarse meal.

And so the first day you grind corn first for your godmother. The next day would be for your aunt. The next day would be for another aunt. The last day would be for your mother. So the first day she went to her godmother's house and told her they were grinding corn, and the godmother knew what she meant. She was glad that the girl was going to grind corn for her. So she shelled some corn, blue corn, and put two or three big handfuls in a basket and wrapped it up with a cloth. And she thanked the girl. Then the girl went back to her house. She put the corn on the coarse grinding stone and sat down and began to grind, grinding it into coarse meal. Pretty soon the other girls came in. They waited for her to finish with the coarse grinding stone. When she was through she took it all out and put it back in the basket again. She'd been doing this in the grinding house. Then she went into her house where her mother was. The grinding house was a smaller house, right next door, connected to their living house. Her mother had already put a pot on the fireplace so it would be warm. This was a big pottery [pot] with handles, with two loops on the side for handles. The girl put her corn-meal into this pot, and she stirred it around and around with a little plaque made for this purpose. She turned the coarse meal over and over until it was brown, then she took it out and put it into another dish. She moved the big pot away from the fire so it wouldn't get too hot. Then she spread the browned meal out on a cloth on the floor to cool, and went back in the grinding room where the other girls were.

The second girl had already started her coarse grinding. It went on like this till they were all through with their coarse grinding. By this time the browned meal inside the house was already cooked. So the girl took it back into the grinding room and put it into one of the fine grinders and started grinding. The other girls did the same thing, and soon they were all grinding corn together. When the first girl was finished with her grinding, she went back to her godmother and got some more coarse meal, which her godmother had already ground. The others did the same. All day long they ground corn like that. Towards evening they stopped and went inside to get cleaned up, because they knew that their godmothers would soon come bringing food for them. Soon somebody came, "Come and get this food." So they ran to the door and opened it, and it was the first girl's godmother. The girl's name was Gyaromana. Her godmother had given her this name when she was initiated, and she refused to be called by her first name—that is, the name given to her when she was a baby. If anyone called her by her baby name she would say, "That is not my name. My name is Gyaromana." (It means Parrot Girl.) Her godmother came first and brought food to them.

They all said thank you, and the woman left. Soon, one by one, all of the girls' godmothers came by with food for them. After they ate, they piled the fine flour they had ground in a basket, and packed it down. After that, they delivered the flour to their godmothers. The next day, each of the girls went to her aunt, and the same thing would be done. The last day was for their mothers. (The second day of grinding is the hardest because the first day of grinding makes you sore and it hurts to move.)

So they finished and were through with this grinding festival. But the girl went through this again every few months as she grew up, till she was a grown girl. Then her girl friends started marrying off. Two of them got married and two of them were left. So Gyaromana and her friend ground corn together, and in the evening when they worked boys would come to visit and talk to them through the little window or air vent in the grinding room. The boys would tell funny jokes to make the girls laugh. They would have fun in this way. Then one day Gyaromana's friend got married and she was left alone. But she did like a certain boy that had been coming all the time. He spoke quietly, and if she didn't want to talk he'd just stay there and watch her grind corn.[1]

She decided that she would marry this boy, because she liked him. So they were married and lived together for several years. About this time she began to want a little excitement. There was a man who'd been coming to their house, and it seemed he'd choose a time when her husband wasn't home, when he was out in the fields working. The man used to talk about exciting things that he did. And one day he said, "Why don't you come with me tonight? I'm going to a place where a lot of things happen." He wanted to take her. He said, "Your husband won't know it; we'll be back before he wakes up." He told her to make some piki.

So she made some that night and put it in the back room.

---

[1]The main story begins at this point. The girls' corn grinding "marathon" does not appear to have any connection with the narrative that follows. Conceivably it was intended to depict good social behavior against which later events might be measured. The corn grinding overture does not appear in other variants of the story.

And when her husband was asleep, she pulled the hairs on his big toe, gave them a little wiggle. He didn't stir, so she knew he was asleep. She got up real quietly and went into the back room and got the piki and went out. The man was waiting for her. They went somewhere, and when she came back her husband didn't know she'd been away. After this she'd make piki every day, or almost every day, and put some away. And the next evening when she'd go out she'd take some of it with her. The husband noticed that she didn't serve him piki any more, but that she'd been making some recently. He said something about it. She said, "Oh, a lady wanted some piki because some men were doing some kind of work for her, and she needed help with the food, that's why I was making some piki." She was always finding an excuse for not serving her husband any piki.

Finally, her husband became suspicious, and he asked around and found that she'd not been telling him the truth. He decided he wouldn't go to sleep that night. When they went to bed, he made her believe that he was asleep, by breathing deeply. So she got up slow and uncovered his feet and gave a tug to the hairs on his toe. He felt it, but he didn't give himself away. He heard someone outside the house say, "It's getting late. You'd better hurry." He saw her going to the back room, and she came back with a stack of piki. She opened the door real quietly and went out. The man said, "What's been keeping you? We're late." She said, "My husband was taking a long time going to sleep." He said, "We must hurry." As soon as they were gone, the husband got up quickly and got dressed and followed them at a safe distance. They traveled quite a ways, and then they went around a little hill. The husband waited for them to come around the other side. When they didn't appear, he sneaked up and found the man embracing his wife, and this made him very angry.

Pretty soon they went on, and at last they came to a mountain. There was all kinds of brush around the foot of the mountain, and the man stepped up at a certain place and put a lot of this brush aside. There was an opening there. She went in first with her piki, then the man followed her and arranged all the brush to hide the opening. The husband waited awhile, then he went in after them. He was in a big place. There was a kiva there and he heard voices down in there. He moved up real slow and peeked in. There were a lot of men and women he knew down there, but the women weren't the men's wives, but secret wives. (Every so often these men and women would meet like that, but the next day [in their village] they would pretend that nothing had taken place.) The husband was surprised, because he knew these people and had never suspected them. He saw his own wife there with this man. He sure didn't like it.

Pretty soon the old man in the middle said, "We have wasted enough time waiting for you, so we'll start right away." There was a hoop right beside him, with a feather tied to it. There were all kinds of pelts and bird skins hanging on the wall. One man and woman stepped up. The woman would be the first one. She got hold of this hoop and rolled over it, and she landed on the floor, and nothing happened. She was still the same person. (Rolling over the hoop was supposed to transform people into animals.) The old man (he was a bear) said, "There's something wrong. Someone must be watching. Is there a stranger in here?" So they looked around and didn't find anybody, only the people who had always been coming. So the girl tried again, and again nothing happened. So the old man ordered a search. They looked everyplace, even outside the kiva. On top of the kiva at the opening where the ladder comes out there are usually logs, and across this is a mat of bamboo sticks. The mat is supposed to keep out rain and sand. Well, the girl's husband had rolled himself into this mat. He could see through the sticks what was going on. One man finally jerked the mat and unrolled it, and the girl's husband was exposed.

So they brought him down into the kiva. He went to his wife and sat down right beside her. His wife was very nice to him. She said, "Why did you come? You're going to be sleepy pretty soon." Then the business in the kiva went on. Anyone who rolled over on the hoop became an owl or some different kind of animal. A man and a woman went up together, in a pair. This went on for hours, and they became tired before they were through. The man's wife [Gyaromana] said, "Put your head on my lap and go to sleep for a while." So he did that and she was stroking his hair. He fell asleep.

When he woke up he was on a high [rock] ledge. It was just wide enough to hold him. He couldn't move or turn over. He lay there in one position all morning. In the afternoon a bird came. The bird said, "You must be thirsty. I will give you some water." He went off and came back with water in a piñon shell. The man thought, "Oh, this is too little, it's not going to do me any good." The bird said, "Drink this and it will satisfy you." So he drank the water, and he was satisfied. It was enough. The bird told him that someone would come soon to try to knock him off the ledge, but he must not move. "First some kachinas will come," the bird said, "and they will throw sweet corn to you. But you must not try to catch it, don't even reach for it or you will fall." Then the bird went off. In a little while he heard sounds of the kachinas, the tinkling of bells. They were up above him on a higher ledge. And they started throwing down baked sweet corn, saying, "Grab this and you won't be hungry." But the man didn't move, didn't try to catch any of the corn. Finally the kachinas went off.

Then the bird came back and told him that the next one to come would be a snake, and that without help the man would surely be knocked off the ledge. "I'm going to give you some medicine to protect you. When the snake starts coming down, chew this real quickly, and when he is close enough blow [spray] it in his face." The bird went off again, and soon there was a rumbling noise [up above], and he saw a great big snake coming down, hanging from something. The man started chewing the medicine, and there was a lot of juice in his mouth, and he blew this at the snake. A strange thing happened. The snake started to wither and then it fell. It fell to the ground below, and then the man heard many voices down there, men's voices and women's voices, and some were crying and some were groaning. This was a man-made snake, there were these people inside of the snake, and now they were at the bottom among the rocks, and some were hurt and crying.

Pretty soon the bird came back and said, "I'm going to get you down from here. I've been to your Grandmother Spider and told her that you're here, that your wife had put you here." The Spider Lady had given the bird some medicine for the man. He was supposed to chew this and swallow the juice. Then the bird went off. So he put the medicine in his mouth and chewed it and swallowed the juice, spitting out the tiny twigs that were left. Then he found himself getting drowsy, and he went to sleep. When he awoke, he was afraid of moving. But the old Spider Lady was beside him. She said, "Don't be afraid, you can get up." (They weren't on the rocky shelf any more.) So he got up, and she led the way and he followed her to her house. She climbed down the ladder into her house. He said, "Oh, the opening is so small I can't get in." She said, "You will. Just get ahold of the ladder and you will climb in." He did, and suddenly the hole was bigger and the ladder was big enough to hold him.

So he went down into the kiva-like place where old Spider Lady lived. She told him to sit down and she would fix something for him to eat. She fixed something and put it on the floor for him. So they sat down. It was a tiny batch of food, and he was thinking that it wouldn't be enough to fill him. He started eating. He put one little bit of food into his mouth and found that it filled his mouth up. Next time he took a smaller bit. He ate like that till he was satisfied, and there was still food left. Old Spider Lady said, "When you are finished eating I will tell you what to do." When he was finished she cleared off the plates and went to a corner where she kept some things in a jar. She pulled out a bundle of something and came back and sat down beside him. She opened the bundle and took out some dried medicine to give him. There were several little bundles in the one big bundle, and what she gave to him came from one of the little bundles. "When you get home," Spider Lady said, "you will act as if nothing happened. Be nice to your wife. And when she is asleep, chew this medicine and rub the juice on your hands and then touch her. Rub your hand on her arm, or leg, or shoulder. You will see what happens." She gave him the medicine. Told him to travel east until he came to a certain hill, then to go south and he would find his village.

So he left Spider Lady's house and went east till he came to the hill, then he turned south and in time he came to his village. His wife was at home, and she seemed happy to see him. Neither of them mentioned what had happened the previous night. He was nice to her and she set food before him. As soon as it became dark they went to bed. When she finally went to sleep he chewed the medicine and rubbed the juice in the palm of his hand, then he rubbed his hand against her shoulder. He waited to see what would happen. Finally she stirred and woke up. She got out of bed and got dressed and started to walk back and forth across the room. Pretty soon she started walking real fast, then started running round and round the room. He pretended he was asleep. Soon she became wild and went out the door. He got up and got dressed and followed her. She was really running out into the open. Then she passed behind a hill, and when she came out on the other side, she had turned into a mule, a white mule. She kicked up her heels and made noises like a mule and ran around wild. Pretty soon she came to a herd of horses and mules and she joined the herd. After a while she calmed down.

Her husband was very surprised. But this was the way Old Lady Spider had said he would pay her back for trying to kill him. The white mule turned around and looked at him, and the tears were running down her face. The husband felt sorry for her but he realized that she and her group had tried to kill him. He had known her as a good woman till this happened.

He went home and went on living.

I forgot to say his name. It was Geleoya; it means Little Hawk.

Tsakaptamana
Moencopi, July 1969

----56----

The Antelope Boy

Aliksai.

This story takes place at the village of Shimopavi [Shongopovi]. There was a man and his wife living there who had only one child, a girl. The girl grew up into a nice, beautiful young lady. She was lonely, didn't have many girl friends. Her hair was long and heavy, and she wore it in big whorls on both sides of her head, meaning that she was of a marrying age. There had been many activities in the village for young people, dances and rabbit hunts. The girls always made somiviki for the rabbit hunts, a Hopi bread made out of blue corn ground real fine.

One day the village crier announced that the following day there would be another rabbit hunt. The girls got busy making somiviki. The mother and father of this girl had been very concerned because she'd been staying by herself very much, and they wanted her to go on this rabbit hunt. She said she wasn't interested, but the next morning she decided to go. Her mother got busy and made bread for her to take. By the time the bread was cool, the other boys and girls were already going down the west side of the mesa, where everyone was supposed to meet. So the girl took the bread, wrapped in a cloth, and went to where the others were waiting. Then they all started off, and they began hunting. The boys would chase a rabbit if they saw one, and whoever caught it would stand there holding it by the hind legs. Then the girls would race toward him, and whoever got there first would get the rabbit, and she'd give him some of her bread in return.

It went on like this. They traveled quite a distance, all the time hunting. Sometimes a boy would wet the end of his stick and put it in a rabbit hole. If he felt something in there he'd give his stick several twists, tangling the rabbit fur real tight on the stick. Then he'd give the stick a quick jerk and have a rabbit at the end of it. They'd kill the rabbit by hitting it on the back of the neck with a chopping motion of the hand. Then the girls would race to take the rabbit away from him. If a rabbit was running, a boy would throw his stick at him and kill him.

In the late afternoon, the girl started having a stomach ache. She'd sit for a while till the pain went away, then she'd follow. Pretty soon she was so far behind she couldn't catch up with them. In a little while she gave birth to a baby. Right close by there was a rabbit hole or a badger hole. She made the hole a little bigger and put the baby into it. By that time the boys and girls had started on their way back to the village, and she was left behind. Nobody had missed her and come looking for her. So she came home alone, the last one in the bunch. She brought two rabbits, and her mother was very happy to receive them.

Her mother didn't have any inkling that the girl had been pregnant. The girl had been wearing her belt [a woven girdle about
four inches wide] very tight and her father and mother hadn't
noticed anything.

Back where she'd left the baby, an old lady coyote was looking for a meal. She was looking for a wounded rabbit that the
boys and girls might have left behind, because it was hard for
her to hunt now that she was old. She heard something crying,
and she went to the badger hole and found the baby there. She
pulled the baby out with her teeth as carefully as she could. It
was a baby boy. She thought that if she were younger and had
milk, she would have certainly taken this boy and raised him for
herself, so that he could hunt for her. But she was too old to
give him any milk. Then she thought about the antelope people
living north of there. She thought that some of them would have
milk, and that they would raise him. So she picked up the baby
and took it to the antelope people. When she got to their kiva
she stomped on it. She didn't want to go in. Somebody called
for her to come down, but she asked for someone to come up.
The man down below sent someone up, and the old lady coyote
told him that she had brought a baby for them. Perhaps one of
their women could raise the baby. The man took the baby and
went down into the kiva and laid the baby next to the fireplace.
The chief was sitting by the fireplace. He got up and knocked
on the door of the next room, opened it, and asked one of the
women to come out. (All the males were in one room, and the
females in the other.)

A woman came out and he told her that someone had
brought a baby. Did she want it? She said yes, she was willing
to take it. She saw the baby on the floor. She took it and washed
it with warm water and wrapped him in a cloth. The baby was
hungry and she nursed it. From then on she took care of the
baby and nursed it whenever it was hungry.

Because it drank antelope milk this baby boy grew as fast as
an antelope. In four days he was taken out of the kiva to test
him in walking. He walked wobbly, but pretty soon he started
really walking. Every day they took him out, and he would walk
around in the sunshine, and soon he was running around with

the rest of the antelope children. After a while he could run real well, like the rest of the antelope, right in the middle of the herd. The way the antelope run is single file, and he was right in the middle.

Time went on, and back at Shimopavi a man decided he would go rabbit hunting by himself. He went down to the foot of the mesa and headed toward the antelope people. He thought he would hunt around that section. When he reached that place, he noticed that there were antelope there in a big herd. He sat down and watched them running around and playing or just grazing. Then he noticed that a boy was running around with them. The boy was very swift. The man was surprised. He wondered where the boy came from, and how he got to be with the herd. He was so fascinated that he forgot all about rabbit hunting, he just stayed there and watched. Before he knew it, it was almost suppertime, so he went back to the village.

He told his wife what he had seen, a small boy running with the antelope. His wife could hardly believe it, but he said it was true, he had seen it himself. After he had eaten, he went down to the kiva. There were many men there, and he told them about the boy running with the antelope. They couldn't believe it. They said, "Oh, you were just seeing things. No one can run as fast as the antelope can." He said, "If you don't believe it, you can go there and see for yourself." A few days after that, another man decided to go and see if it was really so. He went toward that area where the antelope lived. He finally saw the boy in the antelope herd. He saw that the boy was right in the middle of them. So he went back home and told the men about it. Then four more men went, one after the other, and each of them told the same story, that there was a young boy running with the antelope herd. They wondered who the boy could be, but they couldn't think of any boy that was missing from their village.

So they decided something. One man said he would put on a coyote hunt.[1] He went over to the villages of Shipaulovi and Mishongnovi to tell them about it. So they all agreed to go together on the chance that they might catch the boy to find out

[1]That is, organized like a coyote hunt.

who he was. The people of the three villages. They made their
plans. When the time came, the people were to go to their appointed places. When they would get there they would start a
fire to show that they were at the places they were supposed to
be. When the day came, they started moving out, the men and
the women of Shimopovi and the other two villages. When each
group arrived at its place, it started a fire, so that the smoke
would tell the others that they were ready. The people then
spread out and made a circle. This was what they did when they
were on a coyote hunt. They would drive the coyotes to the center, making the circle smaller. This time they were surrounding
the antelope, so they could catch the boy.

The antelope people had already found out that there would
be a hunt, and they knew the purpose of it. So the godfather of
this little antelope boy told him what was going to happen. He
told the boy to stay right behind him, and he'd instruct him what
to do. The circle was formed and the people started moving,
making the circle smaller and smaller. The people could now
see each other and what they had inside their circle. They had
coyotes and foxes in the circle, and also the antelope. The antelope started running around, wanting to get out. As the circle
got smaller, the antelope godfather said to the boy, "Over there
is your mother. Look at her closely to see what she looks like,
notice her clothing [so that you will remember her]. Now I will
point out your father too." So they went around and on the other
side he said, "Now, there is your father." They kept running
around in a circle. The antelope godfather said to the boy, "When
I tell you, run to your mother." The circle got smaller and smaller. The antelope godfather told the boy that the purpose of the
hunt was to catch him. Whoever caught the boy would keep him.
For that reason he was to go to his mother as fast as he could.
Pretty soon the antelope godfather said, "Now!"

The boy ran to his mother. He put his arms around her and
said, "My mother." But his mother didn't say anything. She was
surprised. Then she remembered that she did have a child, and
the boy could be the one she'd left behind out there. He said
again, "My mother." She answered him, "My son," and put her
arms around him. The people all ran to where the boy was. They

wanted to see what he looked like and who he was. The uncle[2] of the girl saw everything. He said, "Is he your son?" She said yes. "And who is his father?" The boy said, "There is my father," and he pointed him out. The young man came up, and the boy said, "My father." And the young man said, "My son."

Then the girl's uncle became very angry because she had been deceiving her folks. He went up to her and pulled down her hair and tied it in a knot the way a woman wears her hair, down under her ear.[3] So they came on home, went back to Shimopavi. Her father and mother were there, and they learned that the antelope boy belonged to their daughter. They took the young man into their house. That is the way it is when a girl marries, her husband is brought into her family.

So they lived there, with the girl's parents. But the boy's father was quick-tempered. He often scolded the boy for little things that he did. And one day he scolded the boy a little too hard, and the boy was very unhappy. So the boy left and went back to the antelope people. The godfather had told him to do that if the people mistreated him. The boy came to the antelope kiva and went down. They were all glad to see him. He told the antelope people that his father scolded him too much, and that he didn't want to live in the village any more. So now he was back among the antelope people. His godfather washed his hair and put his [antelope] pelt on him. In this way the boy became an antelope. He was one of them.

Back in the village, his father missed the boy. Mostly, the grandfather was very worried about him. He asked his daughter what had happened, and she said the boy had been scolded by her husband, and so the boy went away. The father was crying. He said, "We will never see him again, because I know he went back to the antelope people." That day the grandfather made prayer feathers for the boy, and he carried them out to where the antelope people were. When he found the herd, there

---

[2]The girl's maternal uncle, to whose clan she belongs. The mother's brother, among the Hopis, has considerable authority over his sister's children.
[3]The girl had been wearing her hair in whorls, in the style of unmarried young women.

was no boy with them. So he returned home. The mother and father became lonesome for the boy, and the father was sorry for what he had done. The father often went back to the place where they'd found him, but he never saw the boy again because he'd turned into an antelope.

Postscript to the narration: I forgot to say, the morning of the coyote hunt—which was really a hunt to capture the boy—the antelope people fixed the boy up like a Hopi. They washed his hair and dressed him up like a Hopi boy (because he was going back to his mother and father). When the boy's hair was dry, his antelope godfather cut his bangs, then he cut some hair on the side below the ear, in the Hopi fashion, and the rest of his hair hung back. The godfather got a fluffy white eagle feather and tied it on top of the boy's head, and put white cornmeal on his face. He put that woven white skirt [kilt] on the boy and a sash, and then he put leg bands around the boy's ankles. Then he colored his legs yellow. That's the way he was dressed when he was caught.

Tsakaptamana
Moencopi, July 1969

———57———

Honwaima and the Bear People

Aliksai!
Oh!
The people were living in the village. There was a boy there named Honwaima. He had a father, mother, and little sister. He wanted to be a doctor, a medicine man. He wanted to be one of them. One day he thought he'd go out and hunt antelopes. He went out and killed one. Instead of skinning it the right way, he

scraped the meat off the bones, and put the bones in one place. He was sitting there looking at the bones to see how, if anybody broke their arm or their leg, he would fix it up. He was trying to study how he would go about it. While he was sitting there he saw a shadow at the side of him. He looked back to see who was behind him. Sure enough there was somebody there, dressed up in a [kachina ceremonial] costume. The person had a mark across his nose and cheekbones. That's the way they say the Hopis looked when they traveled around. He had a regular [forehead] band, and his hair was cut that [traditional] way. But his hair was loose, just hanging back.

The man asked the boy what he was doing. He said he was studying these bones so he could be a medicine man, to fix people when they broke their arms or legs. So this man told the boy that if he wanted to be a medicine man, he would take him to a place where they taught people like him to be a doctor or medicine man. So the boy got up and they started walking towards the north. There were some bushes there, and the man went behind a bush and just disappeared. When he came out again, he was a bear. The bear told the boy to get on his back. The boy did, and then the bear started running towards north, towards Navajo Mountain, that's Tokonave in the language of the Paiutes. They were going to that place, Tokonave. When they got there, the bear told the boy to get off his back. The bear went ahead and went down in a kiva. So the boy followed the bear and went in the kiva. The bear had just taken his skin off and was just hanging it up when the boy came in. When he looked at the person who'd been wearing the bearskin [he saw] it was a girl.[1] There were old, old, old men, old-timers, sitting around. They were smoking a clay [ceremonial] pipe. They told him that they'd been waiting for him. They asked why it took him so long to get there. They fed him some food. And they asked him if he really wanted to be a medicine man. He said he had his heart set on being one of them. So they told him they would teach him, and when they had taught him he would belong to them. That [place] would be his home.

[1]No explanation given of how or why man turns into a girl.

He was willing to go through with it, so their leader told
two men to go back and bring out a wedding robe—two wedding robes, a large one and a small one. They brought them out
and spread the smaller one on the ground. They told the boy to
lie down [on it], and they covered him with the large wedding
robe. All the old-timers[2] gathered around him and started breaking all his bones, breaking everything. And after they'd done
that they started working on him because they were that group
that knew how to fix broken bones or anything like that. They
were sitting all around him working on him. They had their
hands under the wedding robe, you couldn't see what they were
doing, but they were doing something. After they finished what
they were doing they started moving back to where they'd been
sitting before. Their leader told the boy to get up. So he got up.
He was all right, he was in perfect shape. But he was sweating,
he'd been pretty hot under there.

Well, this leader said that the boy had been taught to be of
service to humans. If they had sickness or any kind of a disease,
or if they broke their legs or arms, he would be the one to fix
them. If there was a sick person, he would go there and [the
sick person] would get well instantly. They told him that when
he got back to his father and mother he should not tell anyone
he had learned [the art of curing] over there [among the old-
timers in this kiva]. Told him not to tell anybody where he had
learned these things, how to be a medicine man. They told him
he would have only a certain limit of time to be a doctor. When
his time was up he would die, and naturally he would go back
to where he had learned to be one of them. But they had taught
him to be a powerful medicine man, because he only needed to
touch a sick person and he'd be well just like that.

They dressed him up just the way the man had been dressed,
the man that had invited him to the kiva. When the boy's time
[to die] came, he was supposed to tell his sister to dress him in
these clothes and bury him. Then the bear took him back to the
place where he'd been looking at the bones, and left him there.
The boy went out and killed another [antelope], and this time

---

[2]The term *old-timers* generally signifies people of earlier generations.

he butchered it the usual way. He put the meat on his back and went home.

Now the boy knew what he was, what he wanted to be. He wasn't married, he was just a young boy, and he slept down in the kiva by himself. His sister went down into the kiva every morning to tell him that breakfast was ready. There were some high steep stone steps that the girl had to go down to get to the kiva. And one morning going to the kiva she tripped on the steps and fell. She went rolling down the stone steps, and when she landed at the bottom she lay there very still. The brother heard something falling up there. He got up and dressed and went out of the kiva, and sure enough his sister was lying there, dead. He picked her up and carried her inside the house. Her mother and father were [agitated] and the father was telling his wife to go look for somebody who could do something.

The boy said, "Let me work on her. Let me try. Don't go after any medicine man." He knew that he was going to try out what he had learned. Over there [at the place where he had learned to be a medicine man] they had told him to go outside and put his hand up toward the mountain [Tokonave] before starting to work on a sick person or someone who'd broken a leg or arm. So that's what he did. He went outside and did this, because when he did it these people who had taught him would know that he was going to work on somebody, and would help him. Then he went back in and started working on his sister. Pretty soon the girl got up and she was all right. His father asked him where he had learned to be a medicine man. The boy wouldn't tell his father where he had learned it. He asked his mother and father not to talk about what happened, but somebody had seen it, that they had carried the girl from the steps and that pretty soon she was walking outside again. So the word got around.

The boy didn't just go around looking to cure people. He didn't try to show that he was a medicine man. But the people had found out, so they started coming for him, and that's the way he began taking care of sick people. He'd just touch a sick person, who'd get well that minute. There were medicine men in all the villages. And there was a medicine man group in Polacca that heard about him. They said they were going to have

a big meeting, a convention, of doctors, medicine men. They
wanted to find out who this person was. The people had been
telling about how good he was, and how you could get well [from
his touch] just like that.

Now, the stories are always like that. They always have a
grandmother.[3] So this grandmother heard about it and she came
to the boy. She told him what was going on and why they wanted
him over there. They'd try him out to see if he was better than
they were. His grandmother told him that if they should ask him
first, he shouldn't do it [demonstrate his knowledge] first. Grandmother told him to be the last one. "They're going to try to show
you up, that you aren't a good medicine man." So they came
after him, but the first time he didn't go with them. He didn't
want to go up there. They kept coming after him. Pretty soon
he went with them. Sure enough, there were all these old-timers
who'd been doing this work from way back. Pretty soon they
asked him to do something, but he said he didn't want to be the
first one. "Let you guys try yours out first."

This one group came out. They were doing this in the big
plaza where they did the dancing, the masked dances.[4] They
went towards the sun and just put their hands up and lightning
came out of their hands.[5] They tried all different things. Then
there was another group. It came out of the kiva. It went up on
top of the highest house. There was a rock pile down at the bottom. They carried a man up to the top of the house, they were
singing, and they threw this man down on the rocks. When he
hit those rocks he was all broken all to pieces. They came down.
They were still singing, just taking their time, coming down the
stone steps singing the song the way it was supposed to be sung.
Then they went back in the kiva and made this medicine and
put it in a bowl, a pottery bowl. And when they came out of the
kiva their leader was carrying that. They were still singing. They
went to where they'd thrown the man down, but somehow the

[3]Probably a reference to Gogyeng Sowuhti, Spider Grandmother.

[4]Though the narrator says the contest took place in Polacca, the dance
plazas are up above in the villages of Walpi and Sichomovi, and in Tewa Village.

[5]This exhibition and the one that follows are said to have been part of the
repertoire of the Yaya Fraternity, now extinct.

man who was carrying the medicine, somehow he dropped it
and the bowl broke all to pieces. So they had to start all over
again. They went down in the kiva. That man they had thrown
on the rocks, he was just getting cold. The second time they
didn't break the pottery. They took the dead man from the
rocks. And these old-timers did something like had been done
in the kiva at Tokonave. Spread the wedding robe, put the
man on it and covered him up, and started to work. But they
couldn't make him come back alive because he had lain there
all that time. Then the young ones [medicine men] started
working on him but they couldn't bring him back alive, so the
old ones started getting in and helping them. But they couldn't
do anything.

This young boy [Honwaima] was the only one that wasn't
taking part; he was just watching to see if they could bring this
man back to life. Pretty soon the old-timers began telling him to
come and do it. So he told the old-timers, "Just let him alone
and let me work on him." The old-timers went back to their seats.
The young boy put his hands under [the covering] and started
feeling around. Pretty soon he took the robe off. The man was
alive and kind of sweating, because he'd been under there a long
time. And then the medicine men believed that his work was
stronger than theirs. They hadn't been able to do anything.
They'd tried all ways to get the best of him, but he was the best
one. The way he had learned how to be a medicine man, they
couldn't outdo him, and that was the end of their convention.

He went home, and after that he worked with all kinds of
sick people or people who had broken their legs or something
like that. Pretty soon he told his sister that his time was getting
close. He told his sister how to dress him up [when he died].
That's the way his godfather[6] had told him. (I forgot to say that
when he was working on a person he made noises like a bear.
That's his group, the bear group.) He still slept in the kiva, he
never did get a wife. One morning his sister went down there to
tell him breakfast was ready, and then she went back to the
house. They were waiting for him, but he never did come to eat.
So his father told the girl to go down to see what was wrong. All

[6]His teacher in the kiva, also called, in translation, "sponsor" or "uncle."

the while, his sister had known that his time was getting short. She went down in the kiva, and sure enough he brother was dead. He was still young, but his time was up.

The girl told his mother and father that he was dead. So they brought his body up. The sister told his father and mother how to dress him up the way the boy had said. And they buried him like that. They buried him, but he was alive and went back to where he'd learned to be a medicine man, in the kiva at Tokonave.

Postscript to the narration: They say that if you are taught to be a medicine man you've got to have a [god]father. Like, one medicine man's godfather would be badger. He wears things and makes noise like that, like badger. Another medicine man would be a snake [person], because his godfather is a snake. This group was bear, the boy's godfather who taught him was in the bear group, and that's why when the boy began working on a sick person he made a noise like a bear.

The wedding robe [ova] used by the medicine men in the curing ceremonies is woven cotton. I can't say why that robe is used. It is used for that purpose. When they make that robe for a girl they don't weave it too tight. It's used like the clouds use it. If it's got holes in it, it will rain more; the rain will come through. The clouds are using that [the ovas] to travel around, so with the holes you'll have more rain. That robe represents the inside of a woman. It's got a string sewed in there; it's kind of blood color—on both sides to the edge. And then there's a corn hanging down, and it's got a little ring. And all these strings that they make go through here, and that's supposed to represent the insides of a woman, how many children she's got. The top part is supposed to represent the placenta or something that has to do with the forming of the child. And there are some strings hanging down that express the hope that she'll have many children. That goes through this corn. Corn is our staff of life. Of course there are prayer feathers on it. Everything has a meaning. There's nothing we do without prayers. But after the bridal robe has been made, and after the girl shows it to the kachinas, it can be used for other purposes. The robe made for my daughter, I can use it for something if I want to. I can cut it up and make something else out of it. It was made for all of us. So that's how the medicine men could use the bridal robe in their curing work.

Uwaikwiota
Moencopi, August 1968

———58———

The Girl and the Kachina

Aliksai!

It is said that many people lived in Oraibi at one time. In this village there were a man and his wife, and they had only a girl child. The man, of course, wanted a son, but his wife could not give him one. When the girl became strong enough, she would want to go with her father down to the fields. And so he would take her down with him to the fields, on the east side of the village.[1] He would tell her many things about the small animals they would see around there, and he would tell her about the different kinds of snakes, those that were poisonous and those that would not hurt anyone.[2] And so from her father she learned many things.

---

[1] The implication here is that a man and his son would work together in the fields, while a girl would normally stay with her mother and help with the house chores. Having no son, the man let his daughter work with him.

[2] The narrator went into details here that tend to interrupt this story, and they have been omitted from the text. The deleted passage is this:

She saw a black and yellow colored snake that she thought was very pretty. Her father said it was harmless, and that she should leave it alone, that it was only there to hunt for its food. And then there was another kind, it was grey and not as pretty as the black and yellow one, but he said it also was there to hunt, and she was to leave it alone. One time she saw another kind of snake. It was small, and it was black and white, ex-

The girl helped her mother shell corn and grind it. The mother made a special mataki for her, a small one that she could hold. The girl would help her mother make bread for their supper, and haul water from the spring on the east side of the village. They made this trip to the spring several times to fill the huge jug that they had in the house. The water in the large jug would last them for some time.

Things went on this way until the girl grew a lot bigger. She was fourteen or fifteen years old. Her father finally died. The mother told the girl that her father had gone home, where he would see his parents. So they were left alone with all the work, at home and in the fields as well. In the spring they planted beans and corn and squash, but it was so much work that each year their fields grew smaller. But even in their hard times they were thankful for what they had. However, they didn't grind as much corn as they used to, and whatever was left from one meal they'd save for the next meal. By the end of the winter they were always out of food, their storehouse was empty. They only saved enough seeds to plant.

One day the mother sent the girl down to the fields to pick squash blossoms. And while the girl was there picking the squash

---

cept that it had red in with it. She would sit there and watch it move along, and she followed it, and when it would stop, she would stop. When it started going, she would go along with it. Her father told her to leave it alone. "They are there to hunt. Sometimes they are in a bad mood and will hurt you." One day she was having a lot of fun with something. Her father noticed her laughing. He asked her what she was doing. She said, "There's a snake here and he's trying to take my stick away from me. He's playing with me." He said, "What does it look like?" "It's just a snake," she said, "but it wiggles at the tail. He has something at the tail, and when he wiggles it, it makes a funny sound. And he tries to take the stick away from me." Her father was alarmed and walked up to her. He noticed that when she put her stick out, the snake would strike at it. He said, "You leave that snake alone and come here." So she finally let the snake go. Then she saw several kinds of spiders. Some would come out of a hole in the ground, and at the top [of the spiders' houses], some of them had a chimney, she thought. Across the chimney there were sticks, and sometimes the spider would come out and move the sticks around and go back in again. The father told her also to leave the spiders alone. But after the incident with the snake, he told her to stay at home and help her mother.

blossoms, she heard a roaring sound, a hissing noise like the wind coming through a small place, and she wondered what it was. Then pretty soon she saw somebody coming. She had never seen anyone looking like this person, and she was frightened. She hid herself behind some rocks. Soon this person came up to her. He said, "Come out, I saw you already. I will not hurt you." So she finally came out of her hiding place, and stood up. This person was a kachina, and he had a pretty kilt on and a sash, and his body was colored [painted], and he had something in his hand that made a noise when he walked.[3] He said, "Well, we have been keeping track of you and your mother. We know that your are having a hard time. So my father and mother have decided that I should be the one to come into your home and take care of you.[4] You are going with me tomorrow [to visit my people]. Go home now and tell your mother what I have told you. Tell her what I look like. Tell her to begin grinding corn.[5] I will come back tomorrow to get you."

He went off then, making noises with the thunderlock, the thing he held in his hand. So the girl went home and told her mother about it, how he was dressed, about the thing he had in his hand. She told her mother what he'd said, that she was supposed to begin grinding corn, and that the boy would be back the next morning. The mother was very glad that at last there would be someone to take over the hard work and take care of them, and she started shelling corn immediately. She said there would not be much flour because they did not have very much corn, but she would do what she could.

So, the next morning the girl went back down to the field, and soon again she heard the roaring sound and the hissing.[6] Pretty soon she saw the kachina coming. He asked her if she had told her mother, and she said yes. He said, "Let us go." He took her by the hand and walked with her over the hill, and she saw there was something there, something round, and they went straight for this thing and got into it. And when they did that,

[3]Described subsequently as a thunderlock. A bullroarer.

[4]That is, he will marry her and live with her in her mother's house.

[5]For the marriage ritual. The ground corn will be given to the young man's parents.

[6]Sound of the bullroarer.

he did something and there was a big roar and soon they were off the ground. The thing they were in seemed to be spinning, and it streaked off. After a while he said, "We are here." They were down on the ground again and the roaring and hissing sound [of the vehicle] stopped. He took her up to his village, to his home. When they got to his house his mother and father were very happy that he had found the girl that they had spoken of.

They brought her into the house and made her welcome. The woman said, "You must be hungry, so I will put this food here for you to eat. But we are going somewhere now to give rain to some people who really need it. While we are gone, you are not to open the door to anyone. Stay in the house and don't go out. There's a man living on the east side of the village who is very bad. He's always going after young girls. So stay inside and don't let anyone come in. Don't be fooled by what that old man tells you." Then the kachina family picked up their water jugs and went out.

Soon after they left there was a pounding at the door. It was someone saying, "I'm an old man and I'm very thirsty, and nobody will give me any water to drink. I know you have lots of water in the house, so I have come here. Please give me some water." The girl sat there not saying anything. He said, "I know you are in there because I saw you. Would you please give me some water, because I'm very thirsty." She thought, "Oh, we have lots of water; it's not going to hurt if I give him some of our water." So she opened the door to him. So in came Goat Man. And he told the girl she was coming with him to his house. She said she didn't want to. She was fighting with him, but nobody heard her and nobody came to her help. Then he took her down to his place. There was a kiva there and he took her inside. He tied her to the ladder, her arms, legs and body. Then he started running around in the kiva. He bumped the wall here and bumped [butted?] the wall there, and each time he came around he touched her. Then he would run around again several times and come back and touch her again.[7] He continued

[7] The narration does not specifically say that the Goat Man raped her, but it seems to be implied. Goat Man's peculiar actions are supposed to suggest the behavior of a goat.

doing this, and she was crying and calling out for someone to come and help her. But for a long time no one came.

Then she saw someone coming into the kiva from the top, and when he got down lower [she saw it was the kachina]. He stood by the ladder, and when the Goat Man came around again, he jumped on him. He fought with the Goat Man and almost killed him. The kachina untied her and took her out of the kiva. They went to his house. He said to her, "Why did you open the door when my mother warned you not to?" The girl said, "He said he was thirsty and nobody would give him any water. I thought it would not hurt to give him some." His mother asked the girl the same question, and the girl said the same thing.

The mother said, "Well, we will have to give you a bath." The girl was smelling very bad [like a goat]. They went out again with their jugs. (The place where the girl was was called the Land of the Cloud People, and the people were kachinas.) The mother told the girl that when it started to rain she should go out and bathe herself. Soon it started sprinkling, and the girl went out and stood in the rain and rubbed herself. Then it began to rain real hard, and she stood in the rain and washed her hair and clothes. When it stopped raining she went back into the house. When the kachina family came back they dried her off and gave her dry clothing.

Well, the boy decided he didn't want to go through with the wedding.[8] He talked it over with his mother and father, and they said they wouldn't blame him. He told them that he was taking her back home. So the next day he took her home. They went down from the mesa and got into this thing that had brought them. It roared and hissed and soon they were in the air. They arrived at a place close to the girl's village. The kachina brought the girl to the place where he had found her. He told her to tell her mother to stop grinding because he was not going to marry her after all.

He told her that she and her mother should go on living as they had before, giving thanks for whatever they had, and one day she would find a husband to take care of them. She went

[8]The exact reason for the boy's change of mind is not stated, but it is implied that the girl's failure to do as she was told and her contact with the Goat Man had made her undesirable.

home and told her mother everything. Her mother was just fin-
ishing the preparation of the corn flour for the wedding. So they
continued to plant their pumpkins and corn the way they had
been doing. They went on, working hard and not complaining.

Tsakaptamana
Moencopi, March 1969

————59————

The Navajo Boy and Death

Aliksai!
West of Leupp a Navajo family was living. There was no
other hogan close by, but they knew of one several miles south.
One afternoon a man came riding in on horseback. He stopped
and got off his horse, tied his horse to a post by the hogan and
visited. The couple living there had one son about fifteen or sixteen. He heard the man say his name was Many Mules and that
he lived many hours east. The boy heard him say that he was on
his way to the Nedah, a squaw dance. The boy was glad, and he
would plan to go. The Nedah was to be the following day. The
Nedah takes place late at night. He thought he might see a pretty
girl and she would ask him to dance. He had not missed a Nedah
in several summers, even if it was far away. Sometimes it would
take him three days to get to a Nedah and three more to get back
home. This one was close by and he wouldn't miss it. When the
man Many Mules had rested he got on his horse and headed
north.

The next evening the boy warmed up the coffee and ate
bread with his cold meat. When he finished eating he started
getting ready. His folks had gone earlier that afternoon, so they
could visit with friends, some they had not seen in many years.
When the moon was up, the boy left. It was a good hour's ride
to Black Falls, where the Nedah was, north of Leupp. When he

had gone about halfway he heard someone riding fast behind him. It was a girl riding a white horse. He knew she was in a hurry to get to the Nedah. He talked with her and they rode together. Soon they heard the singing. (Navajo singing is high-pitched, resembles coyote sounds, and carries a long way.) Every time the boy looked at the girl she turned her face away. He didn't even get to see her face. She said they must not be seen together at the dance, but she would meet him at this place later. He stopped and she rode on to the dance alone. He waited a while and then rode into the camp.

There were many campfires and many people. The dance had started and there were several couples dancing. He saw some girls going after boys and men, trying to catch them. If a boy or a man refused to dance, a girl could take away his beads or bracelet or anything. The boy got off his horse and tied it to a bush. Just as he turned around a girl came up to him and caught his hand and pulled him to the dance area. He was looking for the girl he'd been riding with, hoping he'd see her face, but he didn't see her. She wasn't dancing, she wasn't anywhere around. The girl he was dancing with had a shawl, and they put this around them. They danced backwards and forward taking short steps. When the song ended he paid her, and then another girl got him. He danced with several girls. He felt it was getting late. He wanted to meet the girl on the white horse again. He went to his horse, got on, and rode off.

When he reached the place, she wasn't there, so he waited. Soon afterward she came riding out. He got off his horse, then she too got off. He pulled her down on a rock, where they sat quite a while and talked, but when he touched her hands they were cold. He put his arm around her. Her body was cold, but she said she didn't feel cold. The boy noticed that she was too willing to do what he wanted.

Soon she said she had to be going. She didn't tell him her name or where she came from. She got on her white horse and left him, riding at a fast pace with her skirt flying around her. She went west, and soon he couldn't see her. Well, he thought, he would see her at another squaw dance. The next dance was to be the next night west of Black Falls. That would be the end unless another person would take it over, then it would go on for two more days and nights. When he reached home he put his horse in the corral. He saw two other horses there, meaning his parents had returned. He didn't go inside the hogan. His bed roll was out by the shed, so he unrolled it. (It was made of two sheepskins.) He put a blanket on top of that and crawled in. He thought of the songs and events of the night, but mostly about the girl with the cold hands and body.

Then the next thing he knew the sun was almost up and his mother was calling him to breakfast. While he ate breakfast he told about the girl. He said he was going again tonight to look for her. But in the afternoon he became very sick. He had a fever. All that night he was hot, then cold again. His father and mother sat by him all night, washing his face when he got hot, putting his blanket on when he got cold. They gave him herb medicine. Towards morning he became unconscious. His mother noticed his hair falling off. His skin started to dry on his body. By dawn he was a skeleton. He had no more hair left on his head. When the sky in the east was red he died.

His folks were very sad. Now they were left alone. They dressed him up in fine clothes, put turquoise beads around his neck, bracelets on his wrists, and rings on his fingers, also moccasins with silver buttons. They placed him in the middle of the hogan and put wood on top of him. Then they knocked down the poles of the hogan on top of that, and started a fire. They watched everything burn to the ground, then got on their horses and left. They rode east that morning. They didn't eat anything all day. They stopped when they were tired and slept until morning. That day they gathered posts to start a new hogan. They had to begin everything fresh. Nothing from the old hogan could be used again. It was a chin dee hogan, a devil house.

A few days later a rider came by on his way to a Nedah. He stopped and visited. He told a strange story of a boy who lived close by his hogan who had died the night after attending a Nedah. His body burned with fever that turned his face dark. He shook with cold and soon died. The medicine man's medicine didn't work. The boy's hair all fell off and his skin stretched tight across his bones. The man said the family left that chin dee hogan, and he didn't know where they went. The father of the boy repeated what the boy had told him, about a girl he had met with cold hands and a cold body. The medicine man said this girl was the devil, or death, and he wondered how many young boys had touched her.

Tsakaptamana
Moencopi, March 1969

————60————

The Coyote People

This story takes place around Window Rock. We call it Polok-povi in Hopi. It's a story about the Navajo. At Polokpovi there was a family of Navajo living in a hogan. There were several children and a girl was the oldest. She was about sixteen. She had a boyfriend, and they were always going together to dances, the squaw dances, even if they were a long way off. They would go and dance all night. The boy would dance with other girls, and the girl would dance with other boys and men. (It's always girls' choice at the squaw dances. A man can't refuse, because if you refuse, the girl struggles with you, and her family, her mother or her sister, will come and help. They'll pull the man out to the dancing court and he'll have to dance with her.)

After the dances were over, the girl and her boyfriend would come back home together. This boy was thinking of marrying her. He had talked to her about it and she said she felt the same way. But after a while this girl turned cool. He wondered about it. He didn't like it. He asked her sometimes, and she'd say, "I'm not feeling very well. I don't think I'm going with you tonight." The next time she'd say, "My little sister is sick and I have to stay home with her," or some other excuse not to go with him [to the dances]. He wondered about it, because he didn't believe her. He didn't think she would change like that [unless something was wrong]. But he kept coming to see her.

Then one night when he came to her she said she couldn't

go with him because she wasn't feeling well and was going to bed early. He said, "Couldn't I talk with you for a while? We could just sit here and talk and you can go to bed early." She said, "No, I don't think I'm going to stay out, I'm going to stay inside. You'd better go home and not wait for me." But it was squaw dance time, and he knew that she liked the squaw dances, and he didn't believe her. He came away from the hogan a ways and hid behind a cedar tree, behind the hill, and he lay there on the ground on his stomach watching the hogan. He stayed there a long time, and then he saw her come out of the hogan. She walked around and then she went back in again. Later she came out again, real quietly, through the blanket hanging over the opening. She stood a while, then she started walking away, towards the north, towards a little hill. When she got to the hill on the other side she stopped and stood there a while. Somebody was there. The girl seemed to be talking. The person she was talking to was a man lying on the ground. He stood up. He asked her why she was taking her time when they were late. "Well," she said, "my boyfriend was here. He wouldn't believe that I had a headache and wanted to go to bed early. We were supposed to go to the squaw dance tonight. I think I made him believe I was sick, so he left by himself for the squaw dance." He said, "We have to hurry, because we are late already for the meeting."

So they started out, going north. They walked a long way. This boy [who had been watching them] started following them. They walked far, to a place where there were a lot of trees. They went into this forest, and soon they came to a big mountain. It was all rock and it was high. They went around the bend, and the boy ran up behind them. He looked and saw them going along a ledge. Then they came down from the ledge to a lower ledge, only this one was narrower. Then the boy couldn't see them any more, so he went along the ledge and got down where they did. He couldn't see them. There wasn't anyone there. He went back and forth on the [lower] ledge. He couldn't understand where they went. So he thought maybe he was mistaken, and he went back up to the first ledge and walked around for a while, and then he jumped down again to the second ledge. This time he saw some kind of a bush against the rock. He pushed the rock real hard and there was an opening there. He went into the opening and followed the tunnel. He crawled on his hands and knees, but after he went a little way he could stand up. It was dark, but farther on there was a light coming from somewhere. He followed towards where this light was coming from. He stopped when he heard voices. There was a kind of room up ahead. He stayed in the dark and watched from there.

[There were many people in the big room.] He looked around and saw his girl. There were a lot of men and a lot of women. Some of the men were old men. He saw that his girl was with an old man and he didn't like that. There were other girls there, also with old men. The boy wondered what the girls wanted with these old men. Then he saw a lot of coyote pelts hanging on the wall. The boy's girlfriend and the old man she was with were in the center of the circle where the leader of the group was sitting. The old man [the chief] said, "Why have you taken so long? You have been holding up the meeting. We've been waiting for you." And the girl said, "My boyfriend was there and he wouldn't leave for quite a while. That's why we're late." The old man said, "Well, come up now and we'll get started."

There were two coyote pelts in the circle. They were for the girl and the old man she was with. They put these pelts on [their backs] and made some kind of noises, but nothing happened.[1] So the old man said, "Take them off and try again." They took the pelts off, laid them on the ground, then they started again. Still nothing happened. The old man [the leader] said, "You will all search this place, because there's someone here who should not be here." So everybody got up and searched in the outer room where the boy was hiding. [But they didn't find him.] Pretty soon they all came back and said there wasn't anybody around.

So they started again. They put on the pelts and started to howl like coyotes but again it didn't happen. The old man was impatient. He was very angry. He said, "Everybody get up and search, even outside." And so everybody got up and started

---

[1]They were supposed to turn into coyotes.

searching again. And he said, "Don't come back until you find him." Some of them went outside, and when they didn't find anybody there they came back again. They searched the outer room real thoroughly, and this time they found the boy hiding in the corner. They brought him into the main room, and the old man said to him, "You will stay here and watch." The boy answered, "I will take my place with my girlfriend." He stepped to the center and moved the old man [who was her partner] away. He put himself in the old man's place.

Then they both put on these pelts and started to make noises like coyotes. And pretty soon they were [coyotes]. The old man said, "Well, you know your task, now go. It's getting late." So the two of them went out of the cave. The girl said, "I'll lead the way and you follow me." They started running. They ran at a hard pace. After a while they came to a place where only the day before someone had been buried. The girl [coyote] said to the boy [coyote], "Do exactly as I tell you because all my [coyote] kin are watching me, and if anything goes wrong that will be the end of us." He stayed right behind her when she went to the grave. She howled like coyotes do, and coyotes and wolves from all directions answered her. He did the same thing, howled. She started digging at the fresh grave, and finally she pulled out the body of a man. She sneezed at the body and it became small. Then she picked it up in her mouth and they started running back again. They ran as fast as they could. When they arrived at the cave they went back inside. The old man [the chief] was very pleased. She put the body in the middle of the floor and sneezed at it again, and it returned to its normal size.

They saw that [the corpse] was an elderly man with a lot of jewelry on him, all kinds of bracelets and rings and beads. He was a rich man. The chief said, "All right, come on." And all the people came up and started taking all the jewelry from the corpse. They took the clothes off of it. They ate the flesh of the corpse until it was all gone. When they were through they divided up the jewelry. By then it was very late and dawn was coming soon. They set the date for their next meeting and hurried to get out of the cave. The next meeting was supposed to be the next two moons. They all went to their homes. They wanted to get there before dawn. The boy and the girl went together.[2] He took the girl to her hogan. He found his horse where he had left it, and he went from there to his own hogan.

The boy was unhappy with what he had seen. He wondered about all the people who had been at the meeting. He realized that he hadn't ever seen any of them before. A month or so later the girl became sick, and she died very soon. The girl's family learned that the boy also had died. That is the end of the story.

Tsakaptamana
Moencopi, March 1969

---

[2]The narrator omitted to mention that the boy and girl were restored to their human forms.

4
GAMES
AND PRANKS
OF THE
WARRIOR BROTHERS

The Pokangs
and the Blanket Game

The two brothers, Pokanghoya and Palengahoya, were play-ing one time out on a big hill. They had something wrapped in an old Hopi blanket. They'd just rolled up something and put it inside. And they rolled that thing down the hill, laughing and having a big time. Coyote was out walking near there and he happened to see them. He heard the laughing and he went up close to see what was going on. He saw those two brothers laughing and rolling something around. They were having such a good time Coyote wanted to join them.

So he went up and said, "Hey, what you doing?" "Oh, it's pretty exciting. You want to play with us?" "I think I will." They were rolling their thing around and having a big time. Coyote was wondering what was in there. He asked them, "What you got in there?" They started laughing. They said, "That's our grandmother. Yeah, we killed our grandmother and put her in here and started rolling her." This Coyote said, "I got a grandma too. I'll go get my grandmother so I can play with you."

Coyote left and went home. His grandmother was sitting by the ladder. Coyote grabbed a great big stick and clobbered his grandmother in the head. Killed his own grandmother. He wrapped his grandmother in a blanket, rolled her out, and went up to where the brothers were playing. So the brothers were roll-ing their blanket and Coyote was rolling his blanket. After a while Pokanghoya got tired of it and told Coyote that they didn't really have their grandmother wrapped up in their blanket, it was just a joke. They opened it up and there wasn't anything inside but grass and things like that. And Coyote unwrapped his own grandmother, dead. "Boy, you're foxy, all right," Coyote said, and he started crying.

Kilaoka
Walpi, August 1969

————62————

*The Pokangs'
Rolling Game*

Over at Old Oraibi, about a half mile on this side toward Hotevilla Road, those two kids [Pokanghoya and Palengahoya] were living with their grandma [Spider Grandmother]. Spider Woman, I don't know what to call her [in English], Hopis call her a witch. These kids had no mother, no father, they stayed with their grandma. One time these kids went out to hunt rabbits, toward the east. They found something looking like a buzzard sitting on top of a rock. They hid behind the rocks and watched that thing. He was something like a buzzard. "Let's kill him," they said. "Okay." They got their arrows ready. "Let's shoot him at the same time." "Don't you miss him." "No, I won't miss him." They started to aim. "Now!" They shot him right in the back, and he fell over the big rock. They ran over to see, but they didn't know what it was. "Now what are we going to do with him?" "Take him home, maybe grandma knows what it is."

So they carried him home. He was heavy. So when they got home, there was that ladder going down into the cellar, grandma's kiva. "Let's scare grandma, see what she'll do." They just dropped that thing down. It came down the ladder like a person, rolling down the ladder steps. And grandma got scared.

"What is it?" Something rolling down on her. She thought it was a devil, and old grandma fell down and died. She was lying on the ground, and the kids were laughing. She was already dead. "What are we going to do with grandma?" "Well, we'll take her out somewhere and bury her. We can't keep her here."

They took grandma out and carried her to that other side, by the cliff. There was a sand hill right down to the wash, a kind of slope. "Where are we going to bury her?" "Well, we can bury her at a soft place in the sand, so we don't have to dig all day long." "All right." So they set grandma down at the side and started to dig a hole. They went about two-three feet down. Then grandma became alive again. They weren't watching her. She started to get up. When they saw that, they tied up her hands and legs. Then she started to roll down. She rolled clear down to the wash. The kids were laughing. "Look at grandma rolling down!" They went down and picked her up and carried her back. "That looked funny. Let's roll her down again." So they rolled her down three or four times, and after that they took her home.

That's a kids' story. The kids don't hear these stories much any more.

Louis Numkena, Sr.
Moencopi, August 1968

————63————

*The Pokangs
and the Dance at Terkinovi*

In a certain village there were many people living. It was a large place. And north of this village, a few miles from there, Spider Grandmother was living with her two grandsons, Pokanghoya and the younger one, Palengahoya. The boys were known to be full of life and mischief and were always doing

something that they shouldn't. Their grandmother had taught
them how to set traps for small game like chipmunks, rabbits,
or any small game. The way they set these traps was this: you
get two slabs of rock, one for the floor. You level the ground,
and you put this piece of rock down, say about twelve inches
square. The other one, the heavier one, would be for the top.
And you get a stick, about six inches long maybe, and you tie a
string around the top of it. The string is around three or four
inches long, and at the end you tie your bait, like a piece of apple
or carrot or anything that small animals like. You stand this stick
on the level piece of rock and you lean this other rock [on the
top of the stick] so that it stands at a slant. When the animal
smells this he gets into the place and gives a jerk to the bait. The
top rock will come falling on him. And that's the way they kill
small animals. That's one way of setting the trap, but I don't
know for sure if this is the kind of trap that they used.

The two boys set traps every evening, or every afternoon,
and the next day they would go down to see if their traps had
caught anything. Sometimes they would bring many and sometimes a few [small animals], and their grandmother was always
happy when they brought something. One afternoon they went
to check their traps and [on their way] they heard that there was
to be a dance at Terkinovi[1] and that the people were practicing.
They decided they would go to Terkinovi, and so they started
out. As they neared the village they heard the drums, and they
made a short cut to the village, not bothering to use the trail.
They came to the kiva and stayed on the top watching. They saw
a lot of boys and girls dancing together. They watched for a long
time. Then the man down in the kiva said it was time that the
girls went out and cooled themselves off. The girls started coming up the ladder one by one, and when they all came out they
stood around for a while and then started going back in again.
When they all got back in, the drums and singing started up
and they started dancing again. This went on for a long while,
and then it was over.

[1]Terkinovi is now an extinct Bear Clan village on top of First Mesa, about
a mile northeast of Walpi.

The girls came out and waited at the top of the kiva for two boys who would take them home. The boys came out and the girls went with them. The boys would stop at the first house they came to where a girl lived, and she went inside. Then they went to the next house and left a girl there, then they went to the next house and so on, till they had delivered all the girls. After that the boys went home. The two brothers [Pokanghoya and Palengahoya] started going back down the trail and they heard somebody call after them. "Wait, I want to talk to you." So they came back. It was a boy who had called. He asked them where they were from, if they were from the village north of there, and if they did any kind of dancing there. Yes, they said, they had dances there, but they hadn't had any recently. The boy asked if they would care to come and bring a group and dance with them. The boys said that when they got home they would ask their grandmother.

So they went home and told their grandmother about it. She said, "Did you tell them you would bring dancers with you?" The boys said, "Yes, we told them we would bring dancers and dance with them." "Well," Spider Grandmother said, "you shouldn't have said that, because I don't know who would want to dance." The boys said, "Well, you know a lot of songs and we hear you singing all the time. We thought that maybe we could find some kind of a group that would dance with them." She said, "Well, tomorrow you go over to your uncle's at the north village at Tokonave and ask him if he will help us."[2] And so the next morning they had their breakfast, and their grandmother said, "Now, don't you be playing along the way, because Tokonave is far from here and you'll have to hurry to get there and back." But the boys did not listen. They picked up their [nahoydadatsia] sticks and their ball and went on down the trail. As soon as they reached the foot of the mesa they started playing ball. One would hit it north, and the other one would run after it and hit it south again, and back and forth they went. They were not getting anywhere. Then the older boy, Pokanghoya, remembered what

[2]Tokonave, Navajo Mountain, is 90 to 100 miles north of Terkinovi. Like San Francisco Peak in the south, it has magico-religious connotations. It is only a day's journey for the two Warriors.

their grandmother had said, that it was quite a ways and they should not waste their time. And so they picked up their ball and started running. They ran until they were tired, then they walked for a while, then ran again. Then they came to this village [at] Tokonave and they looked for the kiva. They found it and went inside and found an old man, their uncle, there, sitting all by himself.

The old man looked up and said, "What do you boys want?" They told him that their grandmother had sent them, and that they had promised to take a group of dancers to the village of Terkinovi, and their grandmother wanted to know if he had a group to send to help. The old man said, "No, we cannot help you." That was all he said, and the boys came out of the kiva and started home. When they got home they told their grandmother what the old man had said. They said he was grouchy and very curt with them. The grandmother said, "He is always that way." She said, "Well, tomorrow you will go west to the Mountains of the Snow."

The next morning after breakfast they started out west toward these mountains with the snow on top. When they reached there they looked for the kiva. They found it and went in. They found an old man and several others sitting there, and they said they had come to see their uncle. The old man said, "I am your uncle, the one you came to see. What do you want?" They told the old man what they had promised at the other village. They wondered if he could get a group of people and help them dance. He said no, he didn't think so. He was not very willing to help, so they came out and started back home. When they got there they told their grandmother what their uncle had said to them. She said, "Well, tomorrow you will try your uncle at the village to the south."

The next day they went south to the village of Wenima.[3] They reached the village and found the kiva and went in. There were men in the kiva, and they told their uncle why their grandmother had sent them. He said, "Well, no, we can't come." So they came out again and went home and told their grandmoth-

---

[3]Wenima is now a ruin near the town of Springerville, Arizona.

er. The grandmother told them they had one more place to go. The next morning they would go east, to Kisiwu, to see their other uncle. So after breakfast again the next day they started out east. They found the village, found the kiva and went in. The men there were very cordial, glad to see them. They said, "Come in, sit down." And the old man there said, "What do you boys want?" They said their grandmother had sent them to ask their uncle if he would be willing to send a group of young men and girls to help them dance at Terkinovi. The men talked it over among themselves and said they'd be glad to help. The uncle told the boys to tell their grandmother to tell the boy in charge of the dance at Terkinovi to find two houses for them—to whitewash the walls and clean the house real good. That was for the dancers and the things they would bring along.

The boys were very happy and went on home and told their grandmother. She was happy. That evening they practiced. Their grandmother had a drum, and she would take the drum and start singing, while the boys practiced dancing. This was the dance of the Oyaya, a good dance, and the boys had told their uncle at Kisiwu.

On the evening of the dance, these Kisiwu people came to Terkinovi. The boy in charge of the dance was waiting for them, down at the foot of the mesa, and he escorted them to the houses that had been made ready for them. One house was for the people and the other was for the things that they had brought along. After that they went down to the kiva and danced. They danced so well that the boy in charge decided that the visitors would have the kiva to themselves for the next four days, and the people of Terkinovi would have their own dance after that. The next day the regular dance started. The Kisiwu young people formed a circle, a boy and a girl, a boy and a girl, like that, and they danced moving around in a circle. Then after each dance they would go up to the house and bring out some of the things they had brought for gifts and give them to the people. After a while they'd start up the song again and resume dancing. It went on this way all day. They had another kind of dance, a kind of Somaikoli, that they'd brought along, and he did his dance alone between the other dances. When evening came they started moving toward the end of the village, indicating it was all over. The boy was waiting for them down the trail, and he gave them prayer feathers and cornmeal and sent them on their way home.

These Kisiwu people went first to the house of grandmother and the grandsons and told her how the dance went. She gave them a smoke. They smoked for a while and then departed.

After a few days the people of Terkinovi had their own dance, the one they'd been practicing, a Butterfly Dance. Then they decided they liked the dance the people of Kisiwu had brought, and they started dancing those steps.

That's the story of how the two Pokangs brought a new dance to Terkinovi.

Tsakaptamana
Moencopi, March 1969

5
TALES ABOUT
COYOTE
AND
OTHER ANIMALS

————64————

Coyote
and the Stars

The animals were [in this world] first. They were fixing up this earth the way they wanted it. So they put the trees here, they put the mountains here, and the forests here, and so on. They had fixed the stars the way they wanted them to be [but they had not yet placed them in the sky]. They had them all laid out. Pretty soon coyote came around. He was looking at them. "I wonder what this is?" And he just grabbed them and threw them up in the air like that, and that's why stars are scattered all over.

Uwaikwiota
Moencopi, August 1968

————65————

Coyote Envies
the Turkey's Spots

Aliksai!
Oh!
Yaoyesiwa. In the village people were living. There was a lady turkey [koyeungo] and there was a lady coyote [isauu]. They

were good friends and they lived close to each other, and they each had children. And the lady coyote liked the children that Mrs. Turkey had. They were so pretty. One day she went to visit and she asked the lady turkey, "How is it that your children are so beautiful with those white spots on them?" The lady turkey said that she painted her children with the white clay that we use to paint our walls and then she put them into the pit where the fire was was going. When it was good and hot she put her little children in there. Then [she said] she put a rock on top and then she sealed it with mud around the edges of the stone so it was really sealed good. And then she made a fire on top of it, a big bonfire. And then in the morning [she said] bright and early she opened it up. She lifted the rock and they were all well done. And she took them out one by one and ate off the flesh. She was very careful not to bite into the bones. She put the bones into a yucca basket. She sang a song as she [shook] the bones up and down in her basket. She sang,

> "My children, my children,
> Come back to life."

When she got through singing, [she said to the lady coyote], she threw the bones up in the air and let them land, and they were all alive again, with those little spots on them. And she told Mrs. Coyote that's how she did her children so they were pretty that way.

So Mrs. Coyote went home, and she started a fire in her pit. She painted her children and she put them into the pit. They didn't want to go in, but she said they would be pretty like the little turkeys. And so she put them all in and closed it up, and sealed it up real good and started a big bonfire on top of it. Then the next morning she dug them up, ate off the flesh, and then she put those bones into the basket and did like Mrs. Turkey did. And at last when she finished her song she threw those bones up into the air and let them fall and nothing happened. There were no little coyotes. And so she became real angry and said she would go after those little turkeys; she was going to eat them all up. The lady turkey knew what was going to happen, so she told her children to go ahead into the woods to Flagstaff; they were close to Flagstaff and so she told them to go on ahead. She knew that Mrs. Coyote would be along soon.

Sure enough, here came Mrs. Coyote. She was very angry. Mrs. Turkey left after her children. The lady coyote chased those turkeys in the woods, but they finally flew up into the trees and she couldn't catch any of them.

That's the end of the story, and it means that you are supposed to be satisfied with what you have and not believe what people tell you.

Tsakaptamana
Moencopi, August 1968

————66————

Coyote and Snake
Exchange Visits

Aliksai!

Oh!

Once there lived a coyote at Keuchaptevela, Ashes Hill.[1] Snake lived about a mile from there too. And they were good friends and they kept visiting back and forth. So one time the snake came over to coyote's kiva. "Ha'u!" That's the right way to say when you want to get down in a kiva. "Keuwawata!" (That's a hard word to translate. It means something like "Come in and be welcome.") "Come in," the coyote said, "come in!" So he started going down in there, and you know how long he was. He started curling around. The coyote started to move to the stepladder. There wasn't room for him. He kept doing that, and

[1]Keuchaptevela, Ash Hill, was abandoned when the people moved to the top of the mesa to the present site of Walpi.

pretty soon he got outside of his house. The snake filled his house up, you know how long he is, just curled up there, and the coyote had to sit outside and talk to his friend the snake. Had to sit outside and let the snake take over his house. They talked and talked and finally the snake said that he was going home; it was getting late. So he went home.

When the snake went home the coyote started thinking, "How am I going to pay him back?" He kept thinking all night. He came up with the idea that he would get bark from the cedar trees and tie it up and tie it to his tail. So he tied a lot of it, maybe longer than the snake, and he started going over there. And he said the same thing "Ha'u!" So the snake said, "Come in!" So he started going in there, and pretty soon he crowded the snake out; he had to go out of his house and talk to his friend from the outside. (The coyote was paying his friend back.) They were still talking, and I guess the coyote's tail got close to the fire, and it started burning. The snake called down, "You're on fire!" The coyote took off. He was heading for the lake, he wanted to jump in there. And I guess the coyote is still running, trying to find the water to jump in.

Uwaikwiota
Moencopi, August 1968

————67————

Turtle's Crying Song

Aliksai!
Oh!
The coyote was hunting around to see what she could kill for her little ones. And she heard somebody singing someplace. So she tried to look for him, and she found a little turtle. She came up to the little turtle and said, "You're singing some pretty songs." The turtle said, "I'm not singing, I'm crying." "Why are you crying?" He said because his mother had taken her little turtles out for a walk, and he'd got lost. The little turtle said that

he was lost. The coyote asked him if he would sing his songs.[1] "No, I'm not singing, I'm crying," he said. Then the coyote said, "Well, if you don't sing for me, I'm going to roll you on this hot sand." The little turtle said, "If you roll me on the hot sand it won't hurt me, I'm not afraid of it." Then the coyote said, "Well then I'm going to throw you into that lake over here." And the turtle said, "Don't throw me in the lake. I'm going to drown if you throw me in there." So the coyote ran to the turtle and picked him up in his mouth and threw him in the middle of the lake. Pretty soon the little turtle came up and said that [the lake] was his home. And then the coyote got mad and she jumped in and got drowned. The little coyotes who had lost their mother, when their mother didn't come back, they had to go around and hunt for something to eat. That's why coyotes are good hunters.

The song the little turtle was singing was:

> Ting-a-so!
> Ting-a-so!
> Wa-wa-o-yeh!
> Yakaiendakala!

There are no words to the song, just sounds.

Uwaikwiota
Moencopi, August 1968

———68———

Coyote
and the Dancing Birds

It was a long time ago at Oraibi, the people were living there. On the west side of that village, there was a spring there. And close to that spring a coyote and his grandma were living. This

---

[1]Explained later: The coyote wanted the little turtle to sing the song so that when she got home, she could sing it to her children.

coyote was always going hunting for something to eat, went out every day. One day he went out looking for something to eat again. Of course, Hopis grow pumpkins, watermelons, and such things, and sometimes they leave a few in the fields, and coyote goes looking for them. While he was looking, he heard something that sounded like [singing and] dancing. He went up to the top of the hill to see if he could see somebody. He looked around. He saw some girls [birds] circling around and dancing, and he just watched. He thought, "I wonder if I could go over there and join with them?" Then he went over there. They were going around in a circle, singing and dancing. After a while they quit dancing and all flew away, way up in the air. You couldn't see them. So he just lay down on his back and looked up.

Finally they came down again. They all settled on the ground and started to sing again. Coyote was just watching them. Every bird had something on his back, [about the size of] a basketball. I don't know what kind of bird they were. But they went around and danced some more, then they flew away. Then they all came down and he talked to them, asked them what they were doing. "Oh, we're just playing. Just practicing." "What you got on your back?" They were laughing at him.[1] "Oh, you don't need to know." "I want to know." They laughed. "Can you give me some of your wing feathers, so I can fly with you?" "Oh, it's up to you." They said to Coyote, "The only thing is, you have to have that thing on your back like we do." "What's that?" "That's our grandmothers' heads." "Ahhh, I don't believe that." "Why, sure, if you want to join you have to go back and get your grandmother's head, then you can fly with us." "Sure, I'll get it! I'd like to play with you."

So he went back to the house. His grandma was still fixing the fire in the fireplace. He came down and asked grandma, "Where's that butcher knife we have?" "What you going to do with it?" "I found a pumpkin over there, it's too heavy to carry so I thought I'd cut it in half." "There it is under the sheepskin." He uncovered it, took it out, sharpened it. Then he took hold of grandma's head and chopped it off. He wrapped it up in some

[1]It is not clear whether the birds were actually carrying something on their backs or whether their physical appearance suggested this to coyote.

rags and carried it up there where the girls [birds] were dancing.

They were laughing. "What you got?" "That's grandma's head." Everybody laughed. They started around again. Everybody gave him wing feathers. He just stuck them in there. There were a lot of girls, so there were enough feathers to give him wings and a tail. "Come on, let's go." They started to fly. Coyote went up about this far and got dizzy and dropped down. The rest of them went on up in the air. They came down again. "Why didn't you go with us way up there?" He tried again. He went up, I don't know how many feet, and got dizzy and scared and just fell down. They did that four times. And the fourth time the coyote went up a little ways and the birds came and grabbed their feathers from him, and down came the coyote. That was the end of him.

Louis Numkena, Sr.
Moencopi, August 1968

————69————

Holding Up the Cliff[1]

Coyote was living out there south of Oraibi, and one day he was going around looking for something to eat when he saw a grasshopper clinging to the base of a cliff. Coyote thought the grasshopper looked very peculiar, with its legs against the cliff wall that way, but he was hungry and decided to eat it if he could. As he approached the grasshopper it said, "Thanks that you have come! I have been waiting for help all night."

Coyote said, "Why? Is something the matter?" And the grasshopper answered, "Matter? Yes, everything is the matter.

[1]This tale was not recorded, but set down from memory shortly after the narration.

The cliff wall is about to come down, and if it falls, the whole village will come down with it. I wanted to go up there and warn the people, but there was no time. So I stayed here and braced my feet against the cliff to hold it in place." Coyote said, "Oh, that is something good that you are doing."

The grasshopper said, "Now that you are here, I can warn the people of Oraibi. Come quickly and hold the wall for me." Coyote went at once, lay on his side, and braced all four feet against the rocks. The grasshopper said, "Do you have it held firmly?" Coyote said, "Yes, I am holding it. Go quickly, I don't know how long I can hold it." The grasshopper asked again, "Do you have it?" And Coyote said, "Yes, I have it." Then the grasshopper leaped away.

Coyote lay there for a long time, his feet braced against the cliff wall. He was pushing very hard, and he was getting tired. At last he said, "I can't hold it any longer!" So he jumped up and scrambled away, expecting the cliff to come down on him. But nothing happened. Coyote said, "Well, I did a good thing. I held it until Grasshopper arrived at the village and warned the people. They must have fixed it up above."

Abbott Sekaquaptewa
Kikeuchmovi, July 1968

————70————

*Coyote Envies
the Fawn's Spots*

Aliksai!
There's another coyote story, and at the same place, where Old Oraibi is. This coyote was always hunting animals. And one time this coyote went out again and he found a deer with her little kid with her. The little one was spotted, you know how they look. And this coyote sure like to be like them. He stood

watching them instead of killing the little one, and he came home and told grandma he'd seen that deer over there with its little one. She didn't believe it. "Well, then, let's go over and look at them. I'd like to be like them." They both went over there where the deer were. They were watching them; they [the deer] were eating. They got close to them and they didn't even run off.

So the [coyote] grandma asked the mother, "How did you paint your kid? I'd like to paint mine too." The mother deer said, "Oh, I just paint him good. I just paint him good with that whitewash." "Don't wash off?" "No, it stays on, like that. You like it?" "Sure I like it. I'd like to paint him [her grandson]." So they went home again. And when they got home she started to paint him. She went back again afterward to ask [the mother deer] how she'd done it. That deer told coyote [grandmother], "Oh, I forgot to tell you everything that you should do. After I painted I [made] a hole above the pit and set the fire in there. When it got hot I put in this kid and covered it up with dirt and baked him. When I opened it the paint was all staying on."

"Okay, I'll do that." The coyote grandma went home. She told the kid what she was going to do. He said, "I'd like to be like him." So she started to dig a hole in the ground. She put a fire in. And when it got hot, she put the coyote kid in there and covered him up, till next morning. And opened it, and it was all cooked. She pulled up the head, it was by itself, fell off of the kid. And arms and everything. This coyote [grandma] got mad. Then she ran back, but the deer and its kid had run away from the place. Then the coyote followed them, chasing them clear over to the San Francisco Mountain. This [deer] kid, before they got there he was tired. The mother left him there about five miles before they got to the mountain. The mother ran up to the other deers and told the uncle [of the deers] that there was a coyote chasing them to get the little one, better go over and pick him up and bring him back.

So one of the deers with the big horns started to run over there. That kid was running and crying, and the coyote was coming close. The deer just pick [the young one] up with the horns and began to run with him. [Coyote called out,] "Hey, don't take my boy away! I'm coming after him! They're carrying my boy!" The coyote just followed after them. And there were some other deers over there, and soon as this coyote was there, they picked her up and threw her to each other [on their horns] and killed her.

Louis Numkena, Sr.
Moencopi, August 1968

————71————

Grey Hawk
and the Field Mouse

This is a story told by Masaquaptewa about a field mouse that lived near the Corn Rock over at Second Mesa.

The people at Second Mesa were losing a lot of chickens. They prized chickens very much for their eggs, and the people got worried. They wondered where their chickens had been going. The chief of the village wanted to know what they could do about it. So he went to his war chief to see what the war chief thought about the matter. He took his pipe and tobacco along, and after they had passed the pipe to one another it was time to talk. They laid down the pipe and started to talk. The war chief asked, "What's the purpose of your visit, our father." They always called the kikmongwi "our father."

"Well, son, I came here because people have been coming to me about their chickens. It seems as if somebody is taking them. People are worried. I want you to look into it and find out how the chickens are disappearing."

The war chief said, "All right, I'll detail some boys to go around and see what's happening to the chickens."

Along about noon, one of the boys spotted the old grey hawk on top of Corn Rock. The hawk was fluttering his wings. Soon as he saw a chicken down there in the yard he swooped down, picked it up, and carried it to the top of Corn Rock. Ate a piece of the chicken up there. That evening one of the boys came to the war chief and said, "Now I know where the chickens are going, because I saw it with my own eyes. There's an old grey hawk on top of Corn Rock. He's the one that's been carrying away the chickens. But how can we get at Grey Hawk? You can shoot with bow and arrow, but you can't hit him. If you stand behind the rock your arrow won't reach him. And you can't climb that Corn Rock either. And you can't go up in the crevice." The war chief said, "Well, I'll think about it. Meanwhile we know where the chickens are going."

The field mouse happened to hear about all this, said, "I guess I'll make a visit to the chief myself." So he did. That night he went up to the chief's house, said, "Ha'u!" Chief said, "Come in!" In comes little old field mouse. Now, the chief is the protector, he's supposed to take care of the life and interests of whoever comes to him, even a small creature. He looked at the field mouse, said, "Come in, come in!" Field mouse had his little old pipe and native tobacco. He lit up with a flint before the chief could get his own pipe ready, got ahead of him. (That's one thing you try to do, get ahead of the chief before he hands you his lighted pipe.) Chief took it. After he smoked he passed the pipe, saying, "My son." Field mouse said, "My father." That's the way they're supposed to address one another. The chief said, "Now, what's on your mind?" The field mouse said, "You people seem to be having trouble with your chickens. I've been watching the hawk taking them away. But there's no way you can get rid of that hawk. I guess I'll have to do it for you." The chief said, "Well, son, my child, you're so small, how could you?" The field mouse said, "Oh, there's always a way to help." The chief said, "You can't shoot an arrow up there. You can't throw a spear. I don't see how you could help." The field mouse said, "I have a plan in my mind." "What is it?" "Well, I think I can entice the hawk to come down and try to pick me up. I live down there close to the Corn Rock. I'm going to tempt him to come down and catch me. I can go into my kiva. I'm going to get a sharp stick and put it in the ground. When he comes after me I'll get down next to the sharp stick, and the stick will pierce him."

The chief kind of laughed, said, "All right. I'll let you go ahead with your scheme." So after they agreed, they passed the pipe again. "Well," the field mouse said, "I'll let you know after four days, when I'm ready to have war with the grey hawk."

The field mouse went home, dressed himself like a warrior. On the appointed day he came out singing, mocking the grey hawk. Grey Hawk looked down, said to himself, "There's prize meat, I'm going to get him." So he started to flutter his wings, but field mouse was dancing around close to his hole, and he had a sharp stick sticking up from the ground right there. He kept mocking the grey hawk. Grey Hawk got angry, came down like a bullet to get the field mouse. The field mouse popped into his hole, but the grey hawk was coming down so fast he couldn't check his speed, and he hit the pointed stick head on. He impaled himself. The stick went right through his craw and killed him. Field mouse took the dead hawk to the village chief. "Here you are," he said. "I got rid of your enemy." The chief said, "Did you really kill him?" Said, "Yes. That stick went right through him. Killed him."

Well, the people were so glad that they put up a big feast in honor of the field mouse killing the grey hawk.

That was a story told by Masaquaptewa. Eddie Kennard got it from him and put down the text, then he brought it to me at Keam's Canyon and I corrected the Hopi words.

> Nuvayoiyava (Albert Yava)
> Tewa Village, August 1969

————72————

Mockingbird, Giver of Bird Calls

When the world was young, the birds didn't have any way of communicating because they couldn't talk. Couldn't communicate with one another. The only one that was in a position to teach them was the mockingbird, called yalpa. He was the one who had given people their languages. He sent for all the fowls of the air and asked them to come together. He said to them, "We don't seem to have any language among us. So I'm in a position to teach you something. Now, you all listen to me. I'm going to give you your calls. If I want to call a rock hen, I'll say, 'Tchew tchew tchew,' and the rock hen will hear me. He'll wonder why I'm calling, and he'll come. If I want to have a red-tailed hawk come to the meeting, I'll make that shrill noise, 'Sieuuuu! Sieuuuu! Sieuuuu!' and the red-tailed hawk will know he's supposed to come. If I want to have an owl come to the meeting, I'll kind of cough, 'K-hu! K-hu! K'hu!' Owl will know I want him to come. I'm going to give every bird his call. When they hear these calls they'll know I am holding a meeting. Every bird should listen for his call." Mockingbird assigned all the calls. Whenever a bird heard what his call was supposed to be, he said, "That's all I want to know," and left.

The last bird was still there. He looked like the mockingbird. The mockingbird said, "Seems to me you look like me." It was the catbird. Looks just like the mockingbird. He said, "Yes, I believe I do." Mockingbird said, "Don't you want any call?" Catbird said, "No, I don't think I need to learn a call." "Why?" Catbird said, "Seems like you're not very popular with the other birds. Didn't you notice that as soon as they received their calls they flew right off? I think that the best thing for me is not to know any call. If I want to come to any meeting I can hear you calling the other birds, then I'll come. But I'll just sit quietly and not do any talking."

Mockingbird said, "Well, if you don't have any call, how are you going to make your announcement?" Catbird said, "Oh, I'll just flutter my wings."

Catbirds are the only ones that you hardly ever hear talking. All they say is, "Mieh! Mieh! Mieh!" That's all they say. The catbird decided that he didn't want a real call, because he was ashamed of his cousin, and he didn't want to be mistaken for him. He was afraid that if he had a call, other birds would think he was the mockingbird, who always talked too much.

Nuvayoiyava (Albert Yava)
Tewa Village, August 1969

————73————

The Animals Play
the Shoe Game

The animals that travel at night and the animals that travel at daytime were having a game. They were playing this game where you hide something under the shoes. The night group was on the other side and the day group was on this side. So they kept playing this game. They played all night. They put something under the shoes and sing songs, and an animal comes [from the other group] to try to find which shoe they put it under. So they'd been playing all night. They were supposed to quit when the sun comes up. They were playing so hard that they forgot all about the sun. The sun was ready to come up, and the animals that roam in the daytime noticed that the sun was coming up. They had some colors that they painted themselves with before going home, back to where they live. The sun was about ready to come out, so the bear started running. He was kind of slow and he started running because he might not make it back to the forest before the sun comes out. The sun would do something to them. Before he could get into the forest the sun came up and it struck his fur, that's why his fur is kind of burned, kind of brown. And then this rabbit started running too, but before he got into the forest the sun came up and cut his tail off. He used to have a long tail, and the sun cut his tail off. The crow was the only one that was left there. They had used all the paint, different kinds of paint, and they had left just the black paint. He tried to look for a different kind of paint, but that was the only one they didn't use. He put that on himself and started running. But before he got into the forest the sun came up. And that's why the crow is black. He'd just put the black paint on himself.

That shoe game they played is called sosotakwia. They take their shoes off and line them up. When they're going to hide a stone under one of the shoes, the other group turns around. When they put it under the shoe they start singing, they have songs for that game, two or three songs. Well, they keep singing until [someone] finds the stone. Then they start the game all over again. A person comes from the other group to find the stone, but he can only look under one shoe. If he doesn't find the stone, they start all over. That's the way they play sosotakwia.

Uwaikwiota
Moencopi, August 1968

————74————

Calling the Sun to Rise

The people were living over there at Old Oraibi, a long time ago, before there was any New Oraibi. North of Oraibi a couple of miles are some ruins, and Coyote was living there when this story happened. He was out hunting very early one morning before the daylight came. It was still dark. And he came to a place where he saw a rooster standing on a big rock. That rooster looked very busy, but Coyote couldn't figure out what he was doing. He said, "Ha'u. What are you doing up there?" The rooster said, "I'm doing my work. I am making the sun come up."[1]

Coyote laughed. He said, "That's not anything. Anybody can do that." The rooster said, "No. It's my job." Coyote said, "I'm the one responsible for making the sun rise. I call out to it early in the morning and then it comes up." The rooster said, "Everybody knows I'm the one that does this work. So I'll show you." Coyote said, "I'll do it first." Then he sat down next to the rooster, stuck his nose up in the air and gave a long howl, ending up with a kind of bark. But nothing happened. It was

[1]Although this tale is sheer comedy, it seems dimly to echo the emergence myth, in which Spider Grandmother, or the medicine men under the guidance of a sorcerer, lofts the sun unto the sky.

still dark. The rooster said, "You see? I'll show you how to do it." He crowed to the east and flapped his wings hard, but it was still dark. Coyote said, "This time I'll do it. Watch the sky." He howled real hard. The sky seemed to be just a little lighter, but it wasn't very light. After him, the rooster crowed again, a real loud one. It seemed that the sky was just a little brighter, but there wasn't any sun to be seen.

So they just kept on taking turns, and all the time the sky was getting a little more light, but just grey. Then the rooster gave one more try, gave everything he had, and the forehead of the sun showed up over Second Mesa. The rooster said, "Now you know I am the one who did it." Coyote had to agree the rooster was the one. But he said, "Just the same, I am the one that got it loosened up."

Louis Numkena, Sr.
Moencopi, August 1968

Glossary and Pronunciation Guide

Unchallengeable spellings and pronunciations for many Hopi words are difficult to achieve, since individuals and villages aften disagree. There are vernacular differences between the three mesas and sometimes between villages on a single mesa. Elisions add to the problem. For example, one contributor to these texts pronounces and spells his name Cooyama, a shortened form of Cooyawaiema.

Vernacular differences no doubt were strengthened by the relative isolation of the villages from one another in former times. But it is reasonable to ask whether they might not have come in part from the varied speech elements that entered the settlements with the absorption of ingathering clans and tribal elements. Many ingatherers spoke dialects of Shoshonean akin to, but not necessarily identical with, an earlier form of the Hopi language, and some arrivals appear to have spoken different languages. Incoming groups from the eastern (New Mexican) Pueblos spoke Tiwa, Tewa, Towa, Keresan, and Zunian. While a majority of these easterners returned to their New Mexican settlements after sojourns of various periods of time on the Hopi mesas, some remained behind. Lagunas and Zunis left a linguistic imprint on the Antelope Mesa villages which is still discernable in ceremonial songs brought from Awatovi at the time of its destruction.

Albert Yava, who contributed to this collection of texts, was for many years one of the reservation's most able translators at the Keam's Canyon Indian Agency office, and he had a height-

241

ened awareness of vernacular differences in the villages. In his book, *Big Falling Snow* (pp. 36 and 82), he speaks of some of the linguistic influences on the Hopi language:

The Water Coyote group that came here from the north spoke Paiute or Chemehuevi or some other Shoshonean dialect. . . . We had Pimas coming in from the south. And there's an Apache strain too. Those clans that came here from Palatkwa, such as the Water Clan, the Sand Clan and the Tobacco Clan, brought Pimas and Apaches with them. My father's group, the Water Clan, claims to be Uche—that is, Apache—in origin. . . . According to what we've been told, the Hopis absorbed Pimas, Yumas, Coconinos, Apaches, Paiutes, Utes, Navajos and even some Sioux. Most of that took place in the distant past when the clans were coming in. I think it must have had an influence on the speech of the various villages so that they handled the Hopi language a little differently.

Older Hopis recognize and often comment on speech differences between the villages. Oraibis tend to regard the speech of their mesa as "classical," and the speech heard elsewhere as "rustic." Likewise, some persons in Walpi contend that First Mesa Hopi is the truest form of the language. Investigators of Hopi life have always had problems with the differences. Voth, for example, notes that he heard the place name Kisiwu (as it is usually pronounced on First Mesa) given on Second Mesa and Third Mesa in three different ways: Kí'shiwuu, Kíshiwu, and Kishíwu (*Traditions of the Hopi*, p. 71n). Not only is there variation in the sound of vowels and consonants, but also in accented syllables.

Spellings of Hopi words and proper names in this book generally reflect pronunciations as heard and recorded on tape, though in many instances, for the sake of ready recognition, I have followed spellings already made familiar through wide usage. Pronunciation, indicated in parentheses following each word, was reviewed in sessions with competent Hopis in three different villages in June of 1981. The guide to pronunciation is nontechnical, and is intended only to give the reader a reasonably close idea of how the spoken Hopi words sound.

a is generally soft, as in *father*, and is shown in the pronunciation guide as *ah*.

ai has a long *i* sound, as in *high*, and is shown in the pronunciation guide as *eye* or, following a consonant, as *pye, tye, kye,* etc.

au is sounded as in *maul*, and is shown in the pronunciation guide as *aw*.

e is short, as in *pet*, shown in pronunciation guide as *eh*.

eu is as in French in such words as *neuf, peuple,* etc., and is close to the German *ö* employed in some other writings on the Hopis.

i is short, as in *pit*, or sounded as in French (*ee*).

o is long, as in *hole, mole,* etc.

u is long, as in *rule*, and is shown in the pronunciation guide as *oo*, though in some instances it takes the French *eu* sound.

Glottal stops frequently are elusive and have not always been indicated.

k is sounded as in English, but sometimes is heard as a hard *g*. Thus the word for eagle, *kwahu*, may be heard as *gwahu*.

s is as in English, though sometimes heard as *sh*.

sh is as in English, though sometimes heard as *s*.

ch is as in English *church*, though sometimes softened to *sh* or heard as *ts* (*kachina, katsina*).

v is as in English, but sometimes heard as *b* (*Bakavi, Bakabi*).

y is as in English.

Other consonants are generally as in English.

Aal (AHL or AH-ahl). Horn, name of an important kiva society. Some times called *Aalteu* (AH-ahl-teu), Horn People, or *Aalataka* (AHL-lah-tah-kah), Two Horn Society.

Aliksai (ah-LIHK-sye), sometimes heard as *haliksai* (hah-LIHK-sye). A call or announcement used to begin a story. The listeners respond by saying "oh" or "ho."

Alosoka (AH-lo-so-kah), also heard as *Alosaka* (AH-lo-sah-kah) and sometimes pronounced ah-LO-sah-kah. A deity of the Two Horn Society.

Apovanevi (ah-PO-vah-neh-vee), sometimes heard as *Aponivi* (ah-PO-nee-vee). An old village site on Third Mesa.

Ateu'eu (ah-TEU-eu). A type of red and white shawl worn by unmarried girls.

Auheulani (AW-heu-lahn-ee, OW-heu-lahn-ee, sometimes heard eh-eu-HAH-leh-nee). A kachina who appears in the winter solstice ceremonies.

Awatovi (ah-WAHT-o-vee). An extinct village on Awatovi or Antelope Mesa.

Bahana (bah-HAH-nah). White man, person.

Bakavi, sometimes spelled *Bacavi* (BAH-kah-vee, occasionally heard as BAH-kah-bee or BAH-kah-vay). A Third Mesa village founded after the breakup of Oraibi.

Chakmongwi (CHAHK-mong-wee or cha-AHK-mong-wee). Village crier chief.

Changaieuteika (shang-AI-eu-tay-ih-kah). Seven Houses Point, a site on Second Mesa.

Chimonvasi (chih-MON-vah-see, chih-MAHN-vah-see, or chih-MEUN-veu-seh). In the Corner, an extinct Third Mesa village.

Chindee (chihn-dee, Navajo language). Signifies bad man, sorcerer, devil.

Chuka (DJEU-kah). A personal name meaning mud or clay (indicating his father was member of the Sand Clan, mud and sand being related).

Chung'eu (CHOONG-eu). A personal name meaning Smoking Pipe.

Cooyama (ko-O-yah-mah). A personal name, contracted from Cooyawaiema.

Cooyawaiema (koh-O-yah-wye-eh-mah or ko-YA-wai-eh-mah). Indicates something unspecified in the act of walking.

Deveh(DEH-veh or DEH-EH-veh). A personal name meaning Greasewood.

Dosi (DO-see, TO-see, or TOO-see). A dish prepared from ground sweet corn.

Eototo (EH-o-to-to). Name of a class of kachinas.

Geleoya (geh-LAY-oy-ah, geh-LEH-o-yah, or GEHL-o-hoy-ah). Personal name meaning Red Hawk.

Gogyeng Sowuhti (GO-gyehng so-WEU-tee, sometimes heard as KO-kyehng so-WEU-dee). Spider Grandmother or Spider Old Woman.

Gyaromana (gyahr-O-mah-nah). Personal name meaning Parrot Girl.

Hai (HYE, sometimes heard as HAH-ee). A greeting.

Hano (HAH-no). Hopi name for Tewa Village on First Mesa. Residents of the village disdain the name Hano, a Hopi pronunciation of T'hano, an Eastern Pueblo group that the villagers do not regard as true Tewas.

Hasokata (HAH-so-kah-tah). Gambler, a legendary Hopi personality who gambles with people for their lives. The name is also applied to North Wind Old Man, another legendary figure responsible for bitter winter winds. Some Hopis believe that Gambler and North Wind Old Man are one and the same, while others claim they are different.

Ha'u (HAH-oo). An attention-calling exclamation. A person wanting to enter a kiva may stamp on the ground overhead and call out, "Ha'u!"

Heh'eh (HEH-eh or HEH-eh-eh). The reference in the text may be confusing. Heh'eh or Heh'eh'eh is the name of a certain kachina who wears his hair in girls' style on one side and men's style on the other. Heh'eh is a warrior kachina, generally regarded as a female.

Hogan (HO-gahn). Navajo word for the common Navajo country house with a mounded or somewhat conical top.

Homolovi (ho-MO-lo-vee). An extinct village near Winslow, Arizona, where the clans coming from Palatkwapi are believed to have rested in their migration northward.

Homsuna (HOM-soo-nah, HEUM-so-nah). The haircutter Kachina.

Honwaima (hon-WYE-mah or hoon-WYE-mah). Personal name meaning Bear Walking.

Hopi (HO-pee). Usually translated as "peaceful," hence "peaceful people." To the Hopi, however, the word has more subtle connotations, signifying perfect, pure, irreproachable behavior. Several elder Hopis have said, "We are not perfect yet, but through good behavior we are trying to become Hopi."

Hopitu (HO-pee-too or HO-pee-teu). Plural. Hopi people.

Hotevilla (HOT-vih-lah or HOT-veh-lah). A Third Mesa village. Two interpretations were given for the word: (1) Cedar Slope and (2) Scrape Back.

Huckovi (HOO-ko-vee or HEU-ko-vee). An extinct First Mesa village, the name signifying Wind Top. There was another Huckovi on Third Mesa.

Huruing Wuhti (heu-REU-ing WEU-tee). A Second and Third Mesa creation deity. Her name is generally translated as Hard Substances Old Woman, the hard substances being such things as coral and turquoise.

Iksi (EEK-see, IHK-see and sometimes HIHK-see). Breath, spirit, soul.

Isauu (EE-sow-eu). Coyote.

Kachina (generally kah-CHEE-nah, on rare occasions kat-SEE-nah). Supernatural beings who assist the Hopis in getting rain and good crops. Those who appear in kachina costumes and masks during dances are considered to be kachina personators doing the work of the kachinas.

Kachinmana (kah-CHEEN-mah-nah). Kachina girl. Sometimes refers to a female participant in a ceremony or dance, and is also used as a personal name.

Kaiotakwi (kye-O-tah-kwee or kah-EU-teu-kwee). An extinct village below Second Mesa.

Kaletaka (kah-LEH-tahk-ah). Warrior.

Kaletakmongwi (kah-LEH-tahk-mong-wee). Also heard as Kalatak-mongwi (Kah-LAH-tahk-mong-wee). War chief.

Kawestima (kah-WEHST-ih-mah), sometimes heard as *Kalewistema* (kah-leh-WIHST-eh-mah). A place of old Hopi ruins north of Kayenta in the Betatakin area from where some clans came to the Hopi mesas.

Kawaika (kah-WYE-kah or kah-WYE-kah-ah). An extinct village on Antelope Mesa, and the Hopi name for Laguna people.

Keuchapteika (KEU-chahp-teh-kah or KEU-chahp-teu-ee-kah). Presumably another name for Keuchaptevela (teu-ee-kah means point).

Keuchaptevela (KEU-chahp-teh-veh-lah). The original site of Walpi on a lower shelf of the mesa.

Keuwawata (keu-WAH-wah-tah). "Come in and be welcome," or "Join the festivities." Said when a stranger or a person from a distant place is invited to enter a house or a kiva.

Kiavakovi (kee-AH-vah-ko-vee). "Someone is coming [from a distant village]."

Kikeuchmovi (kee-KEUTS-mo-vee or kee-KEUCH-mo-vee). New Oraibi.

Kikmongwi (KIHK-mong-wee). Village chief.

Kilaoka (KEE-lah-o-kah). Means house builder or building a house. Personal name, in this case a pseudonym.

Kisiwu (KIH-see-weu). An extinct Hopi village northeast of Piñon, said to be a kachina home.

Kiwan (kee-WAHN or keu-WAHN). A class of kachinas.

Koyeungo (ko-YEUNG-o). Turkey.

Kukeuchomo (koo-KEUCH-o-mo or keu-KEUCH-o-mo). An extinct village above the Sikyatki ruins. The name means Hill of Ruined Village.

Kwakwanteu (KWAH-kwahn-teu). One Horn kiva society.

Kwateufteika (kwah-TEUF-teh-ee-kah, also heard as kwah-TEU-y'-kah). Eagle Mesa Point.

Kwitamuh (KWEE-tah-muh). An aggressive, rough person. A hoodlum.

Laangnyam, Le'nyam (LAANG-nyahm. LEH-nyahm). Flute Clan.

Lakone, Lalakone (lah-KON, lah-lah-KON) Ceremony of the women's society, which is called **Lalakontu** (lah-lah-KON-teu).

Lalakontu. See *Lakone.*

Lamehva (lah-MEH-vah). A spring below Second Mesa. According to one informant, the original word was *Neveva* (neh-VEH-vah).

Lansa, Mina (LAHN-sah, MYE-nah). A woman who took over the chieftaincy of Oraibi.

Le'ehu (LEH-eh-hoo, LEH-hoo). A wild grass that produces edible seeds.

Lenachi (LEH-nah-chee). Personal name meaning Flute Banner or Flute Emblem.

Lomaheungva (lo-MAH-heung-vah). Personal name meaning Beautiful Standing Up.

Lomahquahu (lo-MAH-kwah-hoo). Personal name meaning Golden Eagle.

Mas (MAHS). Dead. Also has other meanings.

Masaquaptewa (MAH-sah-kwahp-teh-wah). Personal name meaning Decorating (or Decorated?) With Feathers.

Masauwu (MAHS-ah-oo-woo or MAHS-ah-woo, sometimes MAHS-ah-oo). A dead person or spirit. As a proper name, it signifies Death or the God of Death, who owned the upper world before the people emerged from below.

Maschumo (MAHS-choo-mo). Place name, Dead Person's Hill, near First Mesa.

Masipa (mah-SEE-pah). Gray Spring. Original site of Shongopovi below the present village. The ruins are still visible.

Maski (MAHS-kee). Place where spirits of the dead go to reside.

Maskoteu (MAHS-ko-teu). Skull. A site below First Mesa is known by this name and is interpreted as Skull Mound. Like Maschumo, it has associations with the destruction of Awatovi.

Masturki (MAHS-teur-kee). Dead Persons' Hill. A site near First Mesa associated with the destruction of Awatovi.

Mata (MAH-tah). Metate.

Mataki (mah-TAH-kee). The flat mulling stone held in the hands to grind corn on the mata.

Mishongnovi (mih-SHONG-no-vee). A village on Second Mesa.

Moencopi (MEUN-kah-pee). The westernmost of the Hopi villages, near Tuba City.

Meusiptanga (meu-SIHP-tahng-ah). An extinct village site on the Jeddito Wash.

Moqui (MO-kee). A Spanish term for the Hopis.

Muchovi (MOO-cho-vee, MOO-tso-vee or MOTS-o-vee). An extinct village site near Keam's Canyon.

Muyao (MEU-yah-o). Moon.

Muyingwa (MUY-ing-wah). A deity of fertility.

Muyovi (MOO-yo-vee or MEUH-yo-vee). Hopi name for the Rio Grande Valley.

Nahoydadatsia (nah-HOY-dah-dahts-yah). A ball and stick game similar to shinny.

Namiteika (nah-mee-TAY-ih-kah). Site of a Hopi shrine near Lupton, Arizona.

Nampeyo (nahm-PAY-o). Personal name. A famous potter of Tewa Village.

Nashilehwi (nah-SHEE-leh-wee). Personal name. First chief of Moencopi.

Nedah, Netah (nee-DAH, nee-TAH). Navajo word meaning Squaw Dance.

Niman (NEE-mahn). The going-home ceremony, when the kachinas prepare to return to the San Francisco Mountains.

Numkena (nuhm-KEE-nah). Personal name meaning To Warm Yourself.

Nuvakchina (neu-VAHK-chee-nah). Snow Kachina or Snow Kachina Dance.

Nuvamsa (neu-VAHM-sah). Personal name meaning Flares of Snow.

Nuvangnyam (noo-VAHNG-nyahm or neu-VAHNG-nyahm). Snow Clan.

Nuvatikyao, Nuvatikyaovi (noo-VAH-tihk-yah-o, neu-VAH-tihk-yao-o-vee). San Francisco Peaks. Sometimes loosely used for Flagstaff.

Oraibi (o-RYE-bee). Once the principal village on Third Mesa, but broken up by the Oraibi Split of 1906.

Ova (O-vah). Bridal shawl.

Owakulti (o-WAH-keul-tee, O-wah-keul-teu). The pronunciation ending in *tee* appears to refer to the festival of Owakultu (*-teu*), a women's society.

Pa'ateu. See **Popay.**

Paho, sometimes heard as **Baho** (PAH-ho, BAH-ho). Prayer feather or prayer stick.

Pahoki (PAH-ho-kee, sometimes pah-HO-kee). Shrine, depository for pahos.

Palatkwa (pah-LAHT-kwah), more often **Palatkwapi** (pah-LAHT-kwah-pee). The legendary village in the south from which the Water Clan and related groups migrated to the Hopi mesas.

Palengahoya (pah-LEHNG-ah-hoy-ah). The younger of the two Warrior Brothers in Hopi mythology.

Paleuleukang (pah-LEU-leu-kahng, sometimes heard as PAH-leu-leu-kahng, occasionally with the initial *p* sounded as a *b*. The horned water snake central to the Palatkwapi myth.

Pashumayani (PAHSH-oo-mah-yah-nee, also heard as pas-eu-mah-YAH-nee). "Be careful."

Pautiwa (POW-tee-wah). Personal name. Also the name of a Zuni kachina adopted by the Hopis.

Payupki (pye-OOP-kee). An extinct Second Mesa village named after an Eastern Pueblo people who occupied it.

Peki (PEH-kee). Personal name.

Piki (PEE-kee). Hopi thin-wafer bread, made in various colors.

Pintopakokeuji (PIHN-to-PAH-ko-keu-jee). A dog's name, meaning Spotted Behind.

Pipnyamrieu (PEEP-nyahm-ree-eu). Smoke Clan.

Pivanhonkapi (pee-VAHN-hon-kah-pee). An extinct Third Mesa village.

Pokanghoya (po-KAHNG-hoy-ah). The elder of the two mythological Warrior Brothers.

Pokangs (po-KAHNGS). A Hopi designation of convenience for the two Warrior Brothers.

Polacca (po-LAH-kah). The newest of the First Mesa villages, a roadside offshoot of Walpi and Sichomovi. Named after Tom Polaccaca, a Tewa-Hopi.

Poliquaptewa (po-LEE-kwahp-teh-wah). Personal name. Myron Poliquaptewa was the son of the chief of Oraibi at the time of the breakup of that village.

Popay (PO-pay, Tewa word). A New Mexico Tewa leader in the revolt against the Spanish. In Hopi he was called *Pa'ateu* (PAH-ah-teu), meaning Water Bug.

Povoslowa (PO-vo-slo-wah). A diviner.

Powaka (po-WAH-kah). Sorcerer.

Powamu or **Powamuya** (po-WAH-meu, po-WAH-meu-yah). The Bean Planting ceremony celebrating the return of the kachinas from the San Francisco Peaks.

Puweuvetaka (poo-WEU-veh-tah-kah). A site below First Mesa. "The Dog Chased Them Away."

Queungofovi (kweung-O-fo-vee, also heard as kweung-EU-fo-vee and kweung-EUK-fo-vee). Meaning, Round Stones on Top. Name of a small mesa and an adjoining village whose people are said to have founded Mishongnovi and Shipaulovi.

Sekaquaptewa (sehk-ah-KWAP-teh-wah or sih-kyah-KWAP-tee-wah). Personal name, meaning Yellow Piñon Blossom.

Shiamptiwa or **Siamptiwa** (SHEE-ahmp-tee-wah, SEE-ahmp-tee-wah). Personal name meaning Flowers Budding.

Shimopovi (shih-MO-po-vee) or Shimopavi (shih-MO-pah-vee). See *Shongopovi.*

Shipaulovi (shih-PAW-lo-vee). A Second Mesa village.

Shongopovi, sometimes spelled **Shungopovi** (shong-O-po-vee, shong-O-pah-vee, and frequently heard as shih-MO-pah-vee). A Second Mesa village.

Sichomovi (see-CHO-mo-vee). The middle village on First Mesa, between Walpi and Tewa Village. Name signifies Flower Place or Place of Flowers.

Sihonka (see-HON-kah). Personal name. Matilda Sihonka, though not officially the chief, was given the responsibility of overseeing Sichomovi when it was established by permission of Walpi.

Sikyachiti (sihk-YAH-chee-tee, also heard as sihk-YAH-chih). Personal name meaning Yellow Bird.

Sikyakokuh (sihk-YAH-ko-kuh). Personal name meaning Yellow Feet or Yellow Foot.

Sikyatki (sihk-YAHT-kee). An extinct village below the cliff edge of First Mesa. Its name means Yellow House.

Sipapuni (see-PAH-poo-nee, but also heard as SEE-pah-poo-nee). The opening in the sky of the Third World through which the people emerged into the Fourth World.

Sitaiema (SEE-tye-eh-mah). Personal name meaning Looking for Flowers.

Siwi (SEE-WEE). Onion.

Somaikoli (so-MYE-ko-lee). A kiva fraternity and the name of a kachina which is represented as being blind. The Blind Kachina is associated with ceremonies of the Kaletaka (Warrior Society) and formerly played a role in the ceremonies of the Yaya fraternity, now extinct.

Somiviki (so-MIH-vee-kee). A kind of bread made of finely ground blue corn. The meal is wrapped in corn husks and boiled.

Sowiteuyeuka (so-WEE-teu-yeu-kah). Jackrabbit Point. An extinct (or legendary?) Hopi village.

Sosotakwia (so-SO-tah-kwee-ah, sometimes heard as so-SO-tah-kwee). A Hopi shoe game.

Soyalana (heard variously as SOY-ah-lahn-ah, soy-YAH-lahn, soy-YAH-lahng, soy-eh-LAHNG, and SOY-ah-lahng-weu). Winter solstice ceremony, in which all kiva societies participate.

Soyohim (SO-yo-him). Mixed Kachinas

Soyoko (SO-yo-ko, sometimes SOO-yo-ko). A monster or bogey kachina.

Suchaptekwi (soo-CHAHP-teh-kwee or so-CHAHP-teh-kwee). An extinct village, presumably in New Mexico.

Talavai (tah-LAH-vye, sometimes tah-LAH-vye-eh). The Morning Kachina.

Talayesva (tah-LAH-yehs-vah). Personal name.

Tallahogan (tah-LAH-ho-gahn), sometimes written *Tala Hogan*. The Navajo name for Awatovi, said to mean Singing-House.

Tataukyamu (TAH-tah-ok-yahm-eu). One of the main Hopi kiva societies, sometimes referred to as The Singers.

Tawa (TAH-wah). The sun. Name of the sun god.

Tawakwaptewa (tah-WAH-kwahp-teh-wah). Name of the chief of Oraibi at the time of the fracturing of that village in 1906.

Tawaletstiwa (tah-WAH-lehts-tee-wah). Personal name.

Terkinovi (ter-KEE-no-vee). An extinct First Mesa village on the heights above Sikyatki.

Tesaktumo, Tesakchumo (teh-SAHK-too-mo, teh-SAHK-choo-mo). Site of a Hopi shrine near Williams, Arizona. The name means Grass Hill.

Teukchi (TEUK-chee). A mythological bird.

Teumas (TEU-mahs). Name of a "mother" kachina.

Tewa (TAY-wah). An Eastern Pueblo tribal name.

Tiponi (TEE-po-nee, sometimes heard as TEE-poo-nee). A sacred clan emblem.

Tokonave (to-KO-nah-vay or to-KO-nah-veh). Black Mountain. Hopi name for Navajo Mountain.

Tokpela (TOK-peh-lah or TAWK-peh-lah). Endless space, outer space.

Totolospi (to-TO-lo-spee). A gambling game played by dropping flat sticks, each stick marked on one side and plain on the other. Scores are made by various combinations of odds and evens.

Tsakaptamana (tsah-KAHP-tah-mah-nah). Personal name meaning Pottery Maker or Girl Making Pottery.

Tsaveyo (TSAH-veh-yo, TCHAH-veh-yo, or TCHEH-veh-yo). An ogre kachina.

Tsewageh(tseh-WAH-geh, Tewa word). Name of the New Mexico village from which a large group of Tewas migrated to First Mesa.

Tsikuvi (tsee-KOO-vee, tsee-KEU-vee). An extinct Second Mesa village.

Tuba (City) (TOO-bah). A town near the Hopi village of Moencopi. Named after an early Hopi settler, Teuvi.

Tunwup (teun-WEUP or teun-WEUF). The Whipping Kachina who plays an important role in Kachina Society initiations.

Tuskyata (TEUSK-yah-tah). Exact meaning not given.

Tuvengyamtiwa (too-vehng-YAHM-tee-wah). Personal name.

Tuwahoyioma (too-WAH-hoy-ih-o-mah). Personal name.

Uwaikwiota (oo-WYE-kwee-o-tah). Carrying Stones, a personal name.

Walpi (WAHL-pee). A village on First Mesa. Named after a gap in the terrain.

Wenima (WEHN-ih-mah or WEH-nih-mah). An extinct village, said by one informant to have been located near Springerville, Arizona, and by another to have been closer to St. Johns, Arizona. Some informants say it was a Hopi settlement, while others believe it was a Zuni settlement. There seems to be general agreement, however, that Wenima is used as a home by both Hopi and Zuni Kachinas.

Wepo (WEE-po). A plain on the west side of First Mesa from which a nearby spring, Wepova, takes its name. The word signifies pussy-willow.

Weupa (WEU-pah). A personal name meaning tall or long.

Wuwuchim or **Wuwuchimteu** (WEU-weu-chihm, WEU-weu-chihm-teu). One of the important Hopi kiva societies.

Yachakpa or **Yachakva** (yah-CHAHK-pah, yah-CHAHK-vah). A spring near Awatovi.

Yalpa (YAHL-pah). Mockingbird.

Yaoyesiwa (yah-o-YEH-see-wah). A phrase used to begin a narration, "They were living."

Yaponcha, Yayaponcha (YAH-pon-chah, YAH-yah-pon-chah, or YAH-yah-PON-chah). A wind deity, associated also with fire. A sorcerer who causes fires, particularly prairie fires.

Yava (YAY-vah, shortened from Nuvayoiyava, Big Falling Snow). Personal name.

Yaya (YAH-yah). An extinct fraternal society identified with the Reed (Warrior) Clan on First Mesa.

Yelaha (yeh-LAH-hah). Graphite.

Yoiseumala (yoy-SEU-mah-lah). According to an explanation given in Moencopi, yoiseumala refers to the sound of thunder caused by kachinas rolling little stone wheels or disks in a kind of racing game. An informant in Mishongnovi understood the word to mean "a rain-bringing breeze."

Yukioma (yoo-KEE-o-mah). Name of the leader of the "Hostiles" in Oraibi at the time of the breakup of that village.

Selective Bibliography

Bandelier, Adolph. *Final Report of Investigations Among the Indians of Southwestern United States.* 2 vols. Cambridge, Mass.: Harvard University Press, 1890–92.

Breed, Bill. "The Mountains of Fire." *Arizona Highways,* July 1978.

Courlander, Harold. *The Fourth World of the Hopis.* New York: Crown Publishers, 1971.

———. *People of the Short Blue Corn.* New York: Harcourt Brace Jovanovich, 1970.

Dennis, Wayne. *The Hopi Child.* New York: Science Editions, 1940.

Dozier, Edward P. *The Hopi-Tewa of Arizona.* University of California Publications in American Archeology and Ethnology, No. 44, 1954 (Berkeley).

———. *The Pueblo Indians of North America.* New York: Holt, Rinehart and Winston, 1970.

Fewkes, Jesse Walter. "Archeological Expedition to Arizona in 1895." *Seventeenth Annual Report of the Bureau of American Ethnology.* Washington, D.C. 1898.

———. "Hopi Katcinas Drawn by Native Artists." *Twenty-first Annual Report of the Bureau of American Ethnology.* Washington, D.C., 1903.

———. "Tusayan Migration Traditions." *Nineteenth Annual Report of the Bureau of American Ethnology,* Part 2. Washington, D.C., 1900.

———. "Sun Worship of the Hopi Indians." *Annual Report of the Smithsonian Institution for the Year Ending June 30, 1918.* (Washington, D.C.).

Foster, George M. Entry under "Quetzalcoatl" in *Standard Dictionary of Folklore, Mythology, and Legend,* edited by Maria Leach, Vol. 2, p. 915. New York: Funk and Wagnalls, 1950.

Harrington, John P. "The Ethnogeography of the Tewa Indians." *Twenty-ninth Annual Report of the Bureau of American Ethnology. Washington, D.C. 1916.*

Kennard, Edward A., and Albert Yava. *Field Mouse Goes to War* (Tusan Homichi Tuwvöta). Edited by Willard W. Beatty. Washington, D.C.: Bureau of Indian Affairs, 1944.

Kroeber, A. L. *Native Cultures in the Southwest*. University of California Publications in American Archeology and Ethnology, Vol. 23, 1928 (Berkeley).

Lockett, H. G. "The Unwritten Literature of the Hopi." *University of Arizona Social Science Bulletin*, No. 2, 1933.

Mindeleff, Cosmos. "Localization of Tusayan Clans." *Nineteenth Annual Report of the Bureau of American Ethnology*, Washington, D.C., 1900.

Montgomery, Ross G., Watson Smith, and Joseph Brew. *Franciscan Awatovi*. Papers of the Peabody Museum of Archaeology and Ethnology, Vol. 36, 1949 (Cambridge, Mass.: Harvard University).

Malotki, Ekkehart. *Hopitutuwutsi/(Hopi Tales):* A Bilingual Collection of Hopi Indian Stories. Flagstaff: Museum of Northern Arizona Press, 1978.

Moqui [Hopi] Petition "To the Washington Chiefs." Dated March 27 and 28, 1894. Document in National Archives, Washington, D.C., record no. 14830.

Nequatewa, Edmund. *Truth of a Hopi*. Flagstaff: Museum of Northern Arizona, 1936, 1967.

Parsons, Elsie Clews. *A Pueblo Journal, 1920–1921*. Memoirs of the American Anthropological Association, No. 32, 1925.

Simpson, Ruth DeEtte. *The Hopi Indians*. Los Angeles: Southwest Museum, 1953.

Spence, Lewis. *Myths of Mexico and Peru*. New York: 1913.

Spier, Leslie. *Yuman Tribes of the Gila River*. 1933. Reprint. New York: Cooper Square, 1970.

Stephen. A. M. "Hopi Tales." *Journal of American Folklore*, Vol. 42, 1929.

Talayesva, Don C. *Sun Chief: The Autobiography of a Hopi Indian*. Edited by Leo W. Simmons. New Haven: Yale University Press, 1942.

Thompson, Laura, and Alice Joseph. *The Hopi Way*. Lawrence, Kansas, 1944.

Thompson, Stith. *The Folktale*. New York: Dryden Press, 1946.

Titiev, Mische. "A Hopi Salt Expedition." *American Anthropologist*, Vol. 39, 1937.

Underhill, Ruth. *Pueblo Crafts*. Washington, D.C.: Bureau of Indian Affairs, 1944.

Voth, H. R. *The Traditions of the Hopi*. Chicago: Field Columbian Museum, 1905.

———. "Oraibi Natal Customs and Ceremonies." *Anthropological Series of the Field Museum of Natural History*, Vol. 6, No. 2, 1905.

Waters, Frank, and Oswald White Bear Fredericks. Book of the Hopi. New York: Viking Press, 1963.

Webb, William, and Robert A. Weinstein. *Dwellers at the Source.* New York: Grossman, 1973.

Wallis, W. D. "Folk Tales from Shumopavi, Second Mesa." *Journal of American Folklore*, Vol. 49, 1936.

Yava, Albert. *Big Falling Snow: A Tewa-Hopi Indian's Life and Times and the History and Traditions of his People.* Edited and annotated by Harold Courlander. New York: Crown Publishers, 1978. Reprinted Albuquerque: University of New Mexico Press, 1982.